Magical Tarot, Mystical Tao

ALSO BY DIANE MORGAN

The Best Guide to Eastern Philosophy and Religion

Magical Tarot, Mystical Tao

*Unlocking the Hidden Power of the
Tarot Using the Ancient Secrets
of the Tao Te Ching*

Diane Morgan

ST. MARTIN'S GRIFFIN ≋ NEW YORK

www.stmartins.com

Design by Jennifer Ann Daddio

LIBRARY OF CONGRESS CATALOGING-IN-PUBLICATION DATA
Morgan, Diane, 1947–
Magical Tarot, mystical Tao : unlocking the hidden power of
  the Tarot using the ancient secrets of the Tao Te Ching /
  Diane Morgan.—1st ed.
    p. cm.
  Includes bibliographical references (page 259).
  ISBN 0-312-31221-0
  1. Tarot. 2. Tao. I. Title.

BF1879.T2 M659 2003
133.3'2424—dc21   2002036887

First Edition: March 2003

10   9   8   7   6   5   4   3   2   1

For Nancy Mandowa,
most Magical friend—
and fellow delver into the Mysteries

Contents

Part Three:

Beneath the Waves

Acknowledgments

I would like to thank everyone who helped make this book a reality. To Amanda Pisani, whose vision and wisdom make everything possible. For John Warner, as always my kindest critic and most sensitive reader. And to the people at St. Martin's who can work magic themselves: Marian Lizzi, Julie Mente, Marie Estrada, and Wah-Ming Chang. I owe my deepest appreciation to all of you.

List of Tarot Cards and Corresponding Meditations

CARD		MEDITATION	

CARD		MEDITATION	

Preface

The Tarot is a pack of seventy-eight cards. The Tao Te Ching is a book of eighty-one poems. It seems strange that such slight things can keep such great secrets. It seems stranger still to reflect on how those secrets, once unlocked, reveal the same treasures of the spirit. But it shouldn't be surprising, after all. The spirit of wisdom is too sensible to keep all her jewels in one box.

I have been reading Tarot cards for more than thirty years. Every reading I do reveals a new world. The Tarot's uncanny accuracy in drawing a picture of past events, current conditions, and future probabilities has always amazed me, and sometimes unnerved me as well.

But until recently, I was never able to ground the Tarot's magical vision into a theory of life. It was, if not a party trick, something to do for an afternoon. I would do a reading, and say to myself, "Wow! That's so right on target it's frightening." Then I would forget about it.

It was only when I began teaching and studying the Tao Te Ching more deeply that a strange connection began to develop. At first, it did not seem possible to me that two traditions so diverse in place, time, and outlook could enrich each other. But they do. I soon discovered that the secret of their successful commingling is partly due to their differences. Each speaks to a different part of the human psyche. For while the Tao Te Ching does not "tell fortune," it gives a philosophy to live by every day. Its ancient meditations are full of wisdom. The Tarot picks up that ancient wisdom and points it specifically toward the place where we need to find direction. The Tarot lights up the mysteries of Tao, while the Tao Te Ching deepens the meaning of the Tarot. Together, they draw a plan for joyful living.

Introduction:
The Double Matrix

This is the place where Magic meets Mystery. We could, perhaps, devise other metaphors. This is the crossroads of mind and spirit, the nexus of Yang and Yin. Here prose meets poetry, and words touch silence. In this land, the Wizard meets the Wise. Tarot meets Tao.

We are Westerners, heading East. It is a perilous journey, but one filled with adventure. We seek a new and visionary place where old categories, old modes of thought, and old symbols are reborn into a renewed life. We bring with us our history, our knowledge, and our magic. We'll need them all.

Those who embark on this journey don't hunger for wealth or thirst for fame. They are not spurred by the lust for power. They are merely aflame with the passion for wisdom.

Wisdom, however, is a curious being. She doesn't reside in one mind, in one time, or in one place. She's capricious, whimsical, and full of humor. She's freakish. Sometimes she hides so deeply that only years of serious study can ferret her out. At other times, she appears unbidden, like a wayward child, when you least expect her. Sometimes you glimpse her from far off, shining in the stars. In more domestic moods, she reposes in a card layout on your kitchen table, in a swirl of water, in your daughter's eyes. Sometimes she vanishes altogether, and makes you curse the day you sought her out. She may reappear, however, an hour later, in the chance remark of your next-door neighbor. She doesn't prefer one people, one climate, or one direction to another.

Misunderstanding her flighty nature, some of us Westerners have made a curious mistake. Bored with our own culture, we have decided that a deep, lurking truth awaits us in some other country, some different place, China or India or Tibet. We look Eastward for wisdom, as if only a Hindu temple, Buddhist meditation hall, or Taoist mountain retreat could hold her.

Of course, this is another one of wisdom's tricks, donning the garb of the mystic. She knows how it dazzles our eyes. The Eastern Mystical Tradition is indeed a seductive alien. She stands aloof, but alluring. She promises us untold spiritual riches. She beckons us, and we follow her, breathless from meditation and wild-eyed from Zen riddles. We trudge forward, perhaps gaining entrance to the outer door of her fabulous palace, only to stumble, frustrated and impotent, at the threshold of her most secret chamber. The door is always locked.

This book doesn't have a key to that chamber, but you do, if only you'll reach for it. Your Western heritage is not your burden—it's your suitcase. If you leave it behind, you won't have what you need when you arrive. To get the key to the room—reach deep into the suitcase. What's there? Well, along with a lot of worn and useless articles, you're carrying optimism, faith in the future, and a yearning for perfection. And there's one more thing. Tucked into a seldom-opened inside pocket is an old pack of curious cards. They bear strange names—the Hermit, the Lovers, the Knight of Swords. The very first one is the Magician. That's your card.

To unlock the spirit of the East, it's not necessary to go to China or India, to master classical Sanskrit or Chinese ideograms. You don't need to become an adept at Taoist, Buddhist, or Hindu meditation. You don't have to stare at a wall for nine years, wear rags, live in an unheated hut, or prostrate yourself 360,000 times before an altar.

You have to do something much more radical. To see into the heart of things, you have to transform your vision.

The Transforming Vision

To transform your vision—start seeing. Sherlock Holmes, the archetypal Westerner, the master of logic, once said to Dr. Watson, "You see, but you do not observe." He meant it as a severe criticism. For the seeker of Eastern mysticism, however, his dictum should be reversed, "You observe, but you do not *see*." Students of the West already know how to observe. We examine test tubes and study the stars. We observe laboratory animals and voting behavior. But what do we *see*? How many people spend an entire vacation taking photos, but never *look* at anything with their own eyes, or *imagine* what they see?

The Greek tragic playwright Sophocles gave us another example: Oedipus, great king of Thebes. Oedipus was the master observer, the supreme king of Logos, the archetype of Western thought. He solved the riddle of the Sphinx. "What goes on four feet in the morning, two feet at noon, and three in the evening?" The answer, he thought, was "mankind." He had observed human beings who crawled as babies, walked upright as adults, and hobbled on canes as old men. The answer was correct, as far as it went.

Oedipus, however, fails to apply his clever observations to himself. He cannot *see* that it is he himself who has committed horrible crimes. He becomes truly visionary only when he blinds himself. He recognizes at last that it was he *himself* who had been bound by the ankles as a baby and who crawled, he *himself* who walked proud and tall and spiritually blind among his people. Only at the end of the tragedy, when he hobbles off on his cane, blinded and cursed, does he *see* at last who he really is. Seeing deeply doesn't depend on the eyes—it springs from the spirit.

The Transforming Spirit

Between Tao and Tarot, between the European Magical Tradition and the Eastern Mystical Tradition, there exists an important correspondence. Both deal with Transformation, the radical change between one state and another state. Whether we're doing chemistry, performing magic, celebrating Mass, or meditating in a closet, we are experiencing Transformation—the fundamental transmutation between what is and what can be.

Transformation is the key to all religious traditions and all scientific processes. In the West, we have focused on the alteration of physical matter and events. The Christian rite of communion, an ancient Magical ritual, transforms bread and wine into the literal Body and Blood of Christ. To change matter, we believe, is to change the self. This Western insistence on the stubborn reality of matter and the power inherent in things has produced amazing advances in science and technology, the arts that change the world. We are both matter of fact, and masters of fact. This is what the West has had to offer the East. We hold the power of knowledge.

But it has become apparent to many people that while the West has undoubtedly succeeded in producing a better mousetrap, we may have caught ourselves as well as the mice. We have reduced mystery to what we don't understand—yet. We talk without listening. We observe without seeing. We touch without feeling. We search without finding. In the process, we may have lost ourselves.

The Eastern Mystical Tradition, on the other hand, is not fact; it's metaphor. The East sees the world as an expression of the self, not as a "thing," a self that is the the ultimate riddle and the final mystery. It revels in paradox and contradiction, rather than cause and effect. Mystery is welcomed, not feared. Mystery is what we need to understand in a new way. Mystery expands with every new spiritual discovery; it doesn't shrink with each new scientific advance.

Thus Easterners, and adepts of the Mystical Tradition, begin the transformative process from the inside. To change the self is to change the world. This is the insight (literally) that the East has to offer the West—a view to the inside, into the secret inner workings of the spirit, of which the entire visible cosmos is only a hulking shadow.

To the West, the visible universe is all in all. (We have certainly made more progress in astronomy than in psychology!) The Western world is the world of Logos, or logical discourse. For many Westerners, facts are the only kind of truth, and logic defeats mystery. When logic fails, the mind shuts down. (This is one reason why Western students of philosophy have such a terrible time with Zen riddles.)

The West speaks loudly and clearly. The Eastern world, on the other hand, is the realm of Mythos, which means not to speak, but to murmur with closed lips. This is the essence of mystery, where meaning is not spoken through the word, but enacted in the spirit. This is the power of wisdom.

This doesn't mean that the Western Magical Tradition is shallow and false, while the Eastern Mystical Tradition is deep and true. We must never discard the knowledge of the West for the wisdom of the East.

The Yin and the Yang of things must remain in creative tension. Because, in the end, East and West tell the same story, although they tell it in a very different way. Both traditions are rich, complex, and life enhancing. Sometimes, indeed, the differences between the two are substantial, but just as often it's only a matter of emphasis.

Besides, both traditions have their share of false lights as well as true ones. Just as the Western Magical Tradition has its conjurers, the Eastern Mystical Tradition has its fakirs. Climbing ropes into thin air and sleeping on beds of nails have no more to do with true mysticism than pulling rabbits out of hats does with true magic. These are all illusions for the masses, for people who want to be entertained and bewildered. They are not the food of those who crave to live more deeply.

As human beings, we need both real magic and real mysticism. Each tells us something essential about ourselves. Each is liberating and powerful. If the West is the body, the East is the soul. Both are essential to vital life. Body without soul is empty. Soul without body is pathless. Together, they make one living, pulsating being—and one complex and universal truth.

Part One

The Two Traditions

The Western Magical Tradition

The Western Magical Tradition is great, ancient, and powerful. It has not only given birth to orthodox science, but it has also created its own astrology, alchemy, and systems of divination. It has engendered religions as diverse as Wicca, Paganism, and Christianity. It claims the Tarot as its own.

We can't name the first adepts in the Western Magical Tradition. But as long as there have been human beings, there have been wizards. Call them nerds, physicists, geeks, or inventors. Call them chemists and alchemists. Beneath the white coat, the rumpled shirt, or coveralls, we see the same face—intent, impassioned, a little amused. One and all, they are the makers and un-makers of our world.

The modern scientific worldview is a direct descendant of an ancient practice, and contemporary scientists are merely wizards who have traded their starry hats for telescopes and their magic wands for computers. Their implements of power may sound unromantic—gas chromatographs, cyclotrons, atomic absorption spectrophotometers, magnetic resonance imaging. But their goal is ever the same: to know—and to change.

Look around you—and thank them. They heat your house and water your lawn. They cook your food, do your laundry, iron your clothes. They drove you to work today, and turned on the lights when you came home. They cured your headache, and treated your cancer. They have eradicated smallpox in the world. They have banished goblins. They have touched the stars. They have transformed the very matter of the universe.

But you can curse them, too. The Western Magical Tradition is a heritage of evil, as well as of good. The scientists we worship have denuded our forests and plundered our natural resources. They have polluted our water and choked the air. The gift of longer life and more life has altered the natural balance of the world, and the exploding population has brought with it new diseases, and conditions of untold misery. Along with the banished goblins, the elves and wise spirits of the forest have disappeared. And worse. Our scientist-heroes have created the machinery to kill us all. They can recreate the plagues they "eradicated." The image of the Mad Scientist, the Magician turned Sorcerer, is the contemporary version of the Devil.

Why is this? Perhaps because we in the West have tried to create our own wisdom. We make bridges, construct roads, and erect dams. Our goal has been to change nature, with some disastrous results. The Western Tradition, both in science and magic, has put human beings squarely in the center of the universe. Everything—history, technology, sociology, psychology—all the great studies of the West, are really about *us*. That's comforting. But is that what the universe is all about?

The ageless Tao reminds us: "The universe is sacred. You cannot improve it. If you try to change it, you will ruin it. If you try to hold it, you will lose it." Somehow we know that this is true. What we have gained in our building is balanced by what we have lost in our destroying.

But, for good or ill, the Western Magical Tradition is one of the very greatest powers. No one can deny it; no one can turn aside from it. It's too late for that. This is one magic spell that can't be broken, nor would most of us break it even if we could. The enchantment has us in thrall.

Tarot Magic

The cards we call Tarot are part of this rich heritage. To many, Tarot cards are a parlor game, an evening's entertainment. For others, they seem to hold the key to an unknown and menacing future. Still others regard the Tarot as the Devil's tool. But it isn't any of these things. It's magic.

What is magic? We see a conjurer pull a rabbit from a hat. We know it's not a miracle, but it's not magic either. It's hocus-pocus. It's a conjurer's trick, a sleight-of-hand, a technique, even an art. But it's not magic, any more than technology is science.

Real magic has nothing to do with levitation, love potions, or weird spells. Nor is it some kind of proto- or pseudo-science. Real magic shows us the hidden things of this world. It is a way of reading subtle signs and secret portents. It makes visible the invisible, reveals the obscure, and lights up the dark spaces. It pulls aside the veil. Real magic opens the doors of perception wider than mescaline or LSD, because it enlightens the mind rather than wracking the senses. And the mind is where all real science—and real magic—start.

Divination as Magic and Mystery

The Tarot is real magic and real mystery. But it's also a most practical art, an art that can be learned, cultivated, and used. The old and honorable word for this art is *divination*.

Divination is a way of seeing into the heart of things. The heart of things is not always readily apparent; hence, the notion that the "diviner" has, as the name suggests, a connection with the omniscient divine. The divine is at the heart of all, a fact that magic has long understood. It's no accident that nearly every card in the Tarot pack is resonant with spiritual symbols. No matter how earthly the question: "Will I get a raise next week?" "Should I have an affair with Violet to make Myrtle jealous?" the Tarot directs the seeker to look at the symbol. The symbol points to the world behind, beyond, and beneath the visible.

Although the history of the Tarot is mysterious, nearly everyone agrees that it originated partly as augury, or fortune-telling. For thousands of years we human beings have relied on augurs. Many times, the auguries were objects that were designed (by God or nature) for an entirely different purpose: animal livers and intestines, flights of birds, tea leaves, and tortoise shells. The Tarot, however, like its Chinese counterpart, the I Ching, is a system specifically designed by human beings to answer human questions. But the Tarot is more vividly "real" than the I Ching. The pictures on the cards, with almost no exceptions, show human beings engaged in archetypal human actions—loving, working, fighting, suffering, dying. And just as in life, sometimes the action truly reveals its core meaning; just as often, however, it conceals it. That's where the divination—and the magic—come in.

Unfortunately, many readers, ungifted in the art of true divination, have sought to unravel the truth of Tarot by relying on a purely mechanical, one-to-one correspondence between a card and its "meaning." While gratifyingly easy, such a simplistic approach can never hope to produce profound insights. To compound the problem, most of the "keys" to the Tarot pack are derived from false numerical values. For example, the Major Arcana have no "correct" numerical order. The numbers they bear today were added long after the pack was created, and were altered again in the Rider-Waite deck, which I use in this book. There is nothing *inherently* important or meaningful in their present order. The names of the cards, too, have changed over the centuries. The Hermit was once Father Time, and the Tower was the Arrow. The cards of the Minor Arcana were once imageless, and marked only by Pips. They received individual, revelatory pictures only in the twentieth century with the Rider-Waite deck. Like the Tao, the Tarot is a fluid system whose underlying permanence depends partly on its ever-changing surface. And this is our felt experience of reality: something both changing and changeless.

The History of Tarot

The word *Tarot* itself derives from the Italian word *tarocchi,* meaning "triumph." (We get the English *trump* from this source as well.) Even this source word is mysterious, however. No one knows where it comes from, for the earliest recorded term used to describe the Tarot pack (1442) was *cartes da trionfi,* cards with trumps.

A few people have even made a tentative connection between the words *Tarot* and *Tao.* Although these words do resemble each other superficially in the English alphabet, their pronunciation is nothing alike. *Tao* is pronounced DOW and *Tarot,* while it may be pronounced TAIR-o, Tair-O, Tairit, or almost anything else within reason, may not be pronounced DOW. Or spelled *Tao.* I'm afraid there's no connection, however nice it might be for my thesis.

The word *Tarot* has also been linked to the Egyptian word *Ta-rosh* (the royal way) and to the Hebrew word *Torah* (law). It has been derived from the Arabic word *tariqa* (the way), the Sanskrit word *Tara* (star and savior), the Irish *Tara* (the house of kings), the Buddhist deity *Tara* (the goddess of compassion), and the Latin word *terra* (earth). Geography buffs have even suggested that the name stems from the Taro River, a tributary of the Po. There's also the Greek word *Tartarus,* which means "Hell."

My favorite offering, however, is that of Cynthia Giles, who, in her very interesting and scholarly book *The Tarot: History, Mystery, and Lore,* suggests rather tentatively that "a particular combination of sounds (t/vowel-r/vowel) . . . goes back to a once-universal and now-unknown 'original language.' Or it may be that there is something in the vibration of the sound itself that connects with the basic neurological programming of human beings, linking the sound sequence imaginatively to a certain type of phenomenon" (Giles 4).

The truth is that one doesn't have to draw mysterious connections between ancient, dead, or imaginary languages to find the Tarot fascinating. The most likely explanation is that the word *Tarot* was probably invented just for this particular combination of Major and Minor Arcana cards.

The source of the Tarot cards themselves is another forbidding mystery. Their origin has been attributed by various authors to the Egyptians, the Indians, the Chinese, the Koreans, the Moroccans, the Crusaders, the Gypsies, the Italians, and the Spanish. We do know that the oldest surviving pack dates back only to the early fifteenth century. Cards of *any* kind are only about a hundred years older. It used to be thought that Tarot cards were the ancestors of our current playing decks, but that doesn't seem to be the case, and the relationship between the two is still unclear. The Major Arcana, originally unnumbered, bore obviously allegorical names like Judgment, Temperance, and Death, but as time passed, the cards took on a more richly symbolic meaning. The words *Major Arcana* mean "Greater Secrets," and early Tarot packs consisted only of these cards. Later, they were joined by the popular playing decks, then removed by church officials, who believed the figures represented ancient gods and spirits. (The Fool, of course, reappeared as the Joker in modern decks.) The modern Tarot pack consists of both the Major Arcana and fifty-six other cards, similar to the modern bridge deck.

From their earliest recorded uses, the Tarot cards performed a variety of functions: sometimes to entertain, sometimes to instruct, and sometimes to open an allegorical window into the mind of the Seeker. At one time, specifically during the fifteenth and sixteenth centuries, Tarot was an international pastime, thriving all over Europe. Princes, peers, and peddlers had their Tarot; it was more popular than chess and almost as popular as witch-hunting. No one is really sure how the cards were used, whether for fortune-telling or for ordinary card games—it's a mystery that will probably remain unsolved.

Curiously, some of the earliest references to playing cards are edicts to ban their use. In the fifteenth century, all cards were used for gambling, but Tarot cards were considered by some to be special tools of the Devil. In one sermon, for instance, a Franciscan friar announced that the twenty-one Major Arcana were the twenty-one rungs of a ladder that led the Seeker straight to hell. The good friar seemed particularly enraged that two of the Major Arcana were named after the Pope and the Emperor. Other authorities claimed that the Major Arcana were used to teach heretical ideas throughout Europe. Although this charge is probably false, it's clear that the cards represent more than a collection of intriguing drawings.

Early paintings depict people playing cards, but the faces of the cards are either not visible or unclear. Inventories of noble houses sometimes list "playing cards" among the family possessions, but without further information it's impossible to know if these "playing cards" referred to Tarot or a regular playing deck. For a long time it was believed that the earliest Tarot pack was designed in 1392 by a painter, Jacquemin Gringonneur, for King Charles VI of France. Nowadays, however, many experts think this pack was really an Italian one, dating to about 1470. No matter who designed them, though, the French have still "trumped" the Italians by actually having seventeen of these cards in their Bibliothèque Nationale.

In the sixteenth century, poets penned sonnet sequences in honor of the Tarot. Merlini Cocai (whose real name was Teofilo Folengo) in 1527 and Troilo Pomeran da Cittadela in 1534 published sonnets that mentioned every card in the Major Arcana. (They're not very good poems, which may be why you probably never came across them in your world literature anthology.) Cocai had a political agenda, urging the Pope to free European political prisoners held captive by the Turks, but da Cittadella contented himself with making clever rhymes for Venetian women.

The main point is that the Tarot seems to be an entirely European invention, and represents on its face, at least, European worldviews and values. However, not everyone agrees. Here are some of these other points of view.

The Tarot and Ancient Egypt

A French freemason and Protestant pastor named Antoine Court de Gébelin (1725–1784) devised the fanciful idea that the Tarot was an ancient Egyptian compendium of wisdom contained in the *Book of Thoth.* The fact that the *Book of Thoth* is entirely mythical didn't deter de Gébelin in the slightest. The *Book of Thoth,* he maintained, is presently safely secured underneath the Nile River in a gold box, inside a silver box, inside an ebony and ivory box, inside a bronze box, inside an iron box. (It was de Gébelin who also proposed that the name *Tarot* derived from the Egyptian *Ta-rosh,* the royal way, a far-fetched, but charming etymology.)

Antoine Court de Gébelin was an interesting character in his own right. He had an enormous forehead, a bad wig, and a miserable expression. Even the "de" in his name, an implied claim to aristocratic birth, was an invention of his own. He first encountered the Tarot at a card party, and no sooner had he "glanced at it" than he "recognized the allegory." We have no proof that anyone regarded the Tarot as anything but entertainment and casual "fortune-telling" until that evening, when de Gébelin discovered the mystical "Egyptian" source of the Tarot.

(Some people seem to feel that if you slap the label "ancient wisdom of Egypt" onto any occult system, it suddenly becomes more valid. It's my opinion that if the Egyptians were so wise, they wouldn't have allowed themselves to be beaten up by the Romans, but that's a side issue.)

Perhaps de Gébelin was not so far off, after all. The Egyptian god Thoth was the god of wisdom and learning. By placing the Tarot pack under the aegis of this god, de Gébelin was merely obeying what was surely a correct impulse—that the study of the cards indeed leads to wisdom. Another proof that Wisdom sometimes dons the mask of the jester is that no matter how wrong de Gébelin was about the Tarot being from Egypt, he was eerily on the mark about the symbolism of the cards. The cards do seem to speak a deep language that goes well beyond accidental influence. In a related modern development, Richard Roberts has constructed an interesting hypothesis that describes the Tarot as a kind of European, rather than Egyptian or Tibetan, *Book of the Dead,* wherein the Major Arcana act as soul guides to the departing spirit.

Another proponent of the Tarot-from-Egypt hypothesis was a French wigmaker named Jean-Baptiste Alliette (1738–1791), who told fortunes when the wig industry was in a slump. He elaborated on de Gébelin's theory about the *Book of Thoth,* saying that it was written by seventeen Magi on leaves of gold. Since no one could prove that it wasn't, this was a safe statement.

Alliette, who worked under the name *Etteilla,* a transparent reversal of his real name, renumbered and renamed the cards in the pack. He made some money predicting which of his friends would go to the guillotine, but was thoroughly discredited when he made a further forecast: that the mysteries of Egypt, when unveiled, would reveal the origins of the Tarot. It did no such thing, but the Tarot-as-Egyptian-magic thesis has thoroughly embedded itself in the minds of many who know no better. If the Tarot does have power, its source is much older and deeper than the pyramids—it stems from the structure of the human mind itself.

An Asian Link?

Some Tarot researchers speculate on an Indian connection with the European Tarot. In fact, the earliest scholarly works on the subject, *Researches into the History of Playing Cards with Illustrations of the Origins of Printing and Engraving on Wood* by Samuel Weller Singer in 1816 and *Facts and Superstitions on the Origin and History of Playing Cards* by W. A. Chatto in 1848, came to this conclusion.

The concept of card playing appeared in the East long before such practice came to Europe. In the Indian system, "suits" of cards, representing elephants, chariots, horses, and foot soldiers, were used. Muslims living in India had their own playing cards, with "superior suits" (*bishbur*) of Crowns, Moons, Sabers, and Slaves and "lower suits" (*kunbar*) of Harps, Suns, Royal Diplomas, and Bales of Merchandise. Furthermore, statues of the androgynous god Ardhanari, a combination of

Shiva and his consort Durga or Parvati, hold in their four hands objects that bear a striking resemblance to the four suits of the Minor Arcana— a sword, a cup, and a scepter (the Tarot suit of Wands is also called Scepters), and a circular object that looks like Pentacles or coins. In fairness, it should be pointed out that the object identified with Pentacles may instead be a symbol of fire, a sacred circle, or even the severed head of a victim.

The Indian-Tarot connection is extremely tempting, but it's only conjecture. There's no historical evidence to support such a direct link, but it's certainly possible.

Similar attempts to place the Tarot's origin in China, Arabia, Mongolia, or among the Romany people, called Gypsies, seem equally unprovable. Although the Gypsies may conceivably have brought the Major Arcana to Europe from their homeland in India, there is no real evidence to show that they did so. And though the Gypsies were inveterate fortune-tellers, they usually preferred palm-reading to cards.

The Tarot and Kabbalah

In a somewhat different, but equally mythical vein, Eliphas Levi (1810–1875), whose real name was Alphonse Louis Constant, announced that the Tarot could trace its origins to the Jewish mystical system known as Kabbalah. It can't, but Levi was onto something important nonetheless. He was the first person to draw interpretative connections between the Tarot and a mystical system. It doesn't have to be, as Levi thought, that one derived from the other; in fact, it makes more sense to think of both Kabbalah and Tarot springing from the same mystico/magico source. However, Levi's ideas were so evocative (giving rise to an entire occult cottage industry, in fact) that it's worth the time to look at them in a little more detail.

The word *Kabbalah* itself means "tradition," but it isn't a very old one, as traditions go, emerging in southern France during the twelfth century of our era, a product of the Jewish Diaspora. Kabbalah enthusiasts claim that the ultimate source of Kabbalah lies in the East, but details are sketchy, and we'll probably never know the true roots of this mystic set of beliefs.

Gerard Encausse (1865–1917), who wrote under the pen name Papus, was a French physician who developed the connection between the Tarot and the Kabbalah. He also related the Tarot to numerology, Rosicrucianism, astrology, and color symbolism. The brave reader is invited to sample his *Tarot of the Bohemians* to get the full effect.

Arthur Edward Waite (1857–1942), originator of the classic Rider-Waite pack that we use in this book, was another devotee of the Tarot who believed that the Tarot was connected to Kabbalistic studies (as well as to alchemy). However, Waite was one of the first to maintain that the Tarot draws on universal themes, and is not restricted to one particular system of interpretation. He was also the first person to have the Minor Arcana illustrated with symbolic, storylike pictures, as befitting their true significance. Nearly all modern Tarot decks have followed his example, usually quite closely.

The Kabbalah-as-Tarot (or Tarot-as-Kabbalah) proponents state that a group of Moroccan Kabbalists met in 1200 (or 1300, depending on whom you ask) and designed the Tarot as further explication of their system. As I mentioned earlier, these proponents suggest that the word *tarot* is "derived" from *Torah,* the first five books of the Bible, on which the Kabbalah is based.

The Kabbalah is usually portrayed as a diagram representing the Tree of Life. This "Tree" is ornamented with ten *sephirot* (plural of *sephira,* meaning "figure" or "number"), or emanations, each of which represents a special attribute of the Godhead, such as Beauty, Love, Wisdom, Power, Majesty, or Understanding. God, of course, is really beyond all such categorization, but the *sephirot* are pictorial and symbolic "shorthand" ways that human beings can use to understand the concept of deity. Some say the ten *sephirot* are ten stages of the Tree of Life through which we can approach the Holy.

The *sephirot* are connected to each other by special "paths," of which there are twenty-two, one for each letter of the Hebrew alphabet. Each letter, furthermore, represents not only itself, but also a number and a concept. (Both the Greeks and the ancient Israelites used letters to stand for numbers. The Romans, as we all know, came up with their own system—Roman numerals. People had to wait for the Arabs to invent the handy and now universal system of Arabic numbers.)

At least since the nineteenth century, some Tarot historians have drawn the obvious connections between the twenty-two Major Arcana and the twenty-two letters of the Hebrew alphabet, which themselves have long been treated symbolically. (One card in the Major Arcana, the Fool, has no number. Thus it presents a bit of difficulty, not only for the would-be Kabbalist, but for anyone else using a numerical system to explain Tarot. No doubt this was intended. The Fool is sometimes included as one of the twenty-two Major Arcana. Other times, however, it is considered separately, in which case, of course, there will be only twenty-one Major Arcana.)

Many researchers have speculated that the twenty-two Major Arcana are connected with the twenty-two paths on the Tree of Life of the Hebrew Kabbalah. Still others, primarily adherents of the Golden Dawn, have associated the first Major Arcana with the ten *sephirot* and the first ten letters of the Hebrew alphabet, and next eleven cards with the paths.

The cards were actually drawn by Pamela Colman Smith, a young American scenic artist working at Yeats's famous Abbey Theatre in Dublin. Her work reflects the deeply mystical thinking of the Hermetic Order of the Golden Dawn, founded in 1888. This short-lived, but extremely interesting, mystical society was founded by Waite, Aleister Crowley (the famed magician), and William Butler Yeats, perhaps the greatest poet of the twentieth century. It was based on ideas developed by Rosicrucianism and a manuscript allegedly found in a London book-shop by an English clergyman, the Reverend A.F.A. Woodford, who already belonged to an occult study group. The Order dedicated itself to the study of magic, numerology, alchemy, the Kabbalah, crystal ball gazing (scrying), and astrology. The Order of the Golden Dawn eventually fell apart due to factionalism among the various members, but the importance of the Tarot for magical studies had just begun. Irene Gad, in her *Tarot and Individuation*, has followed the Golden Dawn insofar as connecting the first ten trumps to the Hebrew alphabet and the *sephirot*; however, she chooses to assign the next eleven cards to what she calls the Path of the Serpent (drawing some rather odd but fascinating connections with Kundalini Yoga), or the way of individuation. Dividing the Major Arcana in half is a common and fairly old practice, though its purpose remains unclear.

A further connection has been drawn by Rachel Pollack and others who have noted that the Holy Tetragrammaton, the letters for God (YHWH), consists of four letters. They identify these four letters with the four suits of the Minor Arcana, or, alternatively, with the four Court cards of each suit.

Although the connection between Kabbalah and Tarot is a hoary Western tradition, there's one stumbling block. That is that the Kabbalah doesn't mention Tarot. At all. If there's a connection between them, it is one drawn by Tarotists, not Kabbalists. And the earliest Tarotists didn't do even this much. The whole relationship wasn't "discovered" until the nineteenth century. None of this disturbs the Kabbalah/Tarot fans, however. They claim the connection is an esoteric one known only to a few initiated elites.

True Kabbalists discard this theory altogether. The foremost contemporary scholar of the Kabbalah, Gershom Scholem, entirely rejects any idea that the Tarot cards derive from, or indeed are connected in any but fanciful ways to, legitimate Kabbalistic studies. Scholem specifically attacks the works of Eliphas Levi, Gerard Encausse, Aleister Crowley, and especially Arthur Edward Waite.

This doesn't mean, of course, that these writers had nothing of value to offer; it merely means that, in Scholem's learned opinion, their offerings are not properly derived from "orthodox" Kabbalistic lore. Considering that the Kabbalah, in itself, has always stood pretty well outside orthodox Jewish tradition, this probably doesn't matter. Factually, Scholem is surely right from a scholarly, historical, Western point of view. Still, there's a difference between the scholarly/historical vantage point, and the mythic or occult view. The first aims at factual accuracy, the second at spiritual truth. The two goals and methods are almost always in creative tension, generating an interesting state of affairs that strengthens both. It seems to be true that a combination of Kabbalistic/Tarot studies yields a rich, complex symbology that bears strange yet fruitful results among those learned in these arts. Both Tarot and Kabbalah stubbornly refuse to be limited to their orthodox interpreters. The origin of Tarot remains, as it should be, a deep mystery.

Tarot Pack Design

Hundreds of Tarot packs have been designed over the years, reflecting the continued fascination with these enigmatic cards. Some designs remain close to the original ones, while others have been wildly inventive. One, created by Salvador Dali, reaches the level of high art. (He painted himself as the Magician.) One contemporary artist, Niki de Saint Phalle, has created a Tarot sculpture garden in her home in Tuscany. (She lives in the Empress.)

The Venetian Pack

The prototype of the modern Tarot pack was the Venetian or Piedmontese Tarot, known in France as the Marseilles pack. This deck was created around 1500, with twenty-two Trump cards and fifty-six Minor Arcana. Rival packs, like the Florentine or Bolognese pack, had different numbers of cards, and replaced some of the traditional Trumps with novel designs, such as faith, fire, air, earth, or the twelve signs of the zodiac. Some packs left out the figure of the Pope, either as a nod to piety or from a fear of the Inquisition.

The Marseilles pack resembles the Rider-Waite pack, the most famous pack used today. The main difference is that the Major Arcana are in a somewhat different order, though order was not considered important. In fact, the Trumps of the earliest Tarot packs had no numbers, or even names. When numbers were eventually assigned, they varied, depending on where that particular pack was printed.

Tarot Packs Today

The tradition of novel Tarot design continues through today, with new Tarot packs appearing every year or so. Of all the designs that have been created, however, the pack designed by Arthur Edward Waite and Pamela Colman Smith in 1910 remains the most important, and accessible. (Its artistic merit is less clear, but it has the advantage of simplicity.) Although Waite had some mistaken ideas about the Tarot, his 1910 seminal work, *The Pictorial Key to the Tarot*, was so thoughtful and his insights into Tarot were so deep that they set the standard for nearly all Tarot designs and interpretations since.

Under Waite's close supervision, Colman Smith managed to weld the rich symbology of Yeats's poetic imagination with the deeper truths touched on (if not well understood) by the Golden Dawn. Her brilliant renderings of the timeworn cards still stand as the classic Tarot pack. Waite/Smith also illustrated the Minor Arcana, an innovation since followed by most Tarot pack designers. In fact, many modern Tarot packs, such as the Aquarian Tarot, the Robin Wood Tarot, and the Tarot of the Cloisters, are inspired by the Rider-Waite pack. The same is true of the many Tarot packs that carry the word *Waite* as part of their name.

The "Rider" part of the name comes from Rider & Company, the original issuers. Because the Rider-Waite pack, as it is known, is both popular and elegant (the King James Version of Tarot reading, if you will), we're using that pack as the basis for our work with the Tarot in this book. One reason is simply its familiarity, and deserved popularity. Another (and related) reason is that unlike many of the more modern decks, the Rider-Waite pack is not merely one artist's fancy, some idiosyncratic interpretation drawn from the designer's personal psyche. The Rider-Waite pack is steeped in the most ancient traditions of Western magic and alchemy, and was designed specifically with those elements embedded in its images. That, coupled with the purity and elegant simplicity of its design, gives the pack its unique appeal.

If you choose to use another pack, the same general principles apply; however, certain cards may need reinterpretation.

Waite made one extremely important, hitherto undetected connection—he was the first to notice that the Tarot has extraordinary correspondences with alchemy. Waite was an authority on the Western alchemical tradition. Although he did not develop this particular insight into a full-blown system, Cynthia Giles, Richard Roberts, and others have proposed some interesting paths along which such a study might be conducted.

What is the Tarot?

In accordance with its fascinating history, new Tarot decks spring up every year, just as the Bible is translated over and over again. Some of these new packs are whimsical, even humorous. Some try to make a political or religious point. Some are lovely, some frightening, some obviously derivative. But all of them speak to us of our passionate interest in knowing what lies behind the veil, what secrets are hidden in the symbols.

Is the Tarot a fortune-telling system, an augury into the future? Or it is a complex of symbols that leads us deep into our own minds? Is it the mystical art of meditation—or the magical art of divination? Of course it is all of these, and much more besides. The Tarot is an artifact of history. It reflects our growth as a culture, and absorbs our cultural icons into its symbolism. It gives us our history, and so our future. The future is embedded in the present. By understanding the Now can we create the New.

But the Tarot gives us more than a history lesson. It reaches deep into the collective, archetypal consciousness, as depth psychologist Carl Jung has shown. Reading the Tarot is reading history, but it's also reading ourselves. It is our soul in symbol. It is divinely human.

The Tarot ranges wide as well as deep—it stretches straight across Europe into the East. Personal and cultural history coincide with geography—not just physical geography, but the spiritual, mythic landscape we all inhabit. The ultimate source of Tarot is the sacred, unitary, unnamed Tao, the mystical river that flows beneath, through, and beyond all phenomena. Following the Tao is the first step on the path of wisdom.

The Major Arcana

The Major Arcana are the heart of the Tarot. They were the first part to be designed, and for many years remained the *only* Tarot cards. The evocative names of the Major Arcana and the richly symbolic pictures that accompany each card are so powerful that many books on the Tarot deal only with the Major Arcana. The Magician, the Priestess, the Moon, and the Fool and the others are archetypes that resonate with every reader.

The Minor Arcana

The Minor Arcana, which means "Lesser Secrets," contains fifty-six cards. Fifty-six is the number of possible combinations that can be thrown using three (magic number) dice. In medieval times, occultists often began incantation with a recitation of fifty-six angelic names (frequently followed by reciting twenty-one more angelic names. Twenty-one is the number of the Major Arcana, not counting the unnumbered Fool.)

The Four Suits

The Minor Arcana are divided into four suits: Swords, Cups, Pentacles, and Wands. Each suit further consists of Court cards (face cards) and Pips, or number cards, which run Ace through Ten.

Some scholars believe that the four suits originally indicated the four medieval classes: Swords for the nobility, Cups for the clergy, Pentacles (or coins) for the merchants, and Wands (or clubs) for the churls, the lowest class of society. It's interesting to note that the bidding order of the suits in bridge retain their medieval values from highest to lowest: Spades, Hearts, Diamonds, and Clubs.

As we shall see, a Taoist reading of Tarot assigns a Yin/Yang value to each suit. Each suit falls naturally into a Yin, Yang, Yang/Yin, or Yin/Yang category. In addition, each suit represents one element in the Chinese system of counterbalancing forces and energies: earth, water, wood, or metal. Note: The fifth element, fire, belongs to none of minor suits. As the transforming element/energy, it belongs to the Major Arcana.

2

The Eastern Mystical Tradition

Complementary to the human-oriented, historically based Magical Tradition of Europe is the nature-based, nonhistorical Mystical Tradition of the East. This tradition has come to its most elegant flowering in the mystical tradition of Taoism.

A mystic is primarily interested in things of the spirit, and Taoism has always been more focused on refining the spirit than on refining metal, more dedicated to transforming the self than transforming gold. It doesn't view the universe as a mere stage for the activities of human beings. For Taoists, the state of nature is to be emulated, not abhorred. Neither nature nor humankind is in a state of "fallenness" or depravity. There is no "original sin." Taoism teaches that the fulfillment of humankind lies in finding our place in the world, not changing the world to suit the vagaries of our will. This is in direct opposition to the Confucian ideal, which is to submit to Heaven's decree, or to the Western approach, which prides itself on its power to change the universe. Taoists sail a middle way—they neither change nor are changed; rather, they are one with the flow of the cosmos. In effect, they show themselves as the very cosmos in action, refusing to separate themselves from it.

The West fixes its attention on timebound *events* as sacred history, encounters between human and human, or between human and God. History, by contrast, is irrelevant in Taoism. Taoism looks to the nondatable elements of *nature* and *myth*—rivers, mountains, dragons, and tigers. These symbolize what is enduring in the human spirit. The West tries to control time; the East yields to eternity.

These divergent viewpoints may be called the Yang and Yin ways of life. The Western Tradition is Yang, focusing on the outer world. Magic itself is the practice of Yang; it emphasizes working and action. Furthermore, Yang calls to the Transcendent, to what is "above" us and "beyond" the world. Its language is clear, precise prose. A purely Western reading of Tarot gives us typically Yang responses: "A journey is near." "You will meet a good-looking stranger next week." "Beware the Ides of March."

Mystery, on the other hand, is poetic, not prosaic. It evokes rather than proclaims. It calls upon us to be, rather than to do: in being is our accomplishment. When it speaks, it speaks in verse and paradox. It brings forth the Immanent, and gives birth to Wonder. A Taoist reading of Tarot is complex, even paradoxical. As master tarotist Aleister Crowley wrote, "The truth must be falsehood unless it be the whole truth; and the whole truth is partly inaccessible, partly unintelligible, partly incredible and partly unpublishable." It doesn't reveal itself at the first, or even second, glance. It doesn't give us the answers we expect. But what it whispers to us is deeply true. This is the Yin way of being.

Yin and Yang

Yin and Yang are as old as the universe itself, and are its primary constituents. They aren't elements, but energies that inhere in the world. Traditionally, Yang has been equated with the hot, dry, masculine, bright side of the world. Yin is the cool, moist, feminine, dark element. Yang is above; Yin is below. Yang is sky; Yin is earth. Yang is logic; Yin is intuition. These are relative terms only, complements or polarities rather than opposites. One isn't "good" and the other "evil." They define each other. How can we know what is dark unless we can see what is bright? How can we judge what is cool unless we can experience what is hot? This is, as Alan Watts pointed out in *The Watercourse Way*, duality without dualism.

Taoists understand that the world is not a static place. It's a flowing of Yin and Yang, whose ceaseless ripples make up the universal River we call Tao. It flows through our inner being as well, for we humans are both Yang and Yin. If Yin and Yang are out of balance, sickness results. While the Yang drives our actions and ambitions, the Yin is the secret, hidden, responsive part of every one of us. That's why the Taoists say the deepest Tao is Yin. It is mystery unutterably ancient, but it was "discovered" in China thousands of years ago.

The Birthplace of Wonder

For many, the religion of China means Confucianism—ceremony, etiquette, restraint, propriety, piety, virtue. All that is true. But there's a much older tradition, an untamed and wild vision that reaches back many thousands of years before Confucius was born. This is shamanism.

The world of the shamans is not our world. It's a world of shapeshifters and bear cults, of spirit journeys, and immortality-giving plants. The people of that world gave birth to China's first identifiable culture, the dynasty of Hsia. These very ancient folk lived in northern China. They grew millet rather than rice. They developed the first writing system in China. Their legendary leader, Yü, was part emperor, part shaman, and part bear.

The shaman is one who dances between earth and heaven. The shaman is the first master of the Tao. He—or she—can reveal the hidden mysteries of the sky to the earthbound. To learn the secrets of the cosmos, the shaman usually relies on an augur—a vivid dream, cracks in turtle shells or bones, patterns of colored stones, a toss of coins or yarrow sticks. The movement of the stars. A pack of cards.

Taoism is the heir to the shamanistic tradition. While it has created a sophisticated philosophy and a way of life different from the simpler outlook of shamanism, it has never lost its wild heart. It is full of a vital energy, which, as The Text of Inward Training tells us (verse 2):

> Bright!—as if climbing the firmament.
> Dark! as if pouring into the abyss;
> Vast! as if dwelling in the ocean.
> High! as if leaping on the mountain.

Look deeply into the Tao Te Ching, and you can see it dancing still.

The Written Treasures of Tao

But Taoism is not shamanism, not just nature worship. Not all Taoists are hermits sitting around in thatched huts contemplating waterfalls. Taoism has a developed a rich, intellectual philosophy that applies to the world of humankind as much as to the world of nature. Over thousands of years it has developed a complex literary treasure to give voice to its mysteries.

Presently, the official collection of holy writings, or canon, of Taoism consists of 1,473 texts. (By contrast, the canon of the Jewish, Christian, and Islamic faiths each comprises only one sacred book.) Some of these texts contain ancient rites and incantations, while others lay out formulas for immortality. Still others offer political or military advice. In addition to being large, the Taoist canon is open. This means that new works of value may be admitted at any time. Unlike Christians, Jews, and Muslims, Taoists are not of the opinion that truth is final and can be captured for all time in a single scroll. Truth may be eternal, but she's a fast mover. One has to keep up.

Many of the Taoist classics have exquisitely evocative titles: the Cavern of the Realized, the Cavern of the Mysterious, the Cavern of the Spirit, the Classic of Peace and Balance, the North Star Scripture on Longevity. Some of the titles are downright confusing: the Yellow Emperor's Classic of Yin Convergence, the Seven Bamboo Strips of the Cloud-Hidden Satchel, and the Yellow Court Jade Classic of Internal Images. Included in the canon is the ancient classic of Taoist divination, the Treatise on Celestial Pathways. But of all the Taoist works, the unchallenged masterpiece is the great Tao Te Ching (The Way and the Power), a subtle classic of mystery and wonder. It is the treasure of darkness.

Lao Tzu and the Tao Te Ching
The Tao Te Ching celebrates the glory and mystery of the Tao. It has been translated more often and into more languages than has any other work of Asian literature, yet, like the Tao itself, its 5,000 Chinese characters dance away from would-be interpreters, eluding them. Perhaps it is that very feature that makes the Tao Te Ching such a fitting vehicle for the Tao.

Its author was the man we call Lao Tzu, the Ancient Master. And ancient he was, if we are to believe the legends that credit him with reaching the age of 160,200, or even more. Some reports aver that he lives still. The orthodox account of his life claims that he simply disappeared at the western rim of the world, riding his ox, although rival traditions have produced a couple of tomb sites. His first biographer, Ssu-ma Ch'ien, confesses that Lao Tzu was a "hidden sage," and that we can know for sure almost nothing about him. Ssu-ma Ch'ien was writing about 100 B.C.E., and we haven't learned anything more definite about Lao Tzu's life since then.

However, lack of factual knowledge hasn't stopped speculation about Lao Tzu's origins and life. Of his birth, the *T'ai p'ing ching ch'ao* (Essentials of the Classic of Peace and Balance) says, "The Great Lord of Longevity is named the Great Balance of the One True Wonderful Vigor, the Latter Sacred Lord of the Nine Mysteries of the High Pure Golden Tower of Heaven. . . . He is the fetus of the Great Void of the Jade Emperor. During the Time of the Lord of the Great Mystery and Completeness, in the fifteenth year of the reign of the Great Emperor, when *p'ing-tzu* was the Ruling Star of the year, his vapor was conceived." As for his mother, she was "a virgin . . . who lived in the Chamber of the Nine Mysteries, deep within the shady (Yin) valley. . . . She felt the movement of Yang and knew that she carried within her womb an enlightened being."

The young Lao Tzu expressed his enlightenment in fabulous ways. "At seven he learned to swallow the rays of light, eat the mist, and chew the tendrils of the sun. At the age of twenty-seven, his complexion radiated a golden glow. . . . At thirty-seven, he could use his humility and simplicity to file down sharpness. At forty-seven, he could use his throat to gather harmonious light. At fifty-seven, his saliva became a mysterious nectar and his works of merit became everywhere unhindered. At sixty-seven, he gave a treatise to the Latter Sacred Lord, who was also the Lord who had received the Tao before sky and earth were created. . . . At seventy, his longevity became limitless. . . . He had mastered the arts of immortality."

More prosaically (and probably more historically), it is asserted that he was born around 500 B.C.E., although this is uncertain. He was court librarian and archivist to the emperors of Chou (Zhou), whose dynasty lasted from 1027 to 256 B.C.E. The later Chou period was a fierce and turbulent time; Lao Tzu's life may have spanned the Spring and Autumn Period as well as the Period of Warring States, the worst of it. Both were times of great turmoil. Lao Tzu's homeland, the kingdom of Ch'u, was a strange, even savage place. Perhaps the odd combination of unsettled times and spooky environment provided exactly the right background for some of Lao Tzu's mystical, yet weirdly acute political insights. For although the Tao Te Ching is best known for its mystical speculations, it is also filled with tactical advice for soldiers and people in power.

Of his deeds very little is known. It is claimed (by Taoists) that he debated Confucius and won; it is said that he finally tired of civic life and escaped to the West through the Han-Ku Pass. Here he was stopped by the Gatekeeper of the Pass, Yin Hsi. Yin Hsi refused to let the quirky philosopher through until he wrote down all his wisdom. Lao Tzu, complied, retiring to the forest for three days to gather his thoughts into a little book. That slender volume is the Tao Te Ching. It reveals the essence of the Tao.

The Elusive Tao

What is this thing called Tao? Did you ever take a walk in the woods, and glimpse something from the tail of your eye? You turn quickly to catch it, but it's too late. We may be inclined to say that it's "gone," that it's "a figment of the imagination," or even, if we are schooled in the Celtic path of the Western Magical Tradition, decide that it was a wood sprite, an elf, or a fairy.

But Easterners have a different answer. They say that you've caught a flash of the Tao—not right in front of your eyes, for that's not the way it happens, but just a shadow and a whisper. That's the way the Tao comes to us—in shadows, whispers, and symbols. It is changing, transforming, and flowing. It sparkles, too. But it sparkles not like sunlight on a summer pond, but darkly, like the winter stars against the sky. The Tao is the light of darkness. It exists not to dispel the mysteries of night, but to make them manifest. The Tao is to mysticism what the TOE (Theory of Everything) is to contemporary physics. The Tao is the mothering source, the ultimate Immaterial out of which arose all substance. It is the underground spring, the engendering ocean, and the mirroring lake. It is the powerful, purifying waterfall. Whether invisible as the underground spring, or overwhelming as a storm-swept ocean, the Tao nourishes all beings and flows through all landscapes.

> *The Tao that can be spoken is not the eternal Tao.*
> *The named that be uttered is not the eternal name.*
> *The nameless is the fountain of heaven and earth.*
> *The named is the source of the Ten Thousand Things of Heaven*
> *   and Earth.*

> *Those who don't stare can see into the darkness.*
> *Those who stare see only the darkness.*

> *Manifest and Unmanifest,*
> *Darkness and Darkness within Darkness.*
> *The gate to all mystery.*

Since Taoism understands the world as a duality, in Yin and Yang, it shouldn't come as a surprise that we can think about the Tao in two different ways—a Yang way and a Yin way. The Yang Tao is the Manifest Tao, the Tao-that-can-be-spoken. It characterizes the whole world of becoming. Day and night, male and female, sun and moon are all features of the Manifest Tao, the visible, pulsating, ever-changing, glorious, miraculous world we live in.

But there's another, deeper Tao. This is the Unmanifest Tao, the deep Yin Tao beneath what we see and know, the Tao-that-cannot-be-spoken. The distinction between the Manifest and the Unmanifest Tao is so crucial to understanding Taoism that it comprises the very first chapter of the Tao Te Ching, printed at the beginning of this section. (The whole idea of the relationship between the Manifest and the Unmanifest Tao is strikingly similar to physicist David Bohm's theory of an "implicate/explicate order," in which the former is "enfolded" in the latter. As the implicate order "unfolds," it enters the world of everyday reality.)

All religious traditions yearn toward the Supreme. Christianity, Judaism, and Islam call on a Supreme Being. Hinduism and Buddhism seek a Supreme State of Being. Taoism, on the other hand, understands Being-ness itself, a Supreme Being-ness that pervades the cosmos, and of which all Beings partake. It is not a place, state, god, or condition. It can't be reached by effort or handed out by grace. It's the essential/existential quality of the cosmos itself. In its essential, original state, it is the Unmanifest Tao, unitary, hidden, and holy. In its existential, created condition, it is the Manifest Tao, the individuated Yin and Yang.

The Unmanifest Tao is unknowable. It is unknowable the same way the ultimate particles of the universe are unknowable. They might be deduced, imagined, or even experienced—but not "known" by the senses or even well comprehended by the mind. (As an analogy, we human beings manage to circulate our blood and metabolize our food, without necessarily understanding or even being conscious of the processes involved.)

The Unmanifest Tao is eternal. It isn't part of Time. Time is a process of individuation, the separating out of one instant from another, of naming and characterizing each particular moment. This is a feature of the manifest world, which proceeds instant by instant like a flowing river, symbol of the Manifest Tao. It declares itself, however, within the smallest flower and the largest galaxy. This Manifest Tao is the glory of the universe, the very presence of God. It is pure light, emanating from nonlight. But the Unmanifest Tao is both "one" and "none" and cannot be separated into particles of time or pieces of space.

The Unmanifest Tao is limitless. It knows no boundary; it takes up no space. It is indeed "darkness within darkness." The Unmanifest Tao holds the Manifest Tao as the empty bowl holds the water, and the darkness makes possible the light.

The Unmanifest Tao is nameless, and can be best indicated only by negatives such as "un-manifest," "un-knowable," and "time-less." Names are limitations. By calling something "blue," one excludes "red" and "yellow." The ultimate must forever be beyond names. The Manifest Tao takes on all the names and qualities of the universe: great and small, dark and light, bliss and sorrow.

The Unmanifest Tao is Being-ness without Being. If it were Being itself, it would be manifest. If it were non-Being, it could not be made manifest. It is Being-ness without Being and without non-Being, but bearing the potentiality of all.

The Unmanifest Tao is Yin; the Manifest Tao is Yang. The Unmanifest Tao is potential; the Manifest Tao is power. One proceeds from the other as a child proceeds from its mother. Yang is part of Yin, and Yin is part of Yang. The Unmanifest Tao gives birth to the Manifest, or what we call "Nature."

Nature and Symbol in Taoism

One of the most appealing aspects of Taoism is its celebration of nature. Taoist philosophy, painting, and poetry all view nature as a spiritual treasure, the Tao made visible. The flowing of the rivers and the circulation of the blood, the flight of birds and the flight of time, shining stars and shining deeds are seen as part of the same great and complex pattern. The power of the Manifest Tao blazes forth in the ever-changing, yet eternal rhythms of Nature. "You can never step into the same river twice," declared Heraclitus, that Taoist among the Greeks. But it remains the same river. The flowers of spring and the leaves of autumn reoccur—but not precisely—every year. Every snowflake is different, but we have no problem recognizing one when we see it. The magic of change and the mystery of identity remain delightfully insoluble. And it's delight, more than anything else, that the Tao recognizes as the glorious essential nature of nature.

Europeans saw the world of nature as "fixed" and tried to label it with the four elements of earth, water, air, and fire. But the Chinese saw revealed nature not as stasis, but as ceaseless activity. In fact, the Chinese ideogram *hsing,* used to represent the "elements" of metal, earth, water, wood, and fire, really means "activity." Modern physicists might agree that the basic units of the universe are better defined by what they "do" than by what they "are." This is one reason why reading Tarot using Taoist principles yields results that are both dynamic and in accordance with nature. The card patterns remain constant—but the cards themselves change and reveal their unlimited possibilities.

Taoist Alchemy

In the West, Taoists are most famous for their mysticism—the Yin side of their nature. But Taoists are magicians, as well. They are even alchemists, although their alchemy differs considerably from the Western brand.

Alchemy is classically understood as the magical transformation of one substance into another. In the West, alchemy sought to change lead into gold, an experiment doomed to failure. However, these early attempts at "transubstantiation" were the basis for modern chemistry. Taoist alchemists were also interested in gold, but in their case it was an ingredient—not the goal, which was to achieve immortality, or at least get as close to it as possible. Gold was considered the key substance, because in the words of Ko Hung, author of *Pao P'u Tzu,* "Put in the fire and melted a hundred times, gold never changes. Bury it, and it will not become corrupt, even to the end of time." Early alchemists treasured gold for its purity, its noncorruptibility—not for its market value.

The great philosophical Taoists practiced alchemy for two purposes. First, they used it to understand the processes of nature. In this, they were certainly in basic agreement with their Western counterparts. Their ultimate purpose in doing so, however, was religious and philosophical, not scientific. Taoist adepts had no interest in manipulating the environment to suit themselves. For them, the universe was a holy place.

Certainly not every Taoist practitioner of alchemy was of so high a mind or pure of soul. Petty and limited minds creep into every religious faith, and Taoism was no exception. But those who practiced alchemy to control the elements were as doomed to failure as the Western magicians who were unable to *see* what they merely observed. They swallowed arsenic to prolong their lives and died all the sooner. They placed their faith in the costly treasures of the earth rather than in the free gifts of the spirit.

The alchemists' second purpose was to transform themselves rather than the metals they saw as metaphors for the spirit. These are the true adepts, those who saw beyond lead and mercury and arsenic into the heart of the tiger and the soul of the dragon. They achieved momentous spiritual feats. They left those gifts to us in their paintings, their poetry, their philosophy, their meditation practices, and their arts of divination. These are ours to enjoy.

The most transformative of all substances, however, is not a costly metal like gold or silver, not a powerful one like lead or arsenic. It's water, the humblest and most abundant of all earthly materials. Water transforms itself naturally into steam, liquid, and ice. It needs no alchemist. It merely follows nature. And this is why the Tao Te Ching makes this natural, changeable, humble substance the uttermost symbol of the great Tao itself.

Tarot by Tao

The Tao Te Ching reveals the Unmanifest Tao; the Tarot reveals the Manifest Tao. The Tao makes the Tarot whole, and imbues it with naturalness and suppleness. Tarot without Tao can be rigid and formulaic. When you read Tarot by Tao, you follow the Tao; you let the Tao speak to you through the Tarot. You let the cards bring out what is within you.

Magical Tarot provides the answers the Quester seeks. Mystical Tarot provides the answers the reader does *not* seek, but that will manifest themselves under skillful, one-pointed meditation on the scripture.

This book will use both Eastern Mystical and Western Magical oracular traditions to provide the Tarot reader with a balanced way of divination. Not only does the plan include a way of reading the cards using ancient Taoist divination layouts, but it also supplies for each card a Taoist Meditation section from the Tao Te Ching, the most sacred text of Taoism. This journey will help us understand that the real power of the Tarot lies not only in a magical reading of the future, but also in a mystical understanding of the present.

For a Western reader, the Tao Te Ching seems oddly "structureless." It is a series of meditative poems on the nature of Being. It has no plot, no list of characters. (In this way, it is exquisitely complementary to the Tarot, which appears to have elements of both.) The Tarot presents us with a series of actions frozen in time. The Tao Te Ching flows like a river, from the mountains to the sea. It invites the reader to not merely gaze on it, but to follow.

Part Two

The Running River

3

Setting Forth

It's time to get started. Although it's customary in conventional Tarot readings to present and explain each card in "order" of its place in the Tarot, we are going to take a different path, the path of the Tao.

We'll follow the river of Tao by reading the Tao Te Ching, and looking at the Tarot card that accompanies each chapter or Meditation. The exceptions are the Meditations 1 (Setting Forth), 41 (Turning Point), and 81 (Return). These are focusing points not meant to have an assigned pictorial accompaniment. For these Meditations, the image source must be your own spirit. Like the Tarot, the Tao Te Ching has been edited in ages past—parts of the text were rearranged, and even reversed. But no matter how its chapters are ordered, the essential power of the Tao flows unhindered through the words. All apparent randomness reflects the inviting nature of the Tao; it circles and flows through the cosmos. You can step into it anywhere and follow its flow.

You may also find that a certain Meditation works better with a different Tarot card from the one I have chosen for it. If that's the case, don't be afraid to make the switch (and do the meditative work that connects the Meditation to the image). For the Tarot to work for you, you have to make it your own. When you follow the Tao, you set forth on a flowing river—the Tao Te Ching is your boat, and the Tarot your sail. But you steer the course.

Interpreting the Tarot: Magic and Mysticism

Every Tarot reading yields two interpretations. The first is the outer, magical reading. This can be quickly ascertained by looking at the "Magical Key" I have provided for each card. However, each reading also yields an esoteric, or a mystical, reading that can *only* be revealed by meditation on the cards. I have given a few hints about this meaning as a "Mystical Key."

The interpretations provided here are based on traditional, generally accepted meanings of each Tarot card, combined with the deeper insight offered by the Tao Te Ching. To provide the reader with the most comprehensive reading, I have not only consulted all the standard Tarot texts, but I have also gone to their sources—and beyond. These include Coptic texts of ritual power, and *The Hermetic Museum*, containing twenty-two (corresponding to the number of Major Arcana) of the most famous alchemical texts. This source was edited by A. E. Waite himself. In addition, I have studied the major divinatory and philosophical writings of Taoism, including the Taoist I Ching, the Secret of the Golden Flower, and the Chinese Classic oracle, the Ling Ch'i Ching, among others. A complete listing is provided in the Resources section. The result, I hope, is a precise, clear, and rich reading of the Tarot.

Let's go forth.

Notes on Reading

In certain places I use the words *negative reading* or *unfavorable aspect*. This means that the negative sense of the card should be applied when it appears in a spot designated "Conflicts, Dangers, and Limitations" or the like. A card should not be read for, say, "health" unless it appears in a Health slot, or another relevant position in a reading. For example, if the slot is labeled "Strengths," don't apply the negative reading of the card. If the slot concerns relationships, a negative "health" reading may only indicate that a health issue affects that relationship.

Meditation I

The Tao that can be spoken is not the eternal Tao.
The name that can be uttered is not the eternal name.
The Nameless is the fountain of heaven and earth.
The named is the source of the Ten Thousand Things of Heaven
  and Earth.

Those who don't stare can see into the darkness.
Those who stare see only the darkness.

Manifest and Unmanifest,
Darkness and Darkness within Darkness.
The gate to all mystery.

Mystical Key

The Tao Te Ching opens with a call to adventure, an adventure of the
spirit. Our journey begins with the Call of Mystery (1), the first step into
the journey of the spirit. Traditionally, this journey has been pictured in
terms of darkness and light—a journey from the darkness of ignorance
into the light of knowledge, the darkness of despair into the light of
hope. The Tao Te Ching is wiser than this, and the traveler of the Tao,
the mystic wayfarer, never shuns the shadows. Darkness is no enemy,
but the symbol of the Tao itself, for it reveals its mysteries only to those
who accept it.

This Meditation clearly reveals the Tao Te Ching for what it is—a
radically subversive document that undermines conventional values and
replaces hierarchy with openness, rigidity with fluidity, and answers with
questions—or silence.

For example, both culture and language commonly set up pairs:
white/black; light/dark; man/woman; large/small; strong/weak; day/night;
Yang/Yin; speech/silence. But, as deconstructionist linguistic philosopher Jacques Derrida has pointed out, these pairs are not simply opposites. If you look at each pair carefully, you will discover that the first
word has a "privileged" position in our collective psyche. This privileged
position may be unconscious, but it is surely there. Somehow, we "know"

that in some unfathomable way, light is better than darkness, strength better than weakness, and big better than small. Certainly speech is preferable to silence. These preferences have been ingrained in us for so long that we are barely aware of them—or, if we are, we feel that they are somehow inherent in the nature of things. The Tao Te Ching turns all that on its head.

By elevating the small, the weak, the soft, the dark, and the feminine, it subverts our standard way of looking at things. It makes us think, and question our assumptions. Yet because this viewpoint is so radically opposed to conventional thinking, it doesn't wind up by switching one set of values for another; the reader doesn't end up preferring what she formerly discarded. Rather, the Tao Te Ching's insistence on previously ignored values restores the natural, fluid balance of things as they are. Subversive political movements, like Feminism and Black Power, use the same approach; they exalt values that have been ignored or derided, proclaiming that black is in some ways "preferable to white," and feminine "better" than masculine. The result has been a shift away from the primacy of "white and male" to a richer, more balanced notion of the world. In political issues, however, the restored balance is due to competing interests, rather than to complementary aspects of being.

The Tao Te Ching accomplished the same thing thousands of years ago. It implicitly attacked not merely the Confucian political order, which attempted to repress it, but the very structure of the way we think about the universe. The Tao Te Ching "deconstructs" the "natural" order of the cosmos—not to replace that order with a different hierarchy, but to allow us merely to see that other orders are possible.

It does something else, too. It sets us up right from the beginning for the ultimate paradox, one that it spends the next eighty chapter-poems delineating, circling around, and rejoicing in. "The Tao that can be spoken is not the eternal Tao," it begins, subverting the usual pattern, which asserts that things come into being only with words. "The Tao that can be spoken is *not* the eternal Tao," it insists, disavowing its own achievement. The Tao Te Ching does not merely speak of paradox, it *is* paradox. The Tao Te Ching is the Tao in Words, a state of affairs it claims to be impossible. All the apparent strangeness and oddities of the Tao Te

Ching serve to open itself (and the reality it unfolds) to rich, multilayered interpretations.

The Tarot, too, is a deconstructionist document. Its meaning is not immutably anchored to the cards, but rather, fluid and contextual. The Tarot does pictorially what the Tao does in words: it proclaims the utter mystery of the cosmos, whose core meaning must be interpreted by the reader, not provided by its creator. The Tarot uses character fragments and symbols of universal human myths: the Moon, the High Priestess, the Magician, and so on. It takes these "mythemes," these building blocks of the collective unconscious, and effectively subverts them: Death can mean rebirth, and the Fool can mean wisdom. As the second Meditation says, "Long and short are a matter of perspective." Perspective, by its very nature, is limited and changing. In order to get the fullest possible view, we need to make a journey—and change with the change. This is why we begin with the Moon—the emblem of our changing universe.

THE MOON.

Meditation 2: The Moon (XVIII): Yin

All people under the Moon recognize beauty
When they see ugliness.
They understand that good
Is the other face of evil.

Manifest and unmanifest arise together.
Difficult and easy complement each other.
Long and short are a matter of perspective.
High and low are interdependent.
Voice and note make one melody.
What is behind and what is ahead flow together.

Thus the wise spirit makes his journey without
    traveling,
Teaches without words.

The Ten Thousand Things of this World
Rise and fall as they will.
The wise spirit lays no claim to them.

Creation without possession.
Accomplishment without credit.
Letting go . . .

This is the card of Spiritual Journey.

Mystical Key

We begin our spiritual journey with the Moon as our guide. She rides the highest heavens, yet her spirit is Yin. Because she always moves, always changes, and yet remains one, her element is Water, the symbol of the sacred Tao itself. (Two other common symbols of the Tao are the Infant and the Valley.) Like the Tao, she is sometimes manifest, sometimes hidden. But, visible or invisible, she is never lost to us. She pulls the tides of our blood, and times the rhythms of our bodies. She leads us unfailingly, yet she changes constantly. She reminds us that change lies at the very heart of the cosmos, yet the change is neither arbitrary, nor chaotic, but guided by powerful, incompletely apprehended laws. This is part of what the Chinese mean by *hsiang sheng,* the interdependence of all living things, Yin embracing the Yang, the Moon swallowing the Sun.

All of us, all species, dwell beneath the Moon; we are all brothers. Not only is the howling dog related to the howling fox, but both are brothers to the voiceless lobster—and to us. (The lobsterlike creature in the picture was added in the mid 1500s, as were the more distant towers. The dog and fox showed up a century later.)

Even as the Moon is cradled within the Sun and reflects her light, we are nourished by the selfsame light, and yearn for the same ends. In the same way, the Moon, no matter in what phase she appears to us, is the same Moon.

The wise spirit is one who recognizes the relativity, growth, and change of this universe. She knows that whatever changes cannot be possessed, and that worthwhile work is accomplishment without expectation of reward. One cannot flow with the river by gripping its banks.

Magical Key

Character: The Moon has the most complex and bewildering character of any card in the Tarot. She is intellectually brilliant, has great insight, and may be gifted in music. Although the Moon is usually loving and compassionate, she may be seen as moody, changeable, and faithless by others, who fail to comprehend her true nature.

Current Circumstances: Things are in flux. A woman is being neglected. Bad luck from the East; good luck from the West. It's important now to mix with other people.

Conflicts, Dangers, and Limitations: There is danger and deception from unknown enemies. Caution is advised; things may not be as they appear.

Career: The Moon experiences many different phases in her career, but the overall outlook is good. The Moon should work closely with colleagues, and be careful to explain her thought processes to more literal-minded and less imaginative people.

Friends and Family: Although the Moon is attractive to others, they may view her with suspicion, since she is more complex than they are.

Finances and Possessions: This is a good time to take advantage of the cyclical nature of the market.

Health Concerns: Respiratory system. The Moon should try not to become overexcited.

Romance: This is a wonderful card for love and romance, but not necessarily for permanent union.

Travel: A journey to the ocean or mountains will have many spiritual benefits. An ocean trip is good for romance and healing, while a trip to the mountains may have deeper spiritual benefits.

Decision: Don't waffle any longer. Go ahead and take a chance.

Future Events and Spiritual Achievements: Success in literary endeavors. Expect a benefit in two or three days. The Moon will make a spiritual journey to achieve understanding.

Omens and Talismans: This is a beneficial, protective card for women, and for those engaged in agriculture or marine activities.

> Animal Spirit: Tiger, Wolf
> Bird Spirit: Nighthawk, Eagle
> Color: Red, Orange, Gold
> Plant: Wheat, Moonflower
> Tree: Alder, Pine
> Gemstone: Garnet, Moonstone
> Metal: Silver
> Direction: West
> Place: Sea
> Season: Autumn

QUEEN of WANDS.

Meditation 3: Queen of Wands

Not exalting the talented
Prevents jealous quarreling.
Not hoarding rare treasures
Stills coveting and stealing.
Not tantalizing people with the unattainable
Quenches the ragings of the heart.

The wise leader rules
By emptying the grasping heart
And filling the empty stomach.
By softening ambition
And strengthening bone.

When the mind is empty of knowing
And the heart is free from desire,

The intellectuals will be unable to act.
Then all will be well.

This is the card of Nurturing.

Mystical Key

This wise and ironic Meditation reminds us to put first things first: a full belly and a quiet mind are more conducive to spiritual wellness than ambition, knowledge, and empty actions. The nurturing Queen of Wands rules over natural creation and the creative spirit. The natural world of Yin and Yang is represented by the Sunflower (Yang Sun) and Black Cat (Yin Moon). The Sunflower represents the forces of light and the Black Cat represents the forces of darkness. The lions on her throne and behind her represent her strength.

The Queen of Wands and the accompanying Meditation show us that the spiritual journey starts with the natural body. It is only when the body is at ease that one can transcend attachments, and fulfill oneself in the Tao. Only by "filling the belly" can one be ready to go further. This is a concept very different from religious traditions that stress self-denial, asceticism, and deprivation. From a Taoist view, such practices are unnatural and opposed to the flowing of the Tao. For Taoists, many Hindus and Buddhists and Christians pay too much attention to desires by trying so hard to overcome them. Nurturing the soul and the body is the way to bring them both to perfection, and to walk the path of Tao, which supports body and spirit fully.

Magical Key

Character: This card represents one who knows that the secret of dealing with people is to know their true needs, and to fulfill them. The Queen is philosophical, knowledgeable, and practical. She is generally sympathetic and a good counselor. She may be versed in legal sciences, medicine, or even philosophy. However, the adaptable Queen can turn into a vengeful, dangerous enemy, who may be jealous. Although the Queen is intelligent, she can be led off the path of the Tao.

Current Circumstances: The help of powerful people can turn away overt threats. The past contains wisdom the Queen may have forgotten.

Conflicts, Dangers, and Limitations: The Queen needs to be more objective in her expectations of others.

Career: A partner is turning out to be a disappointment. The time may have come to separate.

Friends and Family: For parents, the card is a reminder to be especially nurturing toward their children.

Finances and Possessions: A gift of money or profit in commercial activities is indicated. However, the Queen should not concentrate on it to the exclusion of her health.

Health Concerns: The Queen should pay attention to her physical health, which at the current time is more important than getting ahead in the world. With proper care, this can be a card of great longevity.

Romance: A loved one is distressed and needs to speak with the Queen.

Travel: Travel to a city is advised. The cultural benefits will be important enough to offset encounters with unpleasant people.

Decision: Consider the welfare of others when making an impending decision.

Future Events and Spiritual Achievements: The Queen will attain pleasure, peace, and comfort.

Omens and Talismans: This is a favorable card for a poet, or for those engaged in agriculture. The Queen will attain spiritual advancement.

    Animal Spirit: Lion, Black Cat
    Bird Spirit: Swallow, Owl
    Color: Pale Rose, Green
    Plant: Sunflower, Holly
    Tree: Elder, Tamarisk
    Gemstone: Yellow Diamond, Ruby
    Metal: Steel
    Direction: East

Place: House
Season: Summer, Autumn

THE MAGICIAN.

Meditation 4: The Magician (I): Yang

The Tao is an empty cup.
It can be filled, but never will it overflow.
It is the utter source of the Ten Thousand Things.
Deep, unfathomable.

Blunt the sharp sword,
Soften the brilliance,
Mingle with earth.

The Tao is the Way
And the source of the Way
Mysterious of birth.
Yet bringing forth the All.

This is the card of Transformation.

Mystical Key

The Magician is the Master of Yang. He opens our way into the Magical world. In the traditional picture, he stands at a table, the tools of his trade laid out before him. These are the elements represented by the four suits of the Minor Arcana—Cups, Pentacles, Swords, and Wands. The red of the Magician's robe stands for Fire, the transforming element of the Major Arcana.

The viewer's eye is drawn away from the implements, as the Magician intends. We follow the Magician's Yang right arm upward toward the magic wand, and thence to the Yang heavens. Infinity rides just over his head. The infinite heavens are both the ultimate source of his power, and his final goal. The serpent, symbol of Wisdom and Life and Death, coils slyly around his waist. His Yin hand, in a classic Eastern gesture, points to earth. "Mingle with earth," says the Meditation, proclaiming the unity of Yin and Yang. In the magical alchemical tradition, the gesture means "As above, so below," not only linking the two spheres, but in effect *commanding* Heaven to do the will of Earth. This may seem very "magical" and indeed it is, but it also reminds us of the Taoist notion of the primacy of the Yin. "Soften the brilliance, mingle with earth."

But there is mystery here, too. The feet of the Magician's table are hidden by an entwined tangle of brilliant red roses and white lilies, which together represent life, death, and the passionate spirituality of the Magician. These are emblems of the Ten Thousand Things of this World, which the Magician, as the embodiment of the Manifest Tao, ushers into being. A richly fruited vine acts as a pulled-up drapery or stage curtain. Although the Magician is on stage, his secrets remain hidden. Around his waist is the Uroborus, the snake that bites its own tail, which symbolizes an eternal circle of renewal. It is also a specific and ancient alchemical symbol, representing the closed, cyclical process of heating, evaporation, cooling, condensation, and purifying of a liquid.

It's no accident that the Magician is the first numbered card of the Tarot. He is the embodiment of the whole Western magical tradition, with its emphasis on outward rather than inward transformation. In a Taoist reading, the Magician is master of the Manifest Tao. He is the master magician, who knows the secret of the empty vessel that is never filled, the dead branch that flowers, the sword whose point is hidden, the pentacle with its blazing star on top and its darkness beneath. (In Taoist ritual, the sword is never sharpened.)

But even the Magician may not understand the true source of his power. He understands, at least theoretically, the Yin and Yang, but may not realize how, as unity, they are the One Force. When the sharp swords are blunted, and the brilliant things of heaven are mingled with the dark things of the earth, the transforming power of the Manifest Tao reveals itself. The obscure overcomes the sharpest weapons. The Magician is brilliant, but not always wise.

Magical Key

Character: The Magician is usually young, with tremendous
potential. He is charismatic, intelligent, creative, self-
confident, self-disciplined, and powerful. Secretly, however,
he is something of an introvert. He is heir to great

intellectual or material wealth. In a negative aspect, obsessed with self or power, he can be manipulative. It is important for the Magician to develop his higher qualities.

Current Circumstances: The Magician is usually a very auspicious sign. However, the Magician must deal with powerful inherent Yang forces that can obscure the inner Yin. The "obvious" answer may not be the correct one. In an unfavorable aspect, the card means that the Magician should pay more attention to detail, and learn to focus the powers of his concentration. Dreams are prophetic.

Conflicts, Dangers, and Limitations: Beware of tricks. Apparent transformations cannot change essential truths.

Career: The Magician is a card of great power, often associated with scientists, physicians, politicians, and people who can make a difference in the physical world.

Friends and Family: The Magician is the dominant member of his family, and the center of a circle of friends, who are somewhat in awe of him. However, he has at most only one or two intimates.

Finances and Possessions: Favorable, but too much success and power can obscure real values.

Health Concerns: Ears and digestive system. The Magician does well under the care of a holistic healer.

Romance: A favorable card for a romantic relationship and marriage.

Travel: The Magician is at home anywhere, a great traveler. Adventure and educational trips are indicated.

Decision: An important, perhaps deceptively simple, choice looms ahead. The Magician must be careful to choose the ethical path.

Future Events and Spiritual Achievements: The Seeker will experience a transformation that will result in tranquillity. Many people will follow his lead.

Omens and Talismans: This is a favorable card for those in the arts and entertainment, as well as for those in science.

    Animal Spirit: Fox, Dragon
    Bird Spirit: Phoenix, Cuckoo

Color: Black, Celadon
Plant: Lotus, Chrysanthemum
Tree: Lemon, Cherry
Gemstones: Alexandrite, Sapphire
Metal: Quicksilver (Mercury)
Direction: East
Place: Cliffs
Season: Summer

Meditation 5: Seven of Wands

The universe is ruthless.
In its regard, the Ten Thousand Things are like
  straw dogs.
The wise spirit, too, is ruthless.
For him, all human beings are straw dogs.

The space between the earth and heaven
Is like a bellows.
As it empties,
It becomes full of power.

As words are spent
The empty self within
Shines forth.

This is the card of Potential.

Mystical Key:
The meaning of this Meditation is complex. The universe seems full of activity, objects, animals, and people. But what are they, really? They are like straw dogs, unreal entities whose appearance masks the cosmos, which is "empty." This may seem like a nihilist doctrine. But in Taoist thought, emptiness is power. And what does it mean to say that the wise spirit regards all human beings as straw dogs? Does it mean that the wise spirit doesn't care? Of course not. (See Med. 27.) It means

that wisdom recognizes the equality of all earthly beings and that the space between things on earth and heaven is an opening. The ruthless wisdom of the wise knows that the way to gain the true self is to lose the false one. For the wise spirit to understand the universe, he must be like the universe. Just as the universe contains all things, the wise spirit contains all beings. Ruthless wisdom means to understand that true Being emerges only as beings empty themselves of their "straw dogs."

The great Taoist text, the Book of Harmony and Balance, has a passage about cultivating this openness, which it identified with bamboo. Bamboo has a hollow ("humble" in the Taoist view) center, but it is this very hollowness that gives it its supple strength. Strength and modesty are both suggested by this card. Openness, says the text, is the "great root of the world."

The way to fight evil is to think of oneself as a bamboo wand, open and flexible, but never breaking. Who is the enemy? Lü Yen once wrote that the unenlightened spent all their days battling with "the six senses." (Just as the Chinese had one more element than did the traditional Western scheme, they also had six rather than five senses. The six senses are represented by the opposing wands.) The battle, suggests Lü Yen, will continue until the fighter recognizes that shapes and forms are completely empty, like bamboo. When the empty self shines forth, the battle is won.

Magical Key

Character: The Seven of Wands is drawn to empirical sciences (the six senses), but needs to look beyond them. He is a very private person, but he has great courage. His values are attacked, but he must maintain them. He is in the right, and will succeed if he can maintain his focus and not give in to doubt. He must remember that the universe is ruthless, and he must be ruthless too. The Seven may also be a gifted speaker or singer.

Current Circumstances: A lot of quarreling, uncertainty, and infighting is present. In order to prevail, the Seven must rise above it. Another way of looking at it is that the Seven is caught among the "straw dogs" of this world; and he must learn to fight them by looking beyond them. A spiritual or moral mentor is of great help now. This may be the time to follow instead of trying to lead.

Conflicts, Dangers, and Limitations: The Seven is very vulnerable right now. Someone is attempting to make trouble, and this card can represent a factional fight—the inevitable struggle among the "Ten Thousand Things." The Seven should not compromise his values.

Career: Good chance for advancement. Supervise subordinates carefully.

Friends and Family: Someone close to the Seven is untrustworthy. It's important to sort out the real from the artificial.

Finances and Possessions: Becoming too attached to possessions will result in their loss.

Health Concerns: Eyes. Someone close to the Seven may be pregnant (it's a girl!). The Seeker is basically healthy and athletic; however, alcohol may present a problem.

Romance: The Seven has many love affairs, but has problems choosing a lifemate.

Travel: A dangerous journey by land is indicated.

Decision: The time to act has not yet come. Think twice about going ahead with this plan. Once the Seven makes the decision, it's important to carry it through.

Future Events and Spiritual Achievements: The Seven will attain satisfaction and power.

Omens and Talismans: The Seven will attain consistency. This is an auspicious card for someone in the military.

> Animal Spirit: Pig, Viper
> Bird Spirit: Crow, Cardinal
> Color: Green, Scarlet, or Crimson
> Plant: Seaweed, Wintergreen
> Tree: Cherry, Bamboo
> Gemstone: Topaz, Sapphire
> Metal: Copper
> Direction: Southeast
> Place: Desert
> Season: Winter, Spring

Meditation 6: The Empress (III): Yin

THE EMPRESS.

The valley spirit never dies.
It is the mysterious Feminine.
Her gateway is the source of heaven
And the root of earth.

It is a gossamer veil
Barely glimpsed.
But just touch it—
It's forever.

This is the card of Nature and Beauty.

Mystical Key

The Empress, who is the embodiment of the feminine Valley Spirit, the mysterious woman, sits on her throne. The Empress is one of the most powerful Yin cards in the pack. She represents nature, fertility, renewal, and abundance. A waterfall, one of the most auspicious of Yin symbols, flows behind her, pouring into the valley. The "veil barely glimpsed" refers us back to the almost hidden, yet transparent waterfall, symbol of the Tao. "Her gateway [which can be seen as a sexual symbol] is the source of heaven and the root of earth." (In Kabbalistic interpretations, the Hebrew letter for this card is "Daleth," which means "gateway" or "door," thus reinforcing the Taoist reading.)

The Empress's dress is adorned with pomegranates, symbol of womanhood, generosity, and fertility. She wears a necklace of pearls, and is crowned with the zodiac stars. The female symbol, inscribed on a heart, rests at her feet. The wheat fields before her symbolize fertility and abundance. (In fact, the figure of the "grain mother" is exceedingly common in mythology.) Grain itself is a symbol of rebirth. Notice the almost invisible rabbit to her left. This is a lunar fertility symbol in both Eastern and Western traditions.

The Empress is the archetypal mother, a generous and powerful person, who holds the keys to spiritual richness and abundant life. She is able to reconcile opposing views (heaven and earth), and is a good mediator.

Magical Key

Character: The Empress may be someone in the medical profession or the arts. She is usually gracious, kind, merciful, life-affirming, peaceful, and loving. She is a source of strength for everyone around her. The Empress is an extrovert, and cares deeply about others. Without correct balance in her life, however, the powerful Empress can be wild, dangerous, and uncontrollable.

Current Circumstances: The Empress creates beauty wherever she goes, even in adverse circumstances.

Conflicts, Dangers, and Limitations: There is danger in the environment. The Empress must not allow subjective desires and trivialities to get in the way of a reasonable choice. More self-discipline is required. There may be deep sorrow, and although the Empress is not responsible for it, she is involved. An older man may be in trouble.

Career: The Empress won't get any help in advancing in her career and will have to rely on herself. It may be better to be content in the position she is in without looking for a more "public" one.

Friends and Family: Marriage and children are important to the Empress, who has the support of, or is representative of, the Great Mother.

Finances and Possessions: Great riches are a possibility. The Empress should take great care of her home now, or she may lose something valuable. Precautions should be taken against fire.

Health Concerns: Spiritual, as well as medical, help for health problems is beneficial. The Empress needs more sleep. Someone close to the Empress is pregnant.

Romance: The Empress may be prey to romantic fantasies.

Travel: A cottage in the mountains or by a river for a relaxing vacation.

Decision: If the decision involves a move, the decision should be yes. All others no.

Future Events and Spiritual Achievements: The Empress will achieve detachment.

Omens and Talismans: This is an auspicious card for a teacher
   or healer.

> Animal Spirit: Salamander, Serpent.
> Bird Spirit: White Eagle, Raven
> Color:Coral, Black
> Plant: Lavender, Buddleia
> Tree: Elder, Apple
> Gemstone: Jade, Aquamarine
> Metal: Gold
> Direction: South
> Place: Ocean
> Season: Summer

Meditation 7: Ten of Wands

Heaven endures forever.
Earth abides always.
What is their secret?
Their secret is this—
They don't exist for themselves,
But for others.

The wise spirit is like this.
He puts himself last.
He moves forward.
He stays centered.
He lets go of his self.
And fulfills his soul.

This is the card of Selflessness.

Mystical Key

At first sight, the figure on the card seems overburdened; his back is
bowed and his head is hidden as he carries his load of wood. But a closer
look and a reading of the Meditation tell us something entirely different.
The Wands are flowering, symbolizing that the burden the figure bears is

the burden of life. The fact that the Wands are crossed shows that the burden is complex and interconnected. One Taoist text, *Twenty-four Essentials for Students,* reminds us not to be afraid of hardship. "If you are afraid of hardship, you will never enter the real."

The figure carries the Wands toward a city, indicating that they are for the use of others. Notice that he does not carry the Wands on his back, as he would a burden, but leans forward, embracing them, as if they are a precious gift. And so they are. His face is hidden in the gift he bears, for his is the face of selflessness.

The number of this Meditation is 7, a number of power and transforming magic. In the same way, those who work for others perform a creative act of transformation. Thus the wise spirit "puts himself last," and at the same time, "moves forward." The eternal sky and earth stretch beyond and below, showing us that the way of selfless action is the way of the Tao.

Magical Key

Character: The Ten of Wands is noble and self-sacrificing, generous to a fault. He may feel abandoned or helpless. New events bring new responsibilities, but he does not fear them. Because he gives fearlessly of himself, the Tao will be reborn within him.

Current Circumstances: There is pain, which can be healed only by spiritual guidance. Affairs are very difficult at the time. There is also a sense of anticipation.

Conflicts, Dangers, and Limitations: A danger of laziness. This card can also represent oppression from others or selfishness within the Ten of Wands. The world may be hostile to the Ten's ideas. Undue severity is causing a problem.

Career: The Ten spends his career serving others. It may be that he is unappreciated by coworkers, although the Ten is too wise to allow this to bother him unduly.

Friends and Family: The family is peaceful and tranquil. A person not of high social status will have a beneficial effect on the Ten.

Finances and Possessions: The Ten will succeed through hard work.

Health Concerns: Digestion. The Ten will recover completely and unexpectedly from an illness. Mineral water, which represents the body in the spirit, is beneficial. If someone close to the Seeker is pregnant, it will be a boy.

Romance: The Ten will be reunited with one from whom he has been separated.

Travel: Travel to the southwest would be auspicious now. It will have many benefits for both health and business.

Decision: This is the time to listen to the opinions of others, and to take a consensus.

Future Events and Spiritual Achievements: Good fortune in small matters.

Omens and Talismans: This is a fortunate card for people in social work or teaching. It is also auspicious for engaged couples.

    Animal Spirit: Wolf, Ox
    Bird Spirit: Swan, Oriole
    Color: Black, Dark Green
    Plant: Clover, Herbs
    Tree: Catalpa, Dogwood
    Gemstone: Quartz, Pearl
    Metal: Quicksilver (Mercury)
    Direction: Southeast
    Place: Plain
    Season: Spring

THE STAR.

Meditation 8: The Star (XVII): Yin

The highest virtue is like water.
It helps all people.
It doesn't set itself up against anyone.
It flows to the lowest places,
Rejected by men.
Thus, it is like the Tao.

When you choose your dwelling
Choose level ground.
In cultivating your spirit
Dive deep.
In relationships with others,
Be soft.

In speech, be honorable.
In ruling, be just.
In business, be competent.
In action—watch your timing.
Those of the greatest virtue
Find no fault with their current place.

This is the card of Hope and Faith.

Mystical Key

This is Meditation Eight, the Eight-Pointed Star. (Note also eight stars in the picture.) The Star is the card of highest and deepest Hope. Eight is the magical number of regeneration.

Although the name of the card is the Star, both the Meditation and the card feature water. This is because both water and star mean life and hope; they are the Yin and Yang of the human condition. "The highest virtue is like water. It helps all people." Thus both the Tarot card and the Meditation link the concept of highest and lowest.

The controlling image of the card is a naked woman kneeling and pouring water. (This is the first naked figure to appear in either the conventional Tarot card order, or in the Taoist Meditation order.) Nakedness represents the pristine human condition of innocence and equality. Her presence indicates that the way of the Tao does not refer only to inanimate nature, but also to the human component of the cosmos, which nonetheless needs to be "like water." Water and starlight stream "downward" to us.

Connecting water and sky in the picture is the green tree; stretching between earth and heaven, it is the tree of life and hope. Its roots are deep in the earth, but it bears on its branches a bird, the primordial symbol of the spirit. The bird's species has been variously drawn by different designers, but Waite chose the ibis for his bird, which represents immortality.

Many Tarot experts consider the Star to be an aspect of the High Priestess. One foot rests on the water, and the other on land, but neither is in real connection with either element. For the Star is a creature of the spirit and the air. She pours the water on the land, and back again to the water, like the rain, for hope will always return to its source. Water flows to the lowest, and even in the darkest circumstances, Hope remains alive. "Rejected by men. Thus, it like the Tao." For the world also rejects the Tao, even if it cannot avoid it. Water gives life to the Ten Thousand Things, including Hope. "When you choose your dwelling, choose level ground. In cultivating your spirit, dive deep." Water is the source of life and strength—the shining Eight-Pointed Star is our goal and aspiration. And it dwells within. "Those of greatest virtue find no fault with their current place."

Whenever the Star appears in a layout, in whatever position, she casts the light of hope on the entire reading.

Magical Key

Character: The Star is loved for her wisdom, steadfastness, and spiritual strength. She has great powers of will, and considerable literary talent. No matter how much the Star works and cooperates with others, she always maintains her individuality. She is a person who inspires everyone with hope and faith.

Current Circumstances: There is much shouting and movement at the current time, but the serene Star is able to rise above it. Many of the problems stem from disorganization. There will be change for the better within three years.

Conflict, Dangers, and Limitations: Unknown to her, the Star is on the brink of the abyss, but her strong faith will pull her through any difficulties. The Star should not believe everything she is told and should not get mixed up in a tangled situation; it will lead to grief.

Career: The Star may be better off in another job, and should pay attention to a good lead in this regard.

Friends and Family: Don't cultivate one friend to the exclusion of others.

Finances and Possessions: Corruption may cause severe losses.

Health Concerns: General weakness. Seek competent medical help.

Romance: This is a fortunate card for love and romance.

Travel: The Star should consider a trip back to her birthplace.

Decision: Options should be kept open. Dreams provide inspiration.

Future Events and Spiritual Achievements: An important opportunity awaits. Good luck comes from the east. Prospects are good and the highest hopes are justified, as long as they follow in accordance with the sacred Tao. In a negative aspect, it means that hopes are wrongly placed, but this card encourages the Star to never give up.

Omens and Talismans: This is an auspicious card for people in the service professions and for students.

    Animal Spirit: Stag, Dragon
    Bird Spirit: Ibis, Crane
    Color: White, Dark Gray
    Plant: Star-Shaped Flowers, Lotus
    Tree: Alder, Birch
    Gemstone: Pearl, Star Sapphire
    Metal: Quicksilver (Mercury)
    Place: Lake, Pool
    Direction: North
    Season: Winter

Meditation 9: Temperance (XIV): Yin

Better to carry a chalice half-filled
Than to let it run over.
If you oversharpen a blade,
You'll soon blunt the edge.

If your home is overloaded
With gold and jade
You cannot protect it.

Riches, honors, and arrogance
Carry the seeds
Of their own destruction.

Enough is enough.
When the work is done,
Retire.

This is the card of Moderation.

Just as the Star is the first naked figure in the deck, Temperance is the first winged figure to appear in either the numbered Tarot pack or in the alternate Taoist path we are taking. This is significant, for although the first card we looked at, the Moon, is a celestial symbol, Temperance, as the first winged figure, is able to *transfer* us from one sphere to another.

Like so many of the Tarot cards, it speaks of transformation. This card has traditionally been linked with alchemy, as can be surmised from the magical pouring of the liquid from one cup into the next. Temperance, too, is an alchemical virtue, since it "tempers" the spirit, and keeps it in balance. The sun in the background is emblematic of fire, the alchemical element.

The winged figure pours liquid from one chalice into another. (In the Marseilles pack, the pouring cup is blue and the receiving cup red, signifying, at least to mythographer Joseph Campbell, the passing of the physical into the spiritual world.) Temperance stands between water and land, earth and sky. The person who practices Temperance touches all three bases (symbolized by the triangle the figure bears on his chest.) The shining disk on the forehead stands for Truth. Notice that the figure seems almost careless as he pours the precious liquid from one cup to another. "If your home is overloaded with gold and jade, you cannot protect it." Thus the Meditation reminds us of the spiritual alchemy that takes place as we shift our attention from outer gold to inner riches, and as we move from one life stage to another.

The figure pours the liquid from one chalice to another, dissolving one into the other, getting rid of the notion of selfish individualism. It is in the blending that the magic comes. Behind the figure grow irises, symbol of the rainbow, itself a mix of colors. The sun in the background is also a crown, suggesting that Temperance is indeed the crowning glory.

Miserly saving is as bad as overindulgence. This means miserly saving up of one's life, too. Temperance is balance. The wise spirit knows when enough is enough.

Temperance is a badly abused virtue in Western culture. We are much fonder of excess. In fact, for much of Western literature, the main paradigm is the journey of the hero, even the over-reacher. For the Tarot, writer Hajo Banzhaf has written a beautiful, scholarly, and exciting book on the subject: *Tarot and the Journey of the Hero.*

Poet William Blake voiced this notion in his "Proverbs of Heaven and Hell": "You never know what is enough until you know what is more than enough." Robert Browning said that "man's reach must exceed his grasp—or what's a heaven for?" ("Andrea Del Sarto.")

The Tao is wiser than this, for it honors this humble, "negative" virtue above all else. (Temperance is also one of the four cardinal virtues of classical times.) By its very restraint, negativity, and emptiness, Temperance is also the virtue of "mixing." The right mix yields the elixirs of life and death; it is the secret of alchemy. When we think of "tempering" a sword, for example, we think of subjecting the blade to the transforming fire, which hardens and purifies the metal. Additionally, the figure here is presented as androgynous, a mixing of the male and female, the Yang and Yin.

The function of Temperance in a person's life is to be the guardian, watchful caretaker of the spirit. "When the work is done, retire." "Retire" can also mean to "hide oneself." Thus it carries two meanings: "retire" in the sense of letting it be and going off to enjoy yourself, or in the sense of hiding oneself from the work so that one doesn't claim possession of it. This is Temperance—not only in refraining from too much alcohol, sex, and food, but also in maintaining a balanced approach to work and acquisitions. This is the ninth Meditation in the Tao Te Ching, and the number nine (three times three) is the most important symbolic number in the Tao. It is fitting, therefore, that Temperance, which plays such a key role in Taoist philosophy, corresponds to Meditation 9. (In the Tarot deck, Temperance bears number 14, which corresponds to the number assigned to the King in the Lesser Arcana. It is a culminating number.)

Like the Star, Temperance has one foot in water and one on land. But here, his foot is actually submersed in the water, indicating a deeper connection with the Tao itself. His other foot, while touching the earth, is on tiptoe—showing his connection with the heavens above. Temperance is the proper mixing of the spheres, and he who knows how to properly temper earth with water and heaven lives wisely indeed. These are not separate realms, but constantly interpenetrating levels.

Magical Key

Character: Temperance is undergoing a transformative process
in the pursuit of higher knowledge. Temperance has always
been kind in the mundane sense, but is now progressing to
a more spiritual, less material state. Balance is important
during this period. Temperance may have artistic ability. In
a negative aspect, Temperance suggests miserliness and
overattachment to and protection of one's possessions.
Temperance may not fully understand his own nature.

Current Circumstances: There is laughter and desire, but
someone is seeking vengeance. The path to fulfillment is
difficult, but infinitely rewarding. Temperance would do
well to join an organization that is dedicated to furthering
the goals he believes in.

Conflicts, Dangers, and Limitations: Someone may be conspiring
against and attempting to tear down Temperance.

Career: For older workers, this is a good time to think about
retirement, and for younger ones, this card is a reminder to
begin making plans for that retirement.

Friends and Family: Temperance is a mysterious figure to friends and family, and is often misunderstood. Harsh language should be avoided.

Finances and Possessions: Using old-fashioned methods will bring about a good income.

Health Concerns: Gastrointestinal system. This is an auspicious card for health, but in an unfavorable aspect, it counsels the Seeker to be more moderate.

Romance: Temperance will enter into a romantic relationship with one who is both good-looking and good.

Travel: Not auspicious right now, but when the time comes, it should be a mind-opening experience.

Decision: Don't hurry; the moment is not ripe.

Future Events and Spiritual Achievements: Temperance will receive a small, but sincere gift, and turn it into something great.

Omens and Talismans: This is an auspicious card for those in finance, visual arts, and the military.

    Animal Spirit: Horse, Sheep
    Bird Spirit: Peacock, Dove
    Color: Yellow, Brown
    Plant: Daylily, Peony
    Tree: Alder, Oak
    Gemstone: Malachite, Beryl
    Metal: Gold
    Direction: West
    Place: Garden
    Season: Late Summer

Meditation 10: Two of Cups

Spirit and body-energy—
By choosing just one,
How can you avoid fission?
Gather them together,
You become supple as a newborn child.

Cleanse the deep water,
Purify the inner vision,
Emerge without stain.

Love all, govern well,
Dispense with clever actions.
Open and close the Gates of Heaven
As a mother bird protects her nest.
Understand all,
Reach far,
Stay still,
Know by not-Knowing.

The Tao gives birth and nourishes us.
It bears, but it does not own.
It works, but it demands no credit.
It leads, but it never dominates.

This is the card of Internal Harmony.

Mystical Key

This card illustrates the perfect relationship between Yin and Yang, woman and man, body and spirit, and the Tao and Humanity. It is the natural result of Temperance, the preceding card. The Taoist says, "Balance is the mainstay of the world, harmony is the way the world arrives at the Tao."

It is essential that spirit and body, represented by the two characters, live in unified harmony. This is a cleansing experience from which the participants can "emerge without stain." They nourish their relationship as a mother bird guards her nest. Bearing without owning, working and demanding no credit, leading but never dominating—this is the way of the river and the Tao. The winged lion's head hovering above the lovers represents the strength of incorporeality or spirit. This is the strength that "leads but never dominates." The caduceus of intertwining serpents crowned by wings represents sexual union.

Magical Key

Character: The Two of Cups is active, energetic, and adaptable. She understands herself well and is comfortable in her knowledge. She is remarkably stable, with a well-deserved sense of her own worth. The Two is also tenderhearted, especially where animals are concerned. The Two cooperates very well with others.

Current Circumstances: The Two must hold on to what she has achieved, which is more valuable than she knows. The Two is rich in spiritual gifts and in the love and honor of those around her. This is a good time to think about their psychological and spiritual needs.

Conflicts, Dangers, and Limitations: An inferior person is trying to undermine the Two gradually. Lies are harmful. The Two is very sensitive to criticism.

Career: The Two can succeed in business, journalism, or politics. The Two of Cups works best in situations where she can be a behind-the-scenes player. The Two does not seek the limelight and is not comfortable in it. The Two makes the best of workers, one who does more than her share, but also one who can get the best from others.

Friends and Family: In general, the Two of Cups makes a great "best friend" and confidante. The Two is loyal, affectionate, and wonderful to be with.

Finances and Possessions: Possible financial trouble. The Two should to talk to her banker.

Health Concerns: Nervous system and muscles; lungs. The Two should take plenty of exercise, and not be lazy.

Romance: This is an auspicious card for a married couple or people in a committed relationship. It shows that the two have achieved a balanced, loving, equal relationship without ownership or domination. In an unfavorable aspect, it might mean trouble in a relationship caused by a parent, or an excessive attachment to a parent. The problems should be easily overcome. "The Tao gives birth and nourishes us. It bears, but it does not own."

Travel: Travel is very dangerous right now.

Decision: Don't hold back—go ahead.

Future Events and Spiritual Achievements: Disaster may be looming in the late autumn, but it can be averted by careful preparation now. The Two of Cups will achieve great longevity, a harmonious life, and love.

Omens and Talismans: An excellent card for those living in the country and for musicians.

    Animal Spirit: Lion, Serpent
    Bird Spirit: Phoenix, Tanager
    Color: Electric Blue, Sea Green
    Plant: Daisy, Rose
    Tree: Apple, Pine
    Gemstone: Diamond, Chalcedony
    Metal: Gold
    Direction: East
    Place: Cliffs
    Season: Spring

Meditation 11: Three of Pentacles

Thirty spokes converge at one hub
But the empty center turns the wheel.

Clay forms a vessel,
But the empty center determines its use.

The doors and windows of a house
Create the empty, useful space.

Profit comes from what is visible,
But the use of the Manifest
Lies in its inner emptiness.

This is the card of Craft and Art.

Mystical Key

The creative void (*k'ung*) at the center of all things gives birth to all things. Only emptiness can engender creation. The pointed Gothic arch is a Christian symbol of hope and spiritual growth. The empty space at the center of each pentacle, and the blackness of the card both symbolize this fruitful emptiness. Only emptiness has potential, which means power. The needs (which are emptiness) driving the creative force are the power that produces the art or product. This card also contains a secret alchemy. The cathedral worker is suggestive of a member of a medieval builder's craft, who reportedly possessed a carved stone necessary for spiritual alchemy. This is a card of spiritual renewal and inspiration.

Magical Key

Character: The witty Three of Pentacles is also a person of deep feeling, who may be highly skilled in music, crafts, or visual arts. However, if the Three ignores his creative impulses, he can become shallow and egocentric. The Three has a strong sexual drive.

Current Circumstances: Slander and intrigue are everywhere. Even though the situation may seem chaotic, the Three has every reason to be optimistic about the final results.

Conflicts, Dangers, and Limitations: Problems arise when the Three becomes lazy or does not allow sufficient room for inspiration—perhaps his life is cluttered with other things. Too much clinging to what is not really stable can result in extreme danger.

Career: The card emphasizes the importance of hard work, while the Meditation underscores the roles of opening oneself to the spirit wind of inspiration. Both are critical to success. A better job should be easy to find, but wait for the right time to break free. Law and education are ideal careers for the Three of Pentacles.

Friends and Family: The Three's friends and family are trying to take control. Abandon their counsel, even though it may mean a painful separation from people who may be working together. Try to find more perceptive people.

Finances and Possessions: The Three can expect an increase in income or a major acquisition for the home. He will get the loan he seeks, but he should probably delay important business for a couple of weeks to see how things play out.

Health Concerns: Head, eyes, large intestine. In general, this is a card of long life.

Romance: It may be difficult to find the perfect partner, who should be strong, practical, and realistic, while at the same time appreciating the Three's unique gifts.

Travel: Stay home, or visit locally.

Decision: Changes are dangerous; things should remain static for the moment.

Future Events and Spiritual Achievements: The Three will achieve strength.

Omens and Talismans: This is a very auspicious card for someone in the arts or building trades.

    Animal Spirit: Wolf, Dragon
    Bird Spirit: Thrush, Finch
    Color: Yellow-White, Red
    Plant: Almond, Hawthorn
    Tree: Cedar, Elm
    Gemstone: Diamond, Star Ruby
    Metal: Silver
    Direction: Southwest
    Place: Canyon
    Season: Autumn

Meditation 12: Seven of Cups

The Five Colors blind the eye.
The Five Tones deafen the ear.
The Five Flavors kill the taste.

Racing, sporting, hunting
Madden the mind,
Rare objects tempt one to evil.

Therefore the wise spirit
Pays heed to that Within,
Not that Without.

This is the card of Delusion.

Mystical Key

According to Chinese thought, the organs of sight and sound are open-
ings, not just receptors. In other words, not only do the organs of sight
and hearing admit light and sound, but they also "leak" bodily energy and
fluid. And of course it is precisely this energy that needs to be retained
and developed if the Seeker is to advance beyond the ordinary. The picture shows a man who is so drawn to the chimerical delights of this
world that his energy, a form of his soul, is leaking out, leaving him only
a shadow. The false world has drained his true self into a dry husk. In
Jungian psychology, the shadow represents a person who is not yet individuated and who cannot achieve true integration with the world.

The creature in the lower right-hand chalice is a basilisk, whose
breath kills everything that comes near. In some symbolic systems, it
represents lust.

Magical Key

Character: The Seven of Cups is both imaginative and a clear
thinker when he is not distracted, which can happen easily.
In an unfavorable reading, the Seven can be led into

debauchery. He has strong beliefs, but does not always justify them rationally.

Current Circumstances: Victory is literally within the Seven's grasp, but current success is illusory. He should take a step back and analyze the situation more carefully. He may have to withdraw or retreat a few steps. Unlike those who are drawn off the path of Tao by cold reason, he is distracted from it by the apparent pleasures that lie to the side. These are delusional. The Seven should not be presumptuous regarding spiritual matters, and should remain very cautious.

Conflicts, Dangers, and Limitations: The Seven of Cups is in danger of being lost in nonproductive desires for goods and material objects. The Seven should pay more attention to the inner self. The Seven can be cynical about others and may also have a guilty conscience.

Career: The Seven is better off realizing the possibilities of the job he has than searching continually for new ones, which may look better from the outside than they really are. Not a good card for students.

Friends and Family: The Seven's friendships should range far beyond a narrow circle.

Finances and Possessions: This is a good card for material success.

Health Concerns: Heart, lungs. Taoist writer Husai Nan Tzu says, "When the perceptions are clear and free from seductive longings, then internal organs are settled."

Romance: The situation is confusing and difficult, because there is something important of which the Seven is unaware. The Seven can seem detached from romantic affairs, but will eventually make an unusual marriage.

Travel: The Seven should travel until he meets someone new and exciting.

Decision: Begin immediately.

Future Events and Spiritual Achievements: The Seven will receive an initiation into a transcendent state and self-mastery.

Omens and Talismans: This is a good card for a youngest
   daughter, or for someone in the sciences.
     Animal Spirit: Serpent, Basilisk
     Bird Spirit: Rooster, Goldfinch
     Color: Dark Gray to Black, Green
     Plant: Rose, Fringed Gentian
     Tree: Pine, Dogwood
     Gemstone: Turquoise, Malachite
     Metal: Tin
     Direction: Northeast
     Place: River
     Season: Winter

Meditation 13: Five of Cups

Accept misfortune and welcome disgrace,
For they are the human condition.
Don't be driven by fear of loss
Or hope of gain.
Love even misfortune
As if it were your own body.

Because having a body
Means being bound to the gain and loss
Of all things.

Love all things
As if they were your own body.

This is the card of Painful Loss.

Mystical Key

This sorrowful Meditation, combining the inauspicious numbers 5 for
the card and 13 for the Meditation, is a difficult one. It counsels us to
accept all of life, the pain as well as the pleasure, for no life is complete
without both. "Having a body means being bound to the gain and loss of

all things." The black-robed figure stands before three overturned cups—two others still remain. It is unclear as to who is responsible for the overturning of the cups—perhaps the figure, or perhaps another person. But this is a moment of realization and ultimate transformation, for loss makes love manifest. The true nature of the liquid in the chalice is not revealed until it is spilled. In this case, the contents of two of the cups are red (life and death) and green (rebirth). This is the cycle of all things. The Five Cups stand for the five elements. When one is tipped, everything is out of balance. "Love all things as if they were your own body." This is the way of the Tao.

Magical Key

Character: The Five of Cups is intuitive and forgiving of others. She has a strong sense of adventure and a desire for freedom.

Current Circumstances: The Five of Cups is facing a severe disappointment, perhaps the loss of a dear friend, but is forgetting to consider what tremendous emotional resources are just behind her. She needs to look with her heart. Despite the seeming despair and cruelty, the loss is only partial. The bridge in the background of the card signifies transition to a better state.

Conflicts, Dangers, and Limitations: The Five is in danger. Disgrace or dishonor are possible, but the Five should bear up under it. It is imperative to be absolutely truthful at the present time, and to obey moral and legal laws. Although the situation is potentially disastrous, there is nothing to do except wait; impatience is counterproductive.

Career: The Five should be sure subordinates are complying with orders, and should also follow instructions from superiors.

Friends and Family: The Five of Cups needs to develop stronger relationships with family members. There is quarreling and dissension within the family. However, the Five of Cups will meet with an unexpected friend.

Finances and Possessions: Put financial matters aside for a time.

Health Concerns: Throat, nerves. Those pregnant will have a girl. It's important to get more sleep.

Romance: A relationship may be treacherous and should be abandoned.

Travel: Not an auspicious time for travel. It is dangerous, even though it seems delightful.

Decision: Defer to someone else in making a decision.

Future Events and Spiritual Achievements: The Five of Cups will learn to take his possessions lightly and his life seriously. The Five will receive a major disappointment.

Omen and Talismans: This is a good card for the second son, and for those in leadership positions.

> Animal Spirit: Rabbit, Fox
> Bird Spirit: Crow, Bunting
> Color: Blue, Black
> Plant: Azalea, Forget-Me-Not
> Tree: Willow, Oak
> Gemstone: Opal, Amber
> Metal: Lead
> Direction: South
> Place: River
> Season: Winter

PAGE of PENTACLES.

Meditation 14: Page of Pentacles

We look at it, but we see nothing.
Call it Invisible.
We listen to it, but we hear nothing.
Call it Inaudible.
We clutch at it, but it slips away.
Call it Intangible.

Invisible, Inaudible, Intangible—
The One Unfathomable.

Its upper side is not bathed in sunlight,
Nor its lower side drowned in shadow.
It flows between being and nonbeing,

Then again returns.
This is the form of the Formless.
The image of the Imageless.
Call it Unnamable.

Encounter it—you find no face.
Follow it—you reach no end.

Inconceivably ancient,
Alive with potential,

The Tao unwinds.

This is the card of Wonder.

Mystical Key

The Page stands holding the Pentacles. One foot is firmly on the ground, the other is on tiptoe, representing the dual aspect of the Tao as both heavenly and earthly. The golden background is a promise of spiritual attainment. The Page of Pentacles stands for invisible light, the secret of the Tao. The Tao is without Form and Substance, yet it pervades every aspect of being. What appears multilayered is a unity. Unlike the visible world, which has both light and shade, the Unmanifest Tao is one. It is missed because people look with their eyes rather than feel with their heart. Yet it affects everyone. The person who draws this card is asked to think about the forever-ancient, always new, constantly unwinding Tao—and the wonders it reveals.

Magical Key

Character: The Page of Pentacles is a person of great
awareness, a person of a scientific or philosophical bent.
The Page is trustworthy, even while absent, but capable of
quick and surprising action. The Page is also a person of
great sensuality.

Current Circumstances: The Page has suffered numerous losses,
but things hold firm at the center. He has the foresight to
envision his own promising future. The Page should not

worry if others seem confused. He should beware of their doubts and stand firm.

Conflicts, Dangers, and Limitations: Currently the Page is trapped by words instead of the concepts they stand for. He may find himself in bad surroundings, to which he is connected by external ties.

Career: This is no time to be self-reliant.

Friends and Family: Former friendships have deteriorated, and they are now characterized by distrust. There are secret plots. Someone dear will return soon.

Finances and Possessions: This is a card of great abundance. However, the Page needs to make his feelings clear to others.

Health Concerns: Teeth, tongue, and gums; stomach. The Page should get rid of any unhealthy habits to which he may be attached.

Romance: Attention to spiritual truths will help in affairs of the heart.

Travel: Summer, not autumn, is the time to travel. Travel by boat will prove especially productive and enjoyable.

Decision: Going ahead with this plan is dangerous and will lead to incomprehensible and negative results.

Future Events and Spiritual Achievements: The Page will achieve victory and the power to see the invisible.

Omens and Talismans: This is a good card for the eldest son.

    Animal Spirit: Wolf, Tiger
    Bird Spirit: Cuckoo, Goldfinch
    Color: White, Red
    Plant: Violet, Daisy
    Tree: Fir, Dogwood
    Gemstone: Pearl
    Metal: Electrum
    Direction: West
    Place: Plains, Hills
    Season: Late Spring

THE HERMIT.

Meditation 15: The Hermit (IX): Yin

The Tao Masters of old
Were deep and subtle,
Responsive, elusive,
Far beyond the learning of men.

We can only say—
They were like winter travelers
Tiptoeing through an icy stream,
Sharp-eyed, skittish,
Alert to danger,
Evanescent as icicles,
Fathomless as blocks of wood,
Hollow as empty valleys.
Mysterious as swirling dark waters.

Who can clear and still this water?
Who can remain still himself
Yet follow the flowing?
Seekers of Tao
Seek no fulfillment.

This is the card of Deep Subtlety.

Mystical Key

The Hermit is a standard figure in both Taoist and Western traditions. The Hermit's Tarot number is 9, the number of fulfillment and completion, a Taoist number of great power.

Early versions of the Hermit sometimes show him with wings, as if to indicate his spiritual nature. Some early Tarot cards showed the Hermit as a hunchback. Tao Master Chuang Tzu emphasizes the great power and virtue inherent in a hunchback, comparing him to a vast and mighty tree, which, because it is old and twisted, is regarded as useless. In other variations he wears rags, or hobbles along on crutches. This gives even more clarity to the connection of this card with this passage, for it emphasizes his apparent unsureness of gait. His half-hidden beard is a sign of the hidden wisdom of the Tao. The Hermit lives alone, yet his wisdom and insight bind him to all being. He is free of petrified dogma.

The Hermit represents the spiritual Seeker who has attained his goal of "unfathomable wisdom." He stands alone, but possesses the gift of good counsel. His wisdom consists not of his words, but of his life. The lamp he holds represents spiritual illumination. The Taoist Hermit shares many features with the Western variety, including wisdom and eccentricity, linked qualities that lift the Hermit above the mundane level and transport him to a more otherworldly and spiritual sphere. Both the wisdom and eccentricity of hermits are reflected in the Meditation.

Over and over, the Tao Te Ching brings forth the examples of elders and babies, the complex mix of innocence and experience. It is the seeking, not the fulfillment, that makes the magic. In a negative aspect, the Hermit could represent loneliness and isolation (in a bad sense) from the world. This is a spiritual separation, not necessarily a physical one. *Understanding Reality*, a basic text of esoteric Taoism attributed to Wang Che (1113–1171), reminds us: "You should know the great Hermit is concealed in the city; what is the necessity of maintaining tranquil solitude deep in the mountains?"

In Chinese tradition, the figure of the hermit is auspicious. He is satisfied with few material possessions; his only goal is to find the Blessed Isles of spiritual happiness.

Magical Key

Character: The Hermit is wise, knowledgeable, eccentric, self-sufficient, and of good counsel. The Hermits seeks wisdom in unlikely places, even from those who seem least likely to possess it. The Hermit is a person of deep feelings. However, sometimes he neglects his own good qualities. This is an error.

Current Circumstances: Older persons who draw this card have had a blessed life. For younger Seekers, it is a promising sign, but may mean a long time before the goal is reached.

However, the Hermit will achieve his objective finally. Change is everywhere.

Conflicts, Dangers, and Limitations: The Hermit has an obstinate opponent.

Career: The Hermit will encounter adversity in his job.

Friends and Family: Many friends have disappeared but the few left are devoted and of higher quality. Despite this, the Hermit may be lonely, but this is essential for spiritual growth.

Finances and Possessions: This is a card of material gain, even though it may be unrecognized.

Health Concerns: Stomach, heart, and headaches.

Romance: This is a favorable card for great love, both spiritual and physical.

Travel: Both traveling and staying home are equally auspicious.

Decision: The Hermit is on the right path.

Future Events and Spiritual Achievements: The Seeker will attain unfathomable wisdom.

Omens and Talismans: This is an auspicious card for all seekers after truth.

    Animal Spirit: Antelope, Leopard
    Bird Spirit: Dove, Junco
    Color: Red, White
    Plant: Viburnum, Rose
    Tree: Holly, Elder
    Gemstone: Quartz, Pearl
    Metal: Silver
    Direction: Northeast
    Place: Ocean
    Season: Winter

Meditation 16: Four of Cups

Empty your spirit,
And let your soul be serene.
The Ten Thousand Things
Swell and fall.
Then they return.
They bloom extravagantly—
Then return to their hidden roots.

To return to one's roots
Is to attain peace.
Knowing peace is wisdom,
For without it, disorder
And confusion rage.
To achieve peace is to accomplish
One's destiny.
To accomplish one's destiny
Is fulfillment, tolerance,
And an open heart.

This is Insight:
The way of kingliness on earth
And divinity in heaven.
This is to be One with Tao.
Though the body dies,
The wise spirit abides for always.

This is the card of Serenity.

Mystical Key

The way of the Ten Thousand Things is to return to their roots. But the wise spirit has the unique consciousness called Insight. The Four of Cups represents the wise spirit, who, while staying close to his roots (note the proximity to the tree), can attain his Oneness through an internal (not an external) alchemy. He rejects the cups handed to him by an airy spirit, and stays close to nourish himself. An ancient Taoist text, the Tsan-tung-chi, (Cultivating Mind) [Wong], a manual of internal alchemy, declares that it is the mind, not the body, that needs nourishment most. It tells the Seeker to "feed yourself internally with quietude, peace, and emptiness. In this way, the secret light of the Beginning will glowingly light up the entire person. . . . The trunk will be upright, and its branches firm." The writer refers to the body, of course, but the Tarot card makes the connection with the spirit clear. The Ten Thousand Things rise and return, but the wise spirit, perfectly empty, lives without attachment, hence without fear. The things of this world (represented by Cups) are meaningless to him. One living this way can expect to live a long time.

Magical Key

Character: The Four of Cups is a strong person of great
    perception, but he also has a sensual nature that must be
    controlled. He communicates truthfully, but sometimes
    feels alone, cut off, and sorrowful. He is loyal and reliable
    under all circumstances.
Current Circumstances: What is being offered looks wonderful,
    but the wise spirit will see through it, and look to his own
    resources. A secret catastrophe, that stems from veering off
    the path, may be brewing. The Four of Cups needs to be
    flexible now.
Conflicts, Dangers, and Limitations: What appears to be luxury
    may contain a hidden danger. It is important to see it.
Career: The Four is working too hard without result, making
    him intolerant and resentful. He needs to step back.
Friends and Family: Not everyone who seems a friend truly is
    one, and conversely, the Four has an unexpected ally.
Finances and Possessions: This is a dangerous time. Only small
    gains can be made safely.
Health Concerns: Circulation, heart, anxiety. The Four of Cups
    may be overanxious, or tired of something—or someone.
    Perhaps he is not sleeping well. If the Four can control the
    stress, he can live a long life. Health will return after illness.
Romance: Outward separation does not affect inner unity.

Someone outside the relationship is trying to cause trouble.

Travel: Travel other than for business is not beneficial at this time. Remaining at home and cultivating one's garden is more profitable.

Decision: Do not make a hasty decision about this matter, but do not turn back.

Future Events and Spiritual Achievements: Pleasure will be attained.

Omens and Talismans: Auspicious for military personnel and their families.

    Animal Spirit: Tiger, Mountain Lion
    Bird Spirit: Eagle, Sparrow
    Color: Black, Yellow
    Plant: Geranium, Phlox
    Tree: Hemlock, Pine
    Gemstone: Ruby, Garnet
    Metal: Tin
    Direction: West
    Place: Garden
    Season: Summer

Meditation 17: Five of Wands

The best leaders are those whose existence
Is barely known to their followers.
The next best are loved and admired.
Bad leaders are feared.
The worst despised.

Those who lack trust in the Tao
Will never be trusted.

The words of the wise spirit are precious
And rare.
He does his work without comment.

When it is finished,
The people claim they did it themselves.

This is the card of Confusion.

Mystical Key

This card is often interpreted as a sign of conflict, but it can just as easily be read as an indicator of cooperation building. The ambiguity of the card reinforces the notion that even in cooperative efforts, squabbles arise. In the same way, many fights occur over nothing. The figures in the card, if they are fighting, seem rather halfhearted about it. Whether in conflict or in building, the figures have no leader, although obviously somebody started all the commotion. The Meditation reminds us that true leaders are almost invisible. They do their work without comment, and lead inconspicuously. Another way of interpreting this card is to consider the five wands as representative of the five elements, which are out of balance or in conflict with each other.

Magical Key

Character: The Five of Wands has great power, strength, and
will. He is competitive, but not necessarily in the best sense
of the word. He is a generous host and a good guest. He is
sensual and hungry for experience, but must be careful
about being led astray.

Current Circumstances: The card can represent a battle between
thought and feeling. Spiritual beliefs will be a safe guide.

Conflicts, Dangers, and Limitations: The Five's current way of
life is impeding him, and a combination of powerful evil
forces is allied against him. Even great virtue may not be
enough to defeat them.

Career: A cooperative project is turning into a battleground.
This is not a good time to angle for a promotion. The Five
should stop trying to promote himself and recognize the
good work of others.

Friends and Family: The Five of Wands has few warm
attachments.

Finances and Possessions: This is a good time to start gathering and saving money; not auspicious for speculative investments.

Health Concerns: Mouth, small intestine.

Romance: Desires are not satisfied. An estrangement will soon be over.

Travel: This is the time to travel, especially to the northwest. Staying home is dangerous.

Decision: This is the time to move forward.

Future Events and Spiritual Achievements: Legal problems may occur.

Omens and Talismans: This is a beneficial card for those who live in the country and for those in mathematical and technical fields.

> Animal Spirit: Unicorn, Ox
> Bird Spirit: Eagle, Lark
> Color: Green, Gold
> Plant: Coreopsis, Dianthus
> Tree: English Yew, Willow
> Gemstone: Chalcedony
> Metal: Bronze
> Direction: Southeast
> Place: Marsh
> Season: Summer

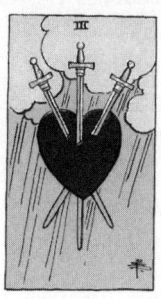

Meditation 18: Three of Swords

When the great Tao is forgotten,
Conventional morality is born.
When cleverness and shrewdness arise,
Pretense and hypocrisy take over.

When the family falls into confusion,
True relationships are replaced
By obedience and condescension.

In the disordered society
The bureaucrats appear.

This is the card of Corruption.

Mystical Key

This passage traces the birth and degradation of modern society, as it falls away from the original Tao. Organized despotism has taken over. The natural way needs no laws, no commandments for loyalty, and especially no bureaucrats! These three are swords in the heart of the Tao. Laws, conventional virtues, and officials were also characteristics of Confucianism, and this passage itself sticks a not-so-subtle knife in Confucian virtues. The weeping clouds signify the sorrows of heaven at the corruption of the Taoist way.

Magical Key

Character: The Three of Swords is a person of great wit, with an intelligence that can wound himself as well as others. However, original purity and native cheerfulness have been destroyed. The Three of Swords has a strong sexual nature and self-mastery is required.

Current Circumstances: There is great danger, but the Three has powerful spiritual protection. The Three of Swords needs to avoid ignorance.

Conflicts, Dangers, and Limitations: Although the Three faces a great deal of pain and injury, he will come to understand the blessing that lies within it. The Three should not resist the course of events. It is important for the Three to cultivate spiritual practices, and return to the principles he knows to be correct.

Career: His career is productive and fruitful. However, the higher the Three advances, the more dangers arise from below.

Friends and Family: This is an inauspicious card in relation to mothers. The Three of Swords is a loyal friend, but sometimes it is necessary to separate from family and friends to attain enlightenment.

Finances and Possessions: Overattachment to money is holding back the Three of Swords spiritually.

Health Concerns: Heart, kidneys. Generally, though, a favorable health card.

Romance: Someone has a dark secret, which must be kept. The Three of Swords is loyal to the point of self-sacrifice, which isn't always a good thing. Separation and infidelity are possible. A marriage will not result in children.

Travel: Travel, even at great expense and personal effort, is necessary for spiritual growth.

Decision: Don't waste any more time.

Future Events and Spiritual Achievements: The Three will achieve a well-deserved success, but it comes after great sorrow. The Three of Swords will achieve material goals in three years; in nine, the Three will see spiritual enlightenment.

Omens and Talismans: This is an auspicious card for people in the literary and musical arts.

Animal Spirit: Bat, Rat
Bird Spirit: Crow, Blue Jay
Color: Luminous Black, Green
Plant: Bleeding Heart, Verbena
Tree: Hemlock, Cypress
Gemstone: Sapphire, Aquamarine

Metal: Iron
Direction: Southwest
Place: Ocean
Season: Late Summer

THE HIEROPHANT.

Meditation 19:

The Hierophant (V): Yang

Renounce your saintliness,
Abandon the pretense to wisdom,
Give up benevolence and fake morality.

Only then can people discover
Honest relationships.

Forget scheming and careful business plans.
Only then will thieves and robbers disappear.

Morality, benevolence, and cleverness
Are not sufficient.

It is more central to know
The source of morality, benevolence, and wisdom.

To see simplicity,
To cast off selfishness,
To realize one's true nature.

This is the card of Conventional Virtue.

Mystical Key
Historically, this card represents the Pope, but Waite changed the name
to Hierophant ("holy teacher"), or Priest. The Hierophant is the spiritual
twin of the Emperor. He carries in his left hand the Papal Cross,
emblem of his office. The two "keys of St. Peter" are at the foot of the

papal throne. They represent the biblical power to "bind and to loose" (Matthew 16:19). The Hierophant represents religion as opposed to spirituality. This is the first card that depicts other humans beings, suggesting the impact of organized religion as opposed to the more solitary spiritual path. Significantly, the other figures kneel before the Hierophant.

In a Taoist reading, this can be a negative card, with the Hierophant as a pretender to virtue, rather than a follower of the Tao.

However, the Hierophant is privy to special knowledge, known only to the elect, the privileged. As Hierophant, the priest mediates between the realm of hidden knowledge and the world of common experience. From his knowledge he derives his authority. His three-tiered crown represents heaven, earth, and the underworld. Powerful forces are at work, but they remain disguised and mysterious.

Magical Key

Character: The Hierophant represents established virtue, position, and authority, especially in matters of morals. The Hierophant is a person of great force, but who nevertheless could be bound in a kind of institutional prison. Hatred is the Hierophant's weak spot.

Current Circumstances: In the most favorable reading, the Hierophant occupies a position of deserved power. However, more commonly, the Hierophant is an example of all that is most wrong with bureaucratic society and structured religion, wherein form supersedes spirit. Cleverness and shrewdness are no substitute for following the Tao, because they tend to subvert the Tao through their own intelligence. As a result, they will inevitably fail. Hanging on to outworn ideas is stultifying; the Hierophant should move on with the times.

Conflicts, Dangers, and Limitations: The Hierophant is in danger and should turn away from it. He must beware of intolerance, vanity, hypocrisy, and fanaticism, or becoming the victim of doctrinal orthodoxy. He must be absolutely circumspect.

Career: Career goals may be inappropriate; the Hierophant should try for more flexibility. This is a bad card for those in middle management. Try doing less, rather than more. The Hierophant may rely too much on popular opinion.

Friends and Family: Friends and family both respect and fear the Hierophant. The Hierophant has one strong, good friend.

Finances and Possessions: The Hierophant is likely to attain wealth on a grand scale, but care should be taken about how it is administered.

Health Concerns: Skin, Bladder.

Romance: The Hierophant is (rather unexpectedly) a good card for passion and love affairs. The right partner can also bring spiritual fulfillment.

Travel: Travel to the west is beneficial at this time.

Decision: It is important for the Hierophant to travel, although the way will be fraught with difficulty.

Future Events and Spiritual Achievements: The card generally means that the perceived authority will conquer. The Hierophant will achieve a measure of material happiness within the year.

Omens and Talismans: This is a fortunate card for those who live alone, for visual artists, and for people who work "behind the scenes." Also fortunate for those connected with religion in an official capacity.

> Animal Spirit: Pig, Frog
> Bird Spirit: Crow, Vireo
> Color: Gray or Silver, Red or Purple
> Plant: Lily, Foxglove
> Tree: Cypress, Oak
> Gemstone: Amethyst
> Metal: Gold
> Direction: South
> Place: River
> Season: Winter

THE FOOL.

Meditation 20: The Fool (0): Yin

Abandon learning and extinguish your problems.
What's the difference between "yes" and "no"?
What's the difference between "good" and "evil"?

Must all people fear the same things?
I don't think so.

I see others sleek and content,
Enjoying themselves in parks and terraces.
I feel apart from them—apathetic, drifting, unsure.
I feel like a baby who has not yet learned to smile.

I feel forlorn, dejected.
No home, no destination.
Destitute.
Possessing nothing.

I am a fool.
I see others looking wise,
Full of insight.
Their minds are on edge.
I feel dull, listless,
Without direction.

But I take my sustenance
From the Tao,
The Great Mother.

This is the card of Infinite Possibilities.

Mystical Key

The Fool is the first antihero in Western history. He stands alone; he is not part of the pack and is set apart from all the other cards. "I see others looking wise, full of insight." He seems unsure of himself, without knowing his goal. "I feel dull, listless, without direction." This is surely not the stereotypical hero of epic and tragedy. But he is uniquely suited for the Tao, for although his destination is still a mystery—his source is sure. It is the Great Mother. One thing is clear: the Fool's adventure is just beginning, and its outcome is unpredictable.

His number is 0—pure potentiality, which is both the seedbed and negation of power. (The zero shape permeates the entire Tarot pack, just as the concept of zero [emptiness] empowers the Tao Te Ching. See Meditations 11 and 43 for specific examples.) Thus he teeters between the Yin and the Yang. He carries a staff (wand) in one hand. This is the symbol of creativity, for this is the beginning. Some readers interpret this wand as the incipient magic wand borne by the Magician, who follows the Fool in traditional Tarot packs. The bag the Fool carries may indicate the collective unconscious that we all carry with us. In his left (unconscious or Yin) hand the Fool carries a white rose, the flowering of Yin. A small dog leaps at the Fool's heels. This dog was an innovation of the Marseilles pack and its clones, some of which substituted a cat for a dog. The nipping dog seems to urge the Fool on—over the precipice? To make a choice? To follow faithfully? To lead on? It is a mystery. (In the Marseilles pack, the dog is actually biting the Fool.)

Equally mysterious and open to interpretation are the many other symbols present on the card: the red plume on the Fool's head, the silver sun at his back, the icy mountains in the background. The feather represents lightness of spirit (or, more negatively, light-headedness.)

"Abandon learning," counsels the Tao. This means don't take everything from books, or outside authority (including this one). Experience for yourself. The Fool, too, prefers to make his own journey.

The Fool is the origin of all mystery and magic, the fountain of the Yin and Yang. He is the shaman—the one possessed by uncontainable magical powers. Until he learns to harness them, he is blown like wind; then he becomes the wind and power and spirit incarnate. For him, all things are possible, since he exists in a state of innocence. Thus, the Fool exposes hypocrisy. Though he stands on a precipice, the Fool should not fear, for there is nothing to be afraid of. If he falls into the precipice, he stumbles into the Valley of the Tao. He is nourished by the Great Mother, the ultimate Tao. This is a surprising discovery. It means that he is not in fact lost, and he never has been. He has always been sustained by the Tao.

The Fool is a Yin voice in a Yang world. He is confused, because he still sees the world as divided between himself and others—between self and not-self. Perhaps he is attempting to impose Yang (outside) values on the inner Yin. Such attempts have negative consequences. The Fool feels aimless, dim, weak, and overlooked, while he views others as "clear and bright," the classic differences between Yin and Yang. But perhaps the difference is not so clear-cut after all. What's the difference between "yes" and "no"?

Like the youngest son in fairy tales, or the young King Arthur, both archetypes of the Western world, the Fool does not even know his own power. In the same way, the Tao is "aimless," "dim," and "weak." It drifts. It is overlooked. The Fool needs to accept his inner Yin and follow the great Tao, which, though it meanders, is never off course, for it charts its own. Once the Fool understands this, he can stop being a Fool. (Paradoxically, to those not in the know, even a Tao Master, especially a Tao Master, appears as a Fool.) But that's all right. That's the way the Tao works. By his open "foolishness," the Fool stands closer to the Tao than many others with pretenses to wisdom. This is a favorable card for young people. For older, more settled people, however, the card can be a warning that the Referent has never grown up.

Magical Key

Character: The Fool is playful, innocent, cheerful, happy, perhaps naïve, adventuresome. Curiously, the Fool has a strong intellectual bent.

Current Circumstances: The Fool is close to being on the right path, very close. Be a Fool, but a Fool in the Wise Way. It is all right to refuse to accept social conventions, but such refusal should be accompanied by keen self-evaluation. In order to preserve the self, virtue must be cultivated. The Fool should find strength in what he already possesses. The Fool should stop worrying about other people's opinions, and not accept others' values as his own. By following the Tao within, wherever it takes him, the Fool will come alive to the world of infinite possibilities.

Conflicts, Dangers, and Limitations: Pride is the Fool's weak point. He encounters strife. There will be difficulty at the beginning. But if he perseveres, he will achieve success.

Career: This is a favorable card for those beginning a new job. However, it is important for the Fool not to overstep his authority or to attempt to advance beyond his capabilities.

Friends and Family: Friends or family may have negative emotions that adversely affect the Fool.

Finances and Possessions: Prosperity is likely to be achieved within two years.

Health Concerns: Liver, kidney. The Fool takes health risks.

Romance: In a relationship slot, this card means the Fool needs to grow up fast. Once this happens, there are excellent prospects for a happy marriage.

Travel: This is a propitious card for journeys.

Decision: A go-between will be important in making this decision. Move slowly.

Future Events and Spiritual Achievements: So far, the Fool has not had the opportunity to make many mistakes, but numerous difficulties lie ahead. Still, there is nothing to be afraid of. The Fool will achieve spiritual victory within eight years, if he attaches himself to a wise person.

Omens and Talismans: This card is auspicious for adventurers, explorers, and all seekers, also for youngest sons and daughters.

> Animal Spirit: Lion, Whale
> Bird Spirit: Ibis, Meadowlark
> Color: Black, Blue, Light Blue
> Plant: Buttercup, Aster
> Tree: Ash, Dogwood
> Metal: Copper, Gold
> Gemstone: Lapis Lazuli, Rock Crystal
> Direction: North
> Place: River
> Season: Spring

Meditation 21: Nine of Pentacles

The greatest power is to follow the Tao.
The Tao is fleeting—elusive.
Leaving just traces . . .

Shadowy, obscure,
But full of spirit.
Truth is in the spirit.
From all time
Its name is constant.

How can we know this?
By Tao.

This is the card of Truth.

Mystical Key

Nine is the Taoist number of Totality. Yet the paradox here is that totality is hooded and fleeting like the falcon of the card. It pauses only for an instant before it escapes again. The only way to follow it is to let it loose—and fly with it.

This is what Lao Tzu meant he wrote that the Tao is "obscure, but full of spirit." This card represents one who can prosper not only in the earthly sphere, but in spiritual ways as well. Truth is also in the spirit. Like a vibrant, living bird, the Tao is not content to stagnate. Yet no matter how far a bird flies, or how close it hovers, or even momentarily rests, its nature remains the same.

Magical Key

> Character: The Nine of Pentacles is a highly emotional and
> sensitive person. But she can rise above her emotions to
> seek knowledge for its own sake. She is tolerant, generous,
> and supportive of others. The courageous Nine follows
> truth wherever it leads and doesn't allow her beliefs to
> stagnate. She has great self-discipline. She is visionary and

altruistic, but tends not to think in terms of details. This can be dangerous, since a lot of truth lies in those details. The Nine can be overzealous.

Current Circumstances: The Nine of Pentacles is in safe territory. Nothing is endangered as long as the Nine does not follow the advice of certain people who are not trustworthy. In the past, things did not proceed the way she hoped. However, things will take a turn for the better now.

Conflicts, Dangers, and Limitations: Desires and passions are the Nine's weak point. Because of her generous and trusting nature, the Nine is also easily manipulated.

Career: No promotion in sight; the way is not currently open. The Nine should stay patient and look over work carefully before passing it along to others.

Friends and Family: This is an important time for the Nine to stick close to family and friends; they need support and advice. A family member should not be pushed too far, even in a good cause. The Nine shouldn't force a change, but should not give up either.

Finances and Possessions: This is the time to acquire mobile, useful possessions, not large unwieldy ones. The Nine will be financially fortunate; in fact, the card indicates a lasting fortune, as long as money is invested prudently.

Health Concerns: Gall bladder.

Romance: If the Nine treats a partner too lightly, the relationship will darken and fade. Patience is important. A faithful attempt to work things out will bear fruit.

Travel: Traveling back home is a good idea now.

Decision: It is important to examine certain details before making this decision. The Nine should not act alone, but should seek help.

Future Events and Spiritual Achievements: The Nine will achieve great material gain. However, the Nine will also encounter unexpected danger in the form of storms, overindulgence, or treachery.

Omens and Talismans: This is a good card for those engaged in agriculture, as well as for artists and poets.

Animal Spirit: Rabbit, Tiger
Bird Spirit: Falcon, Loon
Color: Red, Purple
Plant: Juniper, Grapevine
Tree: Birch, Cypress
Gemstone: Turquoise, White Carnelian
Metal: Silver
Direction: West
Place: House
Season: Autumn, Winter

Meditation 22: Eight of Swords

Break—and be whole.
Yield—and overcome.
Empty—and be full.
Have nothing—and gain everything.

The wise spirit
Holds fast to the One.
She sets an example.
She shines forth.
Not trying to justify herself,
Not boasting,
Not praising herself,
She never falters,
She never competes,
For she is matchless.

Emptiness draws fulfillment.
When you achieve true fullness,
Then all things will come to you.

This is the card of Steadfastness.

Mystical Key

At first glance, this looks like a card of terrible omen. A woman is blind-folded, bound, and surrounded by Swords. The situation looks hopeless until we notice the stream, barely a trickle, running at her feet. And we now remember that the Tao, so small and narrow, supports all things. "Break—and be whole. Yield—and overcome."

Magical Key

Character: The Eight of Swords is person of extreme courage. The Eight could also be politically subversive, but she is highly intelligent. She may not tolerate the presence of inferior people patiently.

Current Circumstances: The Eight is facing a serious crisis. A plan has failed. The shackles that bind her may be the shackles of the law. She may be unjustly accused or punished. Minor, even accidental, events could be a hindrance. This is where it pays to be steadfast, even in the most severe circumstances.

Conflict, Dangers, and Limitations: An obstacle (often in the form of interference) stands in front of the Eight. The Eight of Swords may also feel as if she is trapped, often by trivial problems of her own making. Despite the seriousness of the situation, the Eight should not give up, but seek out the hidden truth and ultimate freedom that the crisis will bring. She will able to draw strength from sorrow and power from her spiritual faith.

Career: Work with others to get the project done.

Friends and Family: Someone is trying to usurp the household.

Finances and Possessions: If the Eight reserves all her wealth for herself, there will be an unfortunate outcome. Otherwise, the Eight has a good chance for material gain. However, she must move forward cautiously.

Health Concerns: Liver.

Romance: The Eight is in a bad relationship and should listen to advice from a true friend.

Travel: This is a good time to embark on a distant journey. The whole world is her home.

Decision: Take no action at the present time.

Future Events and Spiritual Achievements: A great challenge lies ahead. By carefully attending to wise advice, the Eight's whole world will turn to jewels.

Omens and Talismans: This is a good card for military personnel.

    Animal Spirit: Rhinoceros, Dragon
    Bird Spirit: Kingfisher, Parrot
    Color: Yellow, Brown
    Plant: Marigold, Buttercup
    Tree: Willow, Persimmon
    Gemstone: Jade, Opal
    Metal: Iron
    Direction: East
    Place: Mountains
    Season: Late Winter

QUEEN of PENTACLES.

Meditation 23: Queen of Pentacles

Nature's words are few and fleeting.
Even a whirlwind lasts only a morning.
A sudden downpour is soon over.
What creates the wind and rain?
The high heaven and the rich earth.

If even the works of heaven and earth
Don't last,
How can the words of humankind?

The followers of Tao
Belong to the Tao.
The seekers of power
Are one with power.
Those who are lost on the way
Become one with loss.

Surrender to the Tao.
And the Tao is yours.

Give all to Power,
And the Power is yours.
Abandon yourself to Loss
And make it your own.

He who does not trust,
Will never be trusted.

This is the card of Power and Loss.

Mystical Key

The Queen holds in her lap the Pentacle, symbol of earthly things. "The seekers of Power are one with Power." But power, like all things, including loss, is fleeting. "Even a whirlwind lasts only a morning." Human beings and their works are no different. The only way to "handle" power is to hold it gently, and when the time comes, to let it go. This is trust. "He who does not trust, will never be trusted." Trust is the vital bond that connects human beings with the Tao. It puts us in a responsive relationship to it, and allows us to deal with loss and power in the same easy way.

Magical Key

Character: The Queen has power over others and uses it wisely. She has an excellent sense of fair play. She seems well-intentioned, but her innermost nature is obscure and ambiguous, perhaps even cold. In an unfavorable reading she can be lazy, unperceptive, or promiscuous.

Current Circumstances: The Queen has rich and powerful neighbors; they could be dangerous. The way to get along with them is to serve them. A major obstacle has been cleared from the path, but she is not as safe as she may think. The Queen needs to place more trust in other human beings, the Tao, and her own capabilities. She should not make secret plans at this time.

Conflicts, Dangers, and Limitations: The Queen of Pentacles may talk too much, unlike the few and fleeting words of heaven. This can get her in trouble. She needs to exhibit more patience. The Queen is in danger of being persuaded to do something immoral.

Career: The Queen will receive advancement through her talents. Constancy is the key.

Friends and Family: The head of the family is suffering illness. An evil woman is exerting a bad influence.

Finances and Possessions: The Queen is placing too much faith in the power of possessions. Commercial ventures will not turn out well at this time. Lawsuits will be unsuccessful.

Health Concerns: Neck, feet.

Romance: Something is going to happen very soon.

Travel: A trip to the west would be auspicious, but not necessary.

Decision: Principled intuition is a sure guide now.

Future Events and Spiritual Achievements: Danger is drawing closer. The Queen will achieve spiritual wealth and enlightenment.

Omens and Talismans: This is a good card for people in government.

    Animal Spirit: Goat, Tiger
    Bird Spirit: Magpie, Turkey
    Color: Blue, Indigo
    Plant: Rose, Echinacea
    Tree: Birch, Elder
    Gemstone: Carnelian, Turquoise
    Metal: Gold
    Direction: West
    Place: Forest
    Season: Summer, Autumn

KNIGHT of WANDS.

Meditation 24: Knight of Wands

Standing tiptoe is a way to lose balance,
Overstriding exhausts the walker.

Just so, a showoff has nothing to show,
A braggart has nothing to brag of.
A boaster lacks real achievement.

Boasting, bragging, showing off.
The wise spirit regards these things
Like leftover food, extra luggage, tumors of the body.
Something to be avoided.

This is the card of Confidence.

Mystical Key

This Meditation reminds us that talking and doing are two different things. It compares bragging to leftover food, tumors, and extra luggage—things that weigh us down, encumber our actions, and even poison our being. The horse and rider combination, which occurs in the rest of the Knight cards (as well as Death, the Sun, and the Six of Wands) represents psychologically the id (horse) and the (ego) rider. In this case, the Knight barely has control of his id, or impulsive nature. The adjacent cards will clarify the nature of this card.

This card carries the aura of the braggart. Confucius reminds us that exalting the self by denigrating others will lead to loss.

Magical Key

Character: The Knight of Wands can be impulsive, intuitive, and is always unpredictable. It is not always easy to discern his innermost nature, and he can lose his temper very quickly. He is the knightly scholar and the scholarly knight. (The Chinese word *shih* means both.) In a positive aspect, he is generous and active. In a negative aspect, the Knight of Wands is intrusive and evil-minded. He acts out, brags,

and is emotionally demanding. This attitude will get him
into trouble. He always needs to be center stage.

Current Circumstances: Something is frightening the Knight of
Wands. There is great danger. The Knight of Wands should
trust his own abilities and act very carefully here.

Conflicts, Dangers, and Limitations: The Knight may be envious
of others or try to compete with them. The Knight may feel
neglected by others; however, none of them can harm him
in any significant way.

Career: The Knight is surrounded by jealous, crafty people. Too
much ambition right now will land him in trouble.

Friends and Family: The Knight should select friends of noble
character who can help him achieve self-discipline.

Finances and Possessions: Presently a bad outlook for all
business matters.

Health Concerns: Oral, dental, or stomach problems. The
Knight may have a chronic illness that may be difficult to
cure.

Romance: This is the time to draw back a little.

Travel: A journey or move is at hand. The Knight ought not to
neglect this excellent opportunity.

Decision: Be reserved. The time is not yet ripe. An arbitrary
decision will have poor results.

Future Events and Spiritual Achievements: Peace will be
restored.

Omens and Talismans: This is a fortunate card for widowed or
older women, and for people in the legal profession. A
solution that appears very strange will actually work out
quite well.

    Animal Spirit: Salamander, Tiger
    Bird Spirit: Owl, Ibis
    Color: Red, Orange
    Plant: Buttercup, Foxglove
    Tree: Holly, Acacia
    Gemstone: Amethyst, Red Agate
    Metal: Copper
    Direction: East

Place: Water, Mountains
Season: Autumn, Winter

ACE of PENTACLES.

Meditation 25: Ace of Pentacles

Something was
Before Heaven and Earth.
Still. Formless.
Unconditioned. Alone.
All pervasive. All.
Ever moving.

The mother of all things.

We know not its name.
So we call it Tao.
In absence of a better term,
we say it is "great."

The Great Tao flows on,
Goes far,
Returns.

Heaven is likewise great.
Earth is great.
Humanity is great.

So there are four great things.
Humanity follows Earth,
Earth follows heaven,
Heaven follows the Tao.

And the Tao is what it is.

This is the card of Greatness.

Mystical Key

The fruitful land, as well as the vast sky, is prominent in this card, reminding us that "Earth follows heaven." Here, the great single Pentacle stands for the Tao itself. The Meditation tells us that we hold the sacred Tao of the earth in our hand. When we say "Humanity follows Earth," we mean first that humanity is of the earth and must follow its ways. This leads us into the second concept, which is that as earth goes, so go we. We are the caretakers of the earth and can be "great" only insofar as we follow the greatness of earth, which was created by heaven, itself a manifestation of the Tao. "And the Tao is what it is." *Still. Formless. Unconditioned. Alone. All pervasive. All. Ever moving. The mother of all things.*

The sacred Taoist text of inner training tells us that the vital energy inherent in all things "brings all things to life. It generates the five grains below, and becomes the constellated stars above. . . . When stored within the hearts of people, we call them wise spirits."

Magical Key

Character: The Ace of Pentacles has a strong, individual personality. He keeps promises and fulfills undertakings. On the other hand, he can be stubborn and demanding, and his regal air can be off-putting to some. His feelings are more powerful than he cares to admit to others.

Current Circumstances: The current situation may not last. The Ace of Pentacles is slightly in danger; he should attempt to avoid extremes. This is his chance to be "great."

Conflicts, Dangers, and Limitations: Subtle misalignments are causing major problems. The Ace needs to be a better listener. He should disengage himself from quarrels that don't concern him.

Career: The Ace of Pentacles does well as a self-employed artist or entrepreneur.

Friends and Family: People are drawn to the Ace's magnetic personality and generosity. Even bitter enemies will eventually warm up to him. The Ace should be careful not to strive to be the center of attention. Others must be allowed to find their own way.

Finances and Possessions: The outlook is unfavorable at present.

Health Concerns: This is an auspicious card for health, but the Ace has a tendency to work too hard. Headaches are common.

Romance: The prospect of a wedding is difficult and not advantageous at this time. The Ace of Pentacles needs an especially patient mate.

Travel: Travel is extremely difficult now.

Decision: The Ace is still not strong enough to ward off danger. If the decision to go ahead is made, extreme caution is required.

Future Events and Spiritual Achievements: The wreathed arch leads to the high mountains of the future, a sacred realm of immense significance. New possibilities appear in practical life that will offer an unexpected insight into the nature of things.

Omens and Talismans: This is a fortunate card for young women, and for people engaged in the building trades.

    Animal Spirit: Water Snake, Lion
    Bird Spirit: Partridge, Crane
    Color: Purple, Yellow
    Plant: Lily, Rose
    Tree: Alder, Oak
    Gemstone: Garnet, Amethyst
    Metal: Gold
    Direction: West
    Place:Mountains
    Season: Autumn

THE CHARIOT.

Meditation 26:

The Chariot (VII): Yang

Weightiness bears lightness on his shoulders.
Stillness begets swift movement.

The wise spirit
Who travels all day
Stays close to his luggage.

Even though spectacular scenery
Surrounds him,
He remains serene
And still.

Why should the Master
Of ten thousand chariots
Go lightly?
He would lose his connections.
Restlessness means
Loss of self-control.

This is the card of Awareness.

Mystical Key

In classical mythology, the Chariot follows the path of the Sun across the sky. The two Sphinxes—one black, one white—represent the Yang and Yin. The charioteer is master of both; he is the perfectly integrated personality, total consciousness. The wheels of the Chariot represent wholeness and unity, although the rectangle of the Chariot places the Charioteer firmly within the earthly realm. Note the calmness of the Charioteer's expression. Like the Charioteer god Krishna in the Hindu Bhagavad Gita, the Charioteer is the yogi in war, the perfect fighter—the non-attached. The symbol of the chariot and charioteer is an immensely powerful one in many religious traditions. It shows up in Plato's dialogue Phaedrus, "the myth of the charioteer." Even in the otherworldly Katha Yoga Upanishad: "Know thou the soul as the chariot-driver, the body as a chariot. Know thou the intellect as the chariot driver/and the mind as the reins." In the Book of Ezekiel, God's throne-chariot also makes an appearance in Chapter 1, although its connections to the Waite Chariot seem weak at best.

Magical Key

Character: The Chariot is assertive, resourceful, reasonable, and cool-headed. He has enormous willpower, and control of himself.

Current Circumstances: Everything may seem contradictory; influences are conflicting. Things may be moving very fast. The Chariot may be engaged in risky behavior. He may feel constrained and cramped. Dreams are significant and should be heeded.

Conflicts, Dangers, and Limitations: There is anxiety and trouble; be very cautious. The load the Chariot is trying to pull may be too heavy.

Career: Advancement is probable, but any gain may be temporary.

Friends and Family: Someone is telling lies that may lead to harm. Someone else is working for the Chariot's great good.

Finances and Possessions: A commercial venture will be profitable if begun in March or April.

Health Concerns: This is an auspicious card for health.

Romance: This is an inauspicious time for romance.

Travel: The Chariot will soon depart on a long journey, either physical or spiritual. The mountains or lakes are a favorable destination. This is a card of safe travel.

Decision: This is a good time for action, if the action is taken with joy and an open heart.

Future Events and Spiritual Achievements: A test of spiritual strength is not far away. The real nature of a hidden evil will be revealed. The Chariot should be sure his cause is just. Those who are imprisoned will soon be released. Rest from strife is in sight.

Omens and Talismans: Good omen for the eldest child and for gamblers.

    Animal Spirit: Sheep, Jackal
    Bird Spirit: Peacock, Gull
    Color: Yellow, Black, Light Red
    Plant: Hollyhock, Jasmine
    Tree: Pine, Holly
    Gemstone: Moonstone, Yellow Serpentine
    Metal: Steel
    Direction: Northeast
    Place: Trees, Streams
    Season: Mid-autumn

PAGE of WANDS.

Meditation 27: Page of Wands

The skillful walker leaves no track.
The skillful speaker never slips.
The skillful arithmetician needs no markers.

The well-built door springs tight without locks.
Yet no one can break in.
Well-wrought bindings have no knots.
Yet no one can escape them.

The wise spirit cares for all people,
And abandons none.
He looks after all objects,
And neglects none.
We call this following the veiled light.

Skillful people teach those who are still learning.
Virtuous people exemplify good behavior
For those who haven't yet found the right road.

Teacher and student
Must cherish each other.
This is a mysterious truth.

This is the card of Reciprocity.

Mystical Key

The darkness (or "veiled light") of the Tao is still another mystery. Lao Tzu's disciple Chuang Tzu reminds us that "if the Tao turns to brilliance, it ceases to be Tao." Darkness, hiddenness, is its essential characteristic. Following the Tao means exemplifying good behavior for others to follow.

Magical Key

Character: The charming Page can be impulsive and argumentative. The Page is quick to act, but skilled, fond of arguing, mostly for the sake of developing both sides of an issue. The Page is also fair and brave in his opinions with a wonderful sense of humor. He is sometimes dazzled by his own accomplishments. When angry, the Page of Wands can be cruel and cold-hearted.

Current Circumstances: The Page will soon receive an important visitor. This is a good time to take a class in yoga or meditation.

Conflicts, Dangers, and Limitations: Because the Page is reluctant to accept the advice of others, they may not lend support when it is needed. The Page should avoid pride and delusions; these lead to great danger and loss of pleasure. This may be a time of stagnation. The Page may be getting some bad news in relation to the surrounding cards.

Career: The Page makes a good student or teacher, and understands the nature of the relationship between them. There may be difficulties in the beginning, but everything will work out.

Friends and Family: The Page is faithful to friends, significant others, and students, and fulfills his responsibilities. However, he has little chance to influence others right now.

Finances and Possessions: This is a good time for commercial activities. The Page's income will increase markedly. However, an opportunity for gain should not be pursued until he is are sure it is ethical.

Health Concerns: This is an auspicious card for health. Minor skin problems possible.

Romance: This is an inauspicious card for romance.

Travel: It will be more profitable to stay home at this time.

Decision: Wait. Everything must be taken into consideration before a decision is made. The current situation seems to be a trap, but a too hasty attempt to escape can have dire consequences.

Future Events and Spiritual Achievements: This is an auspicious card for those not married, or for the middle son or daughter. The Page will achieve true fellowship with others.

Omens and Talismans: Good card for people in education and skilled trades. The Page will achieve knowledge of things invisible.

Animal Spirit: Wild Dog, Salamander
Bird Spirit: Pelican, Peacock
Color: Black, Blue
Plant: Poppy, Daylily
Tree: Pine, Viburnum Springs
Gemstone: Bloodstone, Ruby, Green Jasper
Metal: Electrum
Direction: East
Place: Desert
Season: Late Autumn

THE HIGH PRIESTESS.

Meditation 28:

The High Priestess (II): Yin

Know the strength of man,
And the yielding flexibility of woman.
Be the river bed—and the river.
By this power you can return
To the stainless purity of a child.

Know the light,
But keep to the shadow.
In this, be a pattern to the world,
A pattern true, quiet, unwavering.

Know honor and glory
But keep your humility.
In this, be the valley and the fountain
Of the universe,
The fountain that creates the waterfall,
And the valley to which all things return.

All things come from the uncarved block.
The master tailor cuts little.

This is the card of Mystery.

Mystical Key

This card is the gateway to the power of the goddess. Although named the High Priestess, there is more of the shaman than the priestess about her. She is wise, holy, and powerful. Unlike the worldly, active Magician who precedes her in the Tarot pack, the High Priestess appears to have withdrawn from the mundane activities of the world. While the Empress emphasizes the power of nature, the High Priestess works in the mystical realm of pure spirit. Yet she has not rejected worldly actions ("Know honor and glory"), but combined them with the reclusive spirit of the

Tao. ("Keep your humility.") She is successful because she has the secret power of the Tao behind her.

The High Priestess sits on her throne, wearing the horned crown of the changing moon. The horned crown she wears with its circular diadem represents both the moon and divine powers. She holds the sacred Jewish law (Torah) in her hands and bears the holy sign of Christianity, the Cross, upon her breast. The crescent moon (very Yin) lies at her feet, while the River of Tao, Mother of the Ten Thousand Things, flows from her gown. She is Shekhinah (the glory of the presence of God). She is Isis. She bears both the Torah (Yang) and the Cross (Yin). (The Crescent Moon is also a symbol of Islam, so in that respect, she bears the signs of the three great Western religions.)

The Jerusalem Temple pillars of Jachin (foundation) and Boaz (strength) stand beside her, representing both stability and duality. The duality is reinforced by their black-and-white color scheme (the pillar in the current printings is gray, although Waite said it should be white) or in some readings, by body and spirit. (One translation of the Meditation reads explicitly, "Know the white, but keep to the black.") At any rate, the pillars represent light and darkness, male and female, symbolizing the Yin and Yang elements. Pillars are a common motif in Tarot; they represent not only strength, but also a gateway into further mysteries.

Atop the pillars are lotus buds, representing the opening of the consciousness from the material to the spiritual realm. The lotus is renowned for growing from the earth, through the water, into the pure air. It is an important symbol in both Hinduism and Buddhism. So in this one card we have the symbols of Judaism, Christianity, Islam, Hinduism, and Buddhism! And the river is the Tao.

The Yin river flows through the crescent moon, another Yin symbol, showing how the Tao is manifested through all nature. The High Priestess wears another form of the crescent moon as a crown.

Behind her throne are pomegranates, which, because of their many seeds, represent feminine fertility. (The pomegranates are shown here split open, revealing the seeds.) Some authorities read the entire picture as a vaginal symbol. In addition, the Bible states that pomegranates were carved on the pillars of King Solomon's Temple. Many experts consider pomegranates to have been the biblical fruit of the Tree of Knowledge, so there is also a connection with Forbidden Lore, the realm of the High Priestess.

The English word *pomegranate* means "apple with many seeds" and may thus account for the common European belief that the fruit of knowledge was the common apple, a fruit unknown in the hot Middle East. The pomegranate is further noted for its flaming red blossoms, and its sweet fruit protected by a rough rind. This is an obvious sexual symbol. The Hebrew word for pomegranate is *rimmon,* which is related to *rim,* meaning to bear a child. In classical mythology, Hera, Juno, Demeter, Persephone, Aphrodite, Athena, and the Phoenician goddess Astarte were all depicted with pomegranates. There is even a Christian shrine dedicated to the Virgin Mary, our Lady with Pomegranates, located near Paestum (in southern Italy) at the site of an ancient statue of Juno. The card also depicts palm fronds (a Yang sign), interspersed among the pomegranates. (The Empress, the following card, also bears a pomegranate design on her person.)

The High Priestess is indeed "the stream of the universe." Yet as the mother of the Ten Thousand things, the High Priestess controls both the Yang and the Yin. She has the qualities of both asceticism and fruitfulness. The High Priestess is the mistress of complexity and paradox, and can be related to Artemis, the virginal goddess who was in charge of women in childbirth. Some theorists connect her with the Sibylline oracle. For Carl Jung, she represented the Anima, the ideal woman, the complete Yin. She represents also the spiritual aspect of love. She is a step beyond the Magician, for she "knows the light, but keeps to the shadows." The High Priestess knows all sides of existence, and honors all. The emphasis is not on magical transformation from one thing into another but on inclusion, not on rejection but on acceptance.

She knows honor (Yang) but keeps humility (Yin) in her heart. She is the uncarved block that contains all potentiality. When the block is carved, it is ready for action. But the more it is carved, the less potential it has. Therefore, "The master tailor cuts little." The more the law is applied, the weaker it becomes. That's why she holds the scroll rolled up, and in reverse. The concepts of virginity, sexuality, asceticism, and motherhood are all woven into this complex symbol.

The same is true for the accompanying Meditation, which must have seemed shocking to the Confucians. It exalted the "feminine," exhorting the Seeker (whether male or female) to keep to the shadow. True power is the power of Yin. Stephen Walter Sterling, in his work *Tarot Awareness*, refers to the High Priestess as the "Eternal Reservoir." (This is quite telling, since Sterling draws no particular connections between Tarot and Tao.)

Magical Key

Character: The High Priestess has a keen ability to teach others. She is intuitive and mysteriously active, like the Tao. In a negative aspect, the High Priestess can indicate short-sightedness and poor judgment.

Current Circumstances: The Priestess must keep hold of the feminine side of her nature, and stay humble in the face of success, which may be illusory. Something important is not yet clear.

Conflicts, Dangers, and Limitations: There is a plot against the High Priestess. She is surrounded by envy. A male inspires fear.

Career: The High Priestess must not abuse the confidence of her employer. Although talents will be severely tested, they will be recognized in the end.

Friends and Family: A young woman to the south needs her help. The High Priestess would do well to help her family learn to get along better.

Finances and Possessions: The business outlook is favorable, especially if the High Priestess is flexible in her timing. If investments are well-balanced, the High Priestess stands to obtain great material wealth.

Health Concerns: Skin and liver. She should be prompt in seeking medical attention.

Romance: Quarreling between partners and separations are possibilities. An older woman may remarry.

Travel: Travel is unnecessary; staying home to enjoy one's home brings surer rewards.

Decision: Major life changes should be avoided.

Future Events and Spiritual Achievements: Dreams hold the key to the future, and should be studied carefully.

Omens and Talismans: This is a good card for gardeners and
people engaged in agriculture.

    Animal Spirit: Hare, Wild Ox
    Bird Spirit: Phoenix, Raven
    Color: White, Dark Green
    Plant: Buttercup, Bee Balm
    Tree: Birch, Pomegranate
    Gemstone: Diamond, Garnet
    Metal: Silver
    Direction: Southeast
    Place: River
    Season: Fall, Winter

THE DEVIL.

Meditation 29: The Devil (XV): Yang

Do you think you can improve the universe
By tampering with it?
It's not possible.

The cosmos is holy and perfect.
If you try to dominate it,
You'll ruin it.
If you try to seize it,
You'll lose it.

For all things are a flowing forth
And a return.
A rising and a sinking.
A heating and a chilling.
A growth and a decay.

The wise spirit
Steers the middle course.
She avoids extremes.

This is the card of Evil Domination.

Mystical Key

Evil is enthroned. The Devil perches on an iron block (representing matter) to which two human figures are chained. He is the Emperor in his darkest, most evil form. Some writers identify the couple as the Lovers, but if they are, there's been a dye job and a different hair dressing applied. The pair probably represent Adam and Eve. Adam's name means "red earth," thus accounting for the hair color. Both man and woman have sprouted a pair of horns and a tail. The woman's tail is a basket of fruit, harking back to the "forbidden fruit" of the Bible, while the man has a tail of flame. An allegorical way of reading this part of the picture is "The fruit of sin is hellfire." The sin is that of pride, of trying to control what cannot be controlled, of trying to take the place of God. The chain represents enslavement to Satan.

The Devil's hand is raised in greeting. The Devil, along with the Tower, was a latecomer to the Tarot pack. Some experts believe that they were suppressed by the church, but there's no evidence of this. It's more likely that they simply hadn't been added yet. The Devil is traditionally the father of lies and deceit, and a person drawing the Devil card was warned against lying and being lied to by others.

But the Meditation reminds us that that the Devil's sin was pride, a pride that made him want to dominate the world—even though at first he may have had good motives. Above the Devil's head is an inverted star. If a star stands for hope, the inverted star means despair, the keynote of the Devil, for hell is a place in which there is no hope.

In Taoism, a lie is not so much a deliberate "falsehood" as the inability to see the fullness of things. When the Devil card appears in a Taoist reading, it means that the reader is not looking at the whole picture, and that his inability to see reality in its fullness is causing him in some sense to "live a lie."

Magical Key

> Character: The Devil is very gifted, but also manipulative and
> dangerous. He appears other than what he really is.
> However, at the deepest core of his being, the Devil is
> closer to the divine than any other card in the deck. The
> Devil's task is to extricate himself from the oppressive traits
> of character that disguise his true nature. The Devil's

arrogance can destroy him. He must strive for more modesty and humility.

Current Circumstances: There is danger of being crushed or dominated by an evil person or habit of mind. He must let go of this crushing influence. Unfortunately, the Seeker may be unaware of the nature of the oppression. He may think the source comes from the outside, when it is actually inside himself—or vice versa. He may believe a powerful person is on his side, when the opposite is really the case.

Conflicts, Dangers, and Limitations: An arrogant enemy will repent. Trouble is caused by doubt and guilt. There is conflict between one male and two females.

Career: Advances are possible if the timing is right. Enthusiasm on the job will help right things.

Friends and Family: The Devil should pay more attention (in every sense of the word) to parents. This is a good card for a married couple. A young person will experience an initiation.

Finances and Possessions: Money and possessions result in possessiveness.

Health Concerns: Heart, ears, or digestive system. Illness or bondage to an evil habit like drugs, tobacco, or alcohol.

Romance: Passion and desire are present, but may not lead to happiness. A concentrated effort to control one's feelings is beneficial (even if it may not seem that way).

Travel: Travel to the east is auspicious; travel to the west is not. Traveling as a wanderer is very auspicious.

Decision: Patience is the key. Overhasty action brings regret.

Future Events and Spiritual Achievements: The Devil will learn that heaven and earth are equally real.

Omens and Talismans: The Devil is an auspicious card for a middle son or daughter, or for those in secretarial and support occupations.

    Animal Spirit: Cat, Bat
    Bird Spirit: Raven, Tern
    Color: Dark Blue, Black, Red, Yellow-Red.

Plant: Red Rose, Burdock
Tree: Pine, Beech
Gemstone: Star Sapphire, Ruby
Metal: Iron
Direction: East
Place: Streams, Forest
Season: Autumn

Meditation 30: Knight of Swords

KNIGHT of SWORDS.

The Tao Master doesn't conquer by force.
It doesn't work.
Wherever an army marches,
Thorns and thistles spring up.
A single war produces years of bad harvest.
Act on only what needs to be done.
Take no advantage of power.
Once you reach your goal,
Cease action.
Don't brag about your accomplishments.
Simply achieve the result.
This is the way of nature.
Excess force leads to unnatural weakness.

That is not the way of Tao.
If you persist in acting this way.
You will perish.

This is the card of Daring.

Mystical Key

This is the only Knight who does not try to control his horse, but rather, lunges forward with him. The true Knight of the Swords is the Knight of the Spirit; he rides like Feng-liu—the flowing of the wind. Riding the wind is merely obeying one's own spirit. To do otherwise is ugly, dangerous, unnecessary, unhealthy. Riding the spirit means casting off the boasting, the bragging, and all similar excrescence that weigh down the traveler. The river of wind strips away everything but his own soul. The true Knight's danger is not to the Seeker of the Tao, but to its enemies, for the true Knight rides with the wind, not against it.

Magical Key

Character: The Knight of Swords is audacious, intense, and brilliant. His character is deep, strong, and subtle. He appears changeable, but his motives are single-minded and fixed. In a negative reading, the Knight of Swords is thoughtless and impulsive. He is possibly very dangerous.

Current Circumstances: The Knight should line up helpers for a charitable project. Some of them may be better able to help than the Knight himself. The Knight will be successful in legal maneuvers, but in love affairs may not attain his goals. The Knight may need to readjust them. This is not a good time is cause a disturbance or to put pressure on others. Let the spirit control the body, not vice versa.

Conflicts, Dangers, and Limitations: Opposition, oppression, and war are possible. The Knight spends too much time arguing with others. The Knight may seek the way outwardly and lose it inwardly. It is very important not to make the least slip. Constant rushing will exhaust the spirit. Someone may be a spy. The Knight is advised to go forth and meet trouble, as long as he is fighting for his principles and the higher good, not for himself. Ignorance is a danger; the Knight struggles with the meaning of sin.

Career: The Knight of Swords will obtain a position suited to his talents and realize his ambitions.

Friends and Family: The Knight should go to the aid of his friends; later, they will be of benefit. The Knight will have many descendants.

Finances and Possessions: The Knight should not rely on the financial advice of others. If the Knight adheres to his principles, he will succeed.

Health Concerns: Heart and blood vessels.

Romance: This is an excellent card for those who are married. For those unmarried, however, it is not a fortunate card.

Travel: Distant travel is dangerous at this time.

Decision: Others should not sway the Knight's decision. It's best to stay firm and avoid this action.

Future Events and Spiritual Achievements: The Knight will obtain spiritual light.

Omens and Talismans: This is a lucky card for the eldest son or a person of maturity.

> Animal Spirit: Horse, Butterfly
> Bird Spirit: Robin, Cardinal
> Color: Black
> Plant: Heather, Anemone
> Tree: Cypress, Magnolia
> Gemstone: Agate, Rubellite
> Metal: Steel
> Direction: West
> Place: Sea
> Season: Late Autumn, Winter

Meditation 31: Six of Wands

Even the most beautiful weapons
Are instruments for killing.
All creatures fear and hate them.
Those who follow the Tao disdain them.

The wise spirit prefers an empty hand
To one that carries a lance.
Only direst necessity compels him
To use a weapon.

Even then he takes no pleasure in it.
To enjoy weapons is to enjoy killing.

To rejoice in victory
Is to rejoice in slaughter.

Those who rejoice in killing
Are no longer part of the human community.
A battlefield is not a place for celebration,
But for funerals.

This is the card of Peace.

Mystical Key

This is the card of mature and sorrowful realization, of one who knows how tragic victory can be. Sometimes it represents a difficult dilemma; the Referent feels that he has acted wrongly, but cannot see how he could have acted in any other way. He has done what he felt was necessary, but also knows the cost.

Magical Key

Character: The Six of Wands is reflective and supportive of others. He is responsible and feels responsible for the well-being of many other people.

Current Circumstances: The Six cannot manage this situation single-handedly. Get help. Students need to study harder. There is something important to be learned by heart. A harmonious change will soon come about, especially if the Six can rise above a false notion of himself.

Conflicts, Dangers, and Limitations: Greed and strong opinions are a danger. The Six experiences a sense of separation from a state or relationship of former security. Through effort, the Six can repair what has been spoiled.

Career: This is a good time to form a partnership, but be careful in the beginning.

Friends and Family: Friends look to the Six for guidance. In a negative reading, a traitor may be present in the Six's life. He may need to cut off dangerous entanglements.

Finances and Possessions: This is not an easy time to borrow money. The Six of Wands may experience a painful financial problem due to his own actions. This doesn't mean that his actions were wrong, but that they carry heavy consequences.

Health Concerns: Bones. Treat any illnesses promptly. This is a good time to go on a diet.

Romance: This is an inauspicious card for romance. The Seeker is suffering a delusion, possibly from trying to re-create a past relationship in the present one.

Travel: Travel to the mountains is beneficial.

Decision: More time and thorough investigation are needed before the right decision can be made.

Future Events and Spiritual Achievements: The Six will experience a bittersweet victory, and learn to see through the things of this world to the things of spirit. The wise Six knows the loss inherent even in the sweetest victory. The Six will find a good mentor and likeminded associates.

Omens and Talismans: This a good card for those in the transportation industry, for poets, and for those in service professions.

    Animal Spirit: Cat, Basilisk
    Bird Spirit: Stork, Cormorant
    Color: Yellow, Green
    Plant: Laurel, Willow
    Tree: Cedar, Tupelo
    Gemstone: White Jade, Chrysoberyl
    Metal: Bronze
    Direction: West
    Place: House, Garden
    Season: Late Summer, Early Fall

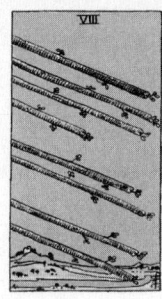

Meditation 32: Eight of Wands

The eternal Tao is without name,
So small it is.
It eludes the grasp.
If the rulers of this world
Knew how to use it,
Earth and heaven
Would come together in bliss
And the sweet dew would nourish all.
Humanity would live as one,
And all things would be in harmony.

But this divided world
Is ruled by names.
We have enough names.
It is time to return,
For the Tao to flow home to the sea.

This is the card of the Ten Thousand Things.

Mystical Key
The Eight of Wands is the only card in the Tarot deck with no human figure, face, or man-made object. It explores the concept that even nature is divided into the "ten thousand things" and suggests the multiplicity of objects in the universe, which, though originally intended to live harmoniously, do not always do so. In a reading, this card gives indications of speed of thought and quick (perhaps inordinately quick) action.

Magical Key
    Character: The Eight of Wands is gifted in speech or communications, and is highly intelligent. However, the Eight is unyielding and tends to rush around too much.
    Current Circumstances: The Eight of Wands has a lot going on; things are happening quickly, perhaps too quickly. Despite

the busy surrounding circumstances, the Eight feels a sense of solitude, and is forced to rely on himself. This may not necessarily be a bad thing. What was formerly mysterious will soon become clear.

Conflicts, Dangers, and Limitations: The Eight needs to slow down, and pay attention to detail. He may be the object of someone's hatred and may receive something that he does not want.

Career: The Eight's career is productive, but ultimate goals may not be reached.

Friends and Family: Something shocking is about to happen, but the shock will be followed by great joy. One family tradition or habit is harmful and should be abandoned.

Finances and Possessions: Not an auspicious card for finance. This is not the time to gamble or indulge in foolish speculations in the financial markets. Such speculation can put wealth in jeopardy. A theft is possible.

Health Concerns: Stomach and sleeping problems. The Eight should be consistent in an exercise program; he should not overtax his strength.

Romance: Things are moving too fast. The Eight should step back from this relationship to reassess it.

Travel: Travel to the hills is beneficial. The trip should be brief.

Decision: The Eight should act early, but not attempt anything big. He should pursue only small goals at the present time.

Future Events and Spiritual Achievements: The Eight will achieve power.

Omens and Talismans: This is a good card for an older person and for people engaged in commercial activities.

    Animal Spirit: Jackal, Crocodile
    Bird Spirit: Swallow, Crow
    Color: Orange, Crimson
    Plant: Jasmine, Lily
    Tree: Pine, Dogwood
    Gemstone: Beryl, Ruby
    Metal: Quicksilver (Mercury)
    Direction: Southwest

Place: Mountains
Season: Summer

Meditation 33: Strength (VIII): Yin

Knowing others is knowledge.
Understanding oneself is wisdom.
Overcoming others requires force.
Mastering oneself requires strength.

One who knows when he has enough
Is rich indeed.
One who keeps to the path is strong.
One who maintains his place is enduring.

To live in the moment is to live without death.

This is the card of Integrity.

Note: In some packs, Strength is number XI, while number VIII is Justice. Waite switched the order of these cards and ever since they have oscillated back and forth. The reasons for Waite's decision are unclear. In his famous *Pictorial Key to the Tarot,* he said simply, "As the variation carries nothing with it which will signify to the reader, there is no cause for explanation." And there we must leave it.

Mystical Key

A woman gently opens (or closes) the mouth of a lion. The overall impression of the card is one of gentleness. Older cards depicted a woman apparently ripping the lion's mouth open, but this kind drawing creates a more evocative and powerful image. The lion is generally considered to be a symbol of wild nature in oneself. The card shows the inherent and indissoluble relationship between our human and our Animal Spirit nature. The point is not to destroy the lion, but to "tame" it by integration into the self. The lion is also a masculine symbol, so this card can be read as the overmastering of the masculine (Yang) by the feminine (Yin).

The woman is crowned with the lemniscate, which stands for infinity. The only other figure so adorned is the Magician. The depiction of Strength as a woman is traditional, a nod to the power of Yin that gives it its true strength. Yin strength is strength over oneself (represented by the Yang lion). It also represents spiritual as opposed to physical strength. True strength is keeping to the path of Tao, and having the ability to live in the moment. It is often said that men need to get in touch with their feminine side. This card shows the importance to women of getting in touch with their masculine side, represented by the maned lion.

Magical Key

Character: Strength is well-integrated, fair, and in touch with her "wild side." She also has great powers of reason.

Negatively, Strength could be a cruel or brutal person, or in danger of becoming such a person.

Current Circumstances: An underlying, perhaps subconscious, fear is stopping Strength from success. Strength must take a firm stand, and move forward slowly but with persistence. Strength must get into touch with the deep wellsprings of her inner power to use it for good and creative ends. Every step is dangerous—both going forward and retreating. Escape is not possible. A course in meditation would be useful for this purpose.

Conflicts, Dangers, and Limitations: Strength may be at a temporary disadvantage against others; strong negative influences are everywhere. She must let the past go and live more in the moment. Ignorance is the greatest danger. There may be a serious challenge next year.

Career: Strength will achieve her goal by using her considerable powers of influence. These are so strong that some modern interpreters of Tarot call Strength the Enchantress. But influence isn't enough. Strength needs to work hard and concentrate.

Friends and Family: There is much opposition; Strength's best friends are in the south and west. For now, she should avoid those in the east and north. A woman overcomes a man.

Finances and Possessions: Business affairs are lackluster at the present time.

Health Concerns: Skin.

Romance: Relationships are gradually improving. To restore them completely requires careful work.

Travel: A river trip would be beneficial. It best to use the trip for meditation and contemplation.

Decision: Proceed with caution. Once the decision is made, it should be adhered to with great determination.

Future Events and Spiritual Achievements: This entire year will be good for Strength, but next year will be a challenge. Strength will achieve victory over others, and, more important, over herself.

Omens and Talismans: This is a good card for those in authority.

    Animal Spirit: Deer, Lion
    Bird Spirit: Pelican, Eagle
    Color: Yellow/Orange, White
    Plant: Rose, Pampas Grass
    Tree: Birch, Ash
    Gemstone: Cat's-Eye, Sapphire
    Metal: Steel
    Direction: South
    Place: Plains
    Season: Winter

Meditation 34: Ten of Pentacles

The great Tao flows everywhere,
Both to the left and to the right.
The Ten Thousand Things of this World
Depend on it, and the Tao never fails them.

Though the Tao is great, it claims no dominion
Over the Ten Thousand Things.
It is so small.
Small—but the Ten Thousand Things

Return to it,
And call it great.

Just so the wise spirit
Fulfills her own greatness
By staying small,
But doing what is great.

This is the card of Happiness.

Mystical Key

This is a card of success, prosperity, and happiness in almost all spheres. It is a recognition of the overflowing of the Tao into all life, including that of the Seeker. "The Ten Thousand Things of this World depend on it, and the Tao never fails them." The presence on the card of three generations and two dogs represents the unity of all beings. The dogs, in addition, play their role of household guardians. (In China, dogs were believed to repel demons.)

Magical Key

Character: The Ten of Pentacles inspires loyalty, and knows how to find the positive side of any situation. The Ten is generally optimistic and cheerful. She has no need to dominate others. However in a negative aspect, the Ten may be stubborn and may lack spiritual purpose, possibly because of an inadequate ethical education.

Current Circumstances: Tensions and complications begin to decrease. There is something very good in life that has been neglected. An end to poverty and misery. What was started should be completed. Teaching should be consistent.

Conflicts, Dangers, and Limitations: The Ten of Pentacles may feel intellectually frustrated. A disturbance needs to be stopped immediately.

Career: A creative retirement lies ahead.

Friends and Family: The Ten should stay open to the gifts and abilities of others. This is a time for the Ten to be especially strict about family responsibilities.

Finances and Possessions: Prosperity and success will come, although they may be late. It is not wise to take a risk.

Health Concerns: Back.

Romance: This is an auspicious card for a fulfilling marriage.

Travel: A trip to the valley would be beneficial.

Decision: Standards are currently changing, and Ten must be careful to make a wise choice—not by acting alone.

Future Events and Spiritual Achievements: The Ten will obtain well-earned wealth, although it may take longer than desired.

Omens and Talismans: This is a fortunate card for those in the healing arts or business. The Ten will achieve the knowledge of the Higher Laws.

    Animal Spirit: Dog, Unicorn
    Bird Spirit: Phoenix, Plover
    Color: Olive, Purple
    Plant: Laurel, Grapevine
    Tree: Elm, Willow
    Gemstone: Tourmaline, Amethyst
    Metal: Gold
    Direction: East
    Place: House, Garden
    Season: Winter

ACE of SWORDS.

Meditation 35: Ace of Swords

He who holds in hand
The great Image of the invisible Tao
Has the power to draw all things to him.
Those who approach find serenity and joy.

At first some may pause
For music, luxuries, and fine food.
Compared to them, the Tao
Seems bland and without flavor,
Without sound or substance.

Yet it is the Inexhaustible Source.
You can never get your fill.

This is the card of Awakening.

Mystical Key

This card signals great things in the artistic, financial, or social sphere. A Taoist poem that envisions the Ace of Swords is "Song to the Lord Within the Clouds" (Wong 12):

> *The Lord-Within-the Clouds comes down to us,*
> *His sacred light shining with eternal brilliance.*

This card combines sexuality invested with deep spiritual qualities, which, paradoxically, may make it difficult for the Seeker to form relationships. Sometimes he is in his "dragon chariot" of spirituality (the dragon represents the higher spiritual realm); sometimes in the more physical realm.

Magical Key

Character: Tremendous power is available to the Ace; he can overcome all obstacles. The Ace tends to be passive, but under the right conditions, he has great determination, and can go to extremes. He is also witty and charming. In a negative reading, he can be willful. It is very important now for him to examine his faults and try to correct them.

Current Circumstances: High levels of spiritual energy are present. There is some grief amid the happiness.

Conflicts, Dangers, and Limitations: Too much ambition can lead to danger. An obstacle in the Ace's life—the focus of anger and hatred—must be renounced. The Ace is beginning to see the limitations of logic.

Career: The current is auspicious, but the Ace should not put too much pressure on others—it could backfire.

Family and Friends: Friends will be loyal, but not all family members can be trusted.

Finances and Possessions: This is an unfavorable card for financial investments.

Health Concerns: Heart, blood pressure, and cholesterol; eyes and ears.

Romance: This card could signal the beginning of a difficult relationship, perhaps the start of enmity or persecution, even great violence. In such a relationship, the Ace may be spiritually or psychologically injured. It may be as long as ten years before the beloved is ready to marry.

Travel: Travel is delayed by an evil event, and travelers will encounter difficulty.

Decision: The Ace should not be impulsive.

Future Events and Spiritual Achievements: Unexpected good luck. It must not be permitted to make the Ace careless. The Ace will eventually find the truth that transcends logic.

Omens and Talismans: This is a good card for people in the military and for women.

> Animal Spirit: Butterfly, Carp
> Bird Spirit: Dove, Snipe
> Color: Yellow, Black
> Plant: Laurel, Palm
> Tree: Birch, Holly
> Gemstone: Pearl, Citrine
> Metal: Steel
> Direction: South
> Place: Sky
> Season: Spring

Meditation 36: Knight of Pentacles

KNIGHT of PENTACLES.

If something is to be shrunken,
It first needs to be stretched.
A breathing out
Is preceded by a breathing in.

Those who are defeated
Once were strong,
Those cast down
Were once exalted.
And those who despoil others
Once made great gifts to them.

This tactic is called "hiding the light."

Just as a fish cannot leave his deep water,
The wise leader keeps his weapons hidden.

This is the card of Clear Perception.

Mystical Key

It is often thought that the Tao counsels only non-action. This is a mistaken idea. As the mother of all things, it engenders action as well as inaction. Wu-wei, the doctrine of no forced action, contains both the sign for action and for non-action, not just inaction. What the Tao does call for is what Nietzsche termed a "transvaluation of values." The greatest actions sometimes lie in non-action. Paradox is the great key.

Magical Key

Character: The Knight of Pentacles is responsible and mature. He is popular, because he doesn't reveal all his talents, and doesn't need to be in control. He may appear to be lazy, but he has an inner restlessness.

Current Circumstances: This is not the time to further one's own ends. The Knight should practice compassion, and learn from a mistake.

Conflicts, Dangers, and Limitations: The Knight may feel secure, but there is still some danger lurking.

Career: Possible unemployment. Talent should not remain hidden; this may be a good time to return to school. Be careful not to alienate your superiors or employees.

Friends and Family: Friends are of like mind.

Finances and Possessions: This is not a favorable time for real estate transactions.

Health Concerns: Problems with the limbs will soon be healed. In general, this card betokens good health, but the Knight should not become overattached to the body.

Romance: Romance will be tempestuous.

Travel: Travel is dangerous at this time.

Decision: Rely on a wise friend to help make this decision.

Future Events and Spiritual Achievements: The Knight will attain his wishes, but it may take longer than expected.

Omens and Talismans: This is an auspicious card for the youngest son or a youngest daughter, and also for those in government service.

Animal Spirit: Elephant, Fox
Bird Spirit: Crow, Sandpiper
Color: White, Deep Purple
Plant: Moss, Elder
Tree: Apple, Plum
Gemstone: Serpentine, Spinel
Metal: Gold
Direction: West
Place: Sea
Season: Summer

Meditation 37: Two of Wands

The Tao is never busy,
But everything gets accomplished.

If those in power could attain the Tao,
The Ten Thousand Things of this World
Would be transformed.

Even if the Ten Thousand Things
Got ahead of themselves,
They would eventually return
To their original state of simple
Natural being.
Without name, form, or desire
Lies peace.

This is the card of Actionless Action.

Mystical Key

This card clearly represents the Penglai Pavilion, at the top of China's Cinnabar Cliff Mountain, a place of great Taoist renown. Penglai stands above the earth and sea, and when one arrives there, one stands above the world and all its honor and disgrace. In fact, one becomes transformed into the immortal world. The Penglai Pavilion stands for the state of consciousness that rises above the Ten Thousand Things of This World, but holds them, too. This supreme state of consciousness has the power and will to transform the world.

Magical Key

Character: The Two is emotionally mature, patient, and
   intuitive. He is often in a position of authority, and is
   known for his generosity and charitable giving. The Two
   favors intuition over intellect and reasoning. He's not afraid
   of hard work, but he may be overly fastidious. For a female,
   the card suggests a woman of unusual boldness. The Two

of Wands may know too much, and tends to manipulate.

Current Circumstances: Continuing on the present path risks humiliation. There may be much regret. Secrets should be kept. Seek the support of other people.

Conflicts, Dangers, and Limitations: There may be an unexpected obstacle, due to someone with a quick-tempered, willful, unforgiving nature. The obstacle can be gradually overcome, but the Two may have to withdraw first.

Career: The Two of Wands has the power to accomplish his goals, but his efforts are erratic. Because the card is a Two, it suggests that this is the perfect time to form a partnership to accomplish those goals. A transfer to a much better job is possible. It will help if the Two encourages others at their own work.

Friends and Family: This is an inauspicious card for family and friends; the Two may not be tolerant of others.

Finances and Possessions: Commercial activities are favorable.

Health Concerns: Throat and jaw. Bad health may prevent the accomplishment of a goal.

Romance: This is an inauspicious card for romance. New attachments should be avoided.

Travel: All travel is favorable now.

Decisions: The Two should take the opportunity offered.

Future Events and Spiritual Achievements: The Two will attain great wisdom and understanding.

Omens and Talismans: The card favors those who take risks.

    Animal Spirit: Dragon, Serpent
    Bird Spirit: Raven, Cormorant
    Color: Brown, Orange
    Plant: Rose, Heal-All
    Tree: Plum, Cherry
    Gemstone: Citrine, Tourmaline
    Metal: Lead
    Direction: Northeast
    Place: Mountains
    Season: Summer

Meditation 38: King of Cups

KING of CUPS.

The Tao Master is unaware
Of his power.
Therein lies his power.

Those who strive after power
Will never attain it.

The wise spirit does nothing.
And accomplishes everything.
Others scramble and fuss,
But achieve nothing.

The truly virtuous
Have no personal goals.
The falsely virtuous
Care only for themselves.
They make a big show
Of ceremony and propriety.
But when that doesn't work,
They reveal their mailed fist.

If we fail Tao,
We are left with "virtue."
If we fail virtue,
We are left with"benevolence."
If we fail benevolence,
We are left with "fairness."
If we fail fairness,
We are left with "propriety" and "ceremony."

Ceremony is an empty husk,
The beginning of disorder.
Just as a quick intelligence

Is only the showy bloom of the Tao,
Not its fruit.
It is the beginning of folly.

The wise spirit,
Abides in the real,
Not the superficial.
He seeks the fruit
And not the flower.
He makes a choice.

This is the card of Discernment.

Mystical Key

The important word in the Meditation is *Te*, which means both power and true virtue. The King of Cups also represents power and virtue. The place where the King resides may be the mystical island of P'u-t'o, where none may dwell but the pure of heart. Behind him to his left is the ship of fortune, while to his right, partly concealed, is the sea serpent or giant sea turtle, representing possible danger. The wise spirit has the same virtue, the same power that the Tao itself has—not something superficial and particular to himself. As virtues become more particularized, they at the same time become more conventional—that which people imagine to be their own particular virtues are really quite commonplace and debased. Paradoxically, the deep virtue available to all is understood and used by only a few.

Taoists believed that all that was needed to rule successfully was to achieve purity in one's soul. While some people might regard this as impractical, it springs from a sound principle—that virtue flows outward. Certainly one cannot expect others to be ethical if one is not ethical oneself.

Magical Key

Character: The King is a secretive, but benevolent friend. He has the power (*Te*) of virtue. He is responsible, malleable, and versed in the arts, law, or sciences. He is known for his equanimity, but he is complex and subtle. He has a penetrating mind. In an unfavorable reading, the King can be overambitious, treacherous, and even violent.

Current Circumstances: The King needs to watch his words carefully.

Conflicts, Dangers, and Limitations: The King of Cups' spiritual pride is very harmful. He may also get into trouble on account of alcohol or sex.

Career: Coworkers, especially underlings, may be plotting against the King of Cups. Their lack of support is extremely harmful. However, this is an inauspicious time to look for a new job.

Friends and Family: The King should be wary of someone.

Finances and Possessions: Loss of property or money is possible.

Health Concerns: Lower back and skin. Diet is important.

Romance: Relationships need hard work now. Marriage is not likely in the near future.

Travel: A trip is indicated. It will be favorable.

Decision: Do not do this.

Future Events and Spiritual Achievements: Remorse disappears. The King will abandon "success," for something better—purity of heart. The Seeker will attain joy.

Omens and Talismans: This is an auspicious card for those in government service.

    Animal Spirit: Elephant, Fish
    Bird Spirit: Eagle, Owl
    Color: Blue-Gray, Purple
    Flower: Bluebell, Lavender
    Tree: Alder, Hackberry
    Gemstone: Beryl, Lapis Lazuli
    Metal: Quicksilver (Mercury)
    Direction: North
    Place: Sea
    Season: Summer

THE SUN.

Meditation 39:

The Sun (XIX): Yang

These ancient, immemorial things
Are from One:
The pure, brilliant sky,
The enduring earth,
The mystic spirit,
The river-jeweled valley,
The Ten Thousand Things of this World.
This is the pattern for kings and princes.
All share the power of the One.

Heaven abides by its purity,
And would crack without it.
Earth abides by its sureness,
And would shake without it.
Spirit abides by its power,
And without it would evaporate.
The valley abides in its fullness
Without which it would run dry.
The Ten Thousand Things of this World
Abide in the One,
Without which they would perish.
Kings and princes abide in that virtue
Without which their reign would lack legitimacy.

Just so, the root bears the flower and fruit.
The exalted stands on the humble.
Kings and princes realize
Without the people
They would be orphans, widowed,
And without worth.

We honor jade for being precious
But its strength is in being rock.

This is the card of Stability.

Mystical Key

The Sun is the daytime star, the principal light of the sky. The Sunflowers on the card are reminiscent of the Golden Flower of Taoist alchemy, which symbolizes the immortal soul. They also represent the earthly, as complementary to the heavenly, Sun. The child rides the horse without saddle or bridle, reminding us of the power of the innocent and the value in being able to let go. Guidance never needs whip or spur or bit. The child's nakedness and outstretched limbs show he has nothing to hide. This is the manifest Tao at its most glorious, and most innocent. The child in the picture reminds us of the steady counsel of both the Tao Te Ching and Jesus that regaining one's innocence is essential to spiritual achievement.

Of all the Major Arcana, the Sun may be the most powerful and beneficent. Almost without exception it is a sign of the greatest fortune and of auspicious portent. The Sun illuminates all other cards in a layout and casts a more favorable light on them. It is so dazzling, however, that we can ignore its real power, a power that can injure as well as help. Just as in the natural world we see the sun as an object of nearly incomprehensible beauty, we can forget that its true value lies is its power and strength to bring forth life. It is the One, the mystic spirit, the pattern for kings, and the giver of life. No wonder the ancients worshipped it as a god. Yet the Meditation reminds us that the value of the Sun is not its beauty or symbolic importance, but its life-giving warmth.

Even the Sun, however, the most Yang of cards, has its "dark side." It can destroy by its power what it has brought forth.

Magical Key

Character: The Sun has a powerful life force. He is inwardly
tranquil, and does whatever he can to be helpful to others.
Freedom of motion is important to him. The Sun may have
musical or artistic abilities.

Current Circumstances: This card signifies a joyful and happy period. The Sun has made an important promise and must keep it. He must reconcile with all previous enemies and come to terms with difficult times in the past.

Conflicts, Dangers, and Limitations: Mental instability. Some things may be a matter of chance right now, not something the Sun can control. This is a time to be calm.

Career: Subordinates need to understand clearly their assigned tasks.

Friends and Family: The Sun will make a new friend. A powerful, restless man has a great influence. There is separation from the mother.

Finances and Possessions: Commercial activities are favorable. However, this is not a good time to make a major purchase.

Health Concerns: Special care of the neck, digestion, or hip is important now. Older people should forget their worries about living a longer life. Medication now being taken has not been shown to be entirely beneficial.

Romance: Craving is leading to delusion. Divorce, a broken engagement, or the end of a romantic relationship is possible. Someone has been badly hurt.

Travel: Travel is not necessary at this time.

Decision: The welfare of others is paramount in making this decision.

Future Events and Spiritual Achievements: The Sun will be able to conquer the powers of evil and achieve stability and a high degree of consciousness.

Omens and Talismans: This is an auspicious card for scholars and students.

> Animal Spirit: Frog, Lion
> Bird Spirit: Dove, Hawk
> Color: Green, Smoky Gray
> Plant: Columbine, Azalea
> Tree: Buckthorn, Hornbeam
> Gemstone: Turquoise, Zircon

Metal: Gold
Direction: Northeast
Place: Castle
Season: Spring, Summer

THE LOVERS.

Meditation 40: The Lovers (VI): Yang

The Tao proceeds by contraries
But always returns.
Its way is the way of yielding.

Heaven, Earth,
And the Ten Thousand Things
Are born of being.
But being is born of nothing.

This is the card of Desire.

Mystical Key

This is the last card on the Going Forth part of the Tao Te Ching. It is another card in which Waite made some major changes from older packs. Male and female figures stand beneath the angel. This angel is the first winged character in the Major Arcana. (The others are found in Temperance and Judgment.) The wings are a reminder of the spiritual dimension that lies behind every choice.

The story of Adam and Eve is alluded to by the depiction of the tree with the serpent. Some believe the fruits stand for the five senses, the source of temptation. Behind the male figure is a tree with flamelike blossoms, suggestive of both hell and passionate desire. The lovers stand apart from each other, possibly aware of their nakedness for the first time. Adam and Eve got into trouble partly by blaming each other (and the serpent) for their mistakes.

The serpent is a complex symbol that has both Yin and Yang characteristics. Preclassic Mediterranean civilization regarded women and serpents as fellow generators of life; hence the appearance of the serpent on the caduceus. In Tantra, the goal of the practitioner is to raise the serpent within himself to reach a state of divine knowledge and bliss. The serpent has long represented mystical knowledge as well; hence its connection with the Tree of the Knowledge of Good and Evil. This combines both elements of serpent lore—wisdom and life, as trees are always the symbol of life.

There is explicitly a Tree of Life in the Garden of Eden as well, which is sometimes identified as the Tree of the Knowledge of Good and Evil. In this Tarot card, the Tree of Life may be represented by the Tree to the right, behind Adam. Its blossoms may be the blood-red, flaming blossoms of the pomegranate—in which case both trees may be of the same variety. (Some ancient traditions make the case that the Tree of the Knowledge of Good and Evil is a pomegranate tree, which would accord with the design of this Tarot card.)

The Lovers card has traditionally been held to represent choice, just as Eve and Adam had to make a choice. The Tao Te Ching is full of verses that urge the reader to "choose" the Tao. "He lets go of that and chooses this" is another way of talking about the individuation process. But the Lovers also obviously represent sexuality and desire. Sexuality is the source of the Ten Thousand Things, and the Lovers are connected to the curiously ambiguous individuation process, which is the essence of love. For lovers love not in general, but one person alone. Yet at the same time, the Lovers seek union, which is the destruction of individuation. This is strongly stated in the meditation.

> The Tao proceeds by contraries
> But always returns.
> Its way is the way of yielding.

But desire goes much further than simply sexual desire, and the desire that both elevated and doomed the First Couple was a desire for the knowledge of "good and evil." In Hebrew, the phrase *good and evil* meant not literally "good and evil" but "everything in the world"—the same meaning as the Chinese "Ten Thousand Things."

The number of this Meditation is 40, a number sacred in the Western world. The forty days of Jesus' fast and temptation and the forty days of the Flood are typical examples.

Magical Key

Character: The Seeker is attractive to others, strong, respected, and honored. However, the Seeker is also beset by duality, the flowing of Yin and Yang, which is sometimes in balance, and sometimes not.

Current Circumstances: Youthful folly has unexpectedly brought about success. The Seeker is coming to a major turning point—(see Meditation 41). He *must* make a choice. The choice may be between movement and staying still—the Manifest and Unmanifest Tao. It may also mean that it is time for the Referent to leave his childhood family and set out on his own adventures, though the path will be fraught with peril. Appearances can be deceiving. Neither the card nor the Meditation suggest which is right for the Seeker at this point, but it emphasizes that both are part of the nature of things.

Conflicts, Dangers, and Limitations: Many minor quarrels, disobedience, and willfulness occur when the Yin and Yang are out of balance. Alcohol may be a problem. Some acquaintances are jealous, but they can do no real harm. The Seeker should not give way to anger.

Career: Required tasks are proving onerous. Possible unemployment or career troubles lie ahead. It is important to make use of all the resources available.

Friends and Family: Friends are envious.

Finances and Possessions: This is a good time for a thorough housecleaning, both of the Seeker's home and accounts. His greatest profit lies in joining with others.

Health Concerns: Take special care of the skin, teeth, jaw, or tongue. Be careful not to eat too much or too richly.

Romance: Pride or complacency can get in the way of a good relationship.

Travel: It is better to stay home right now.

Decision: A change is beneficial now, but care must be taken. Once the choice is made, it will be difficult to retreat. Whatever the Seeker chooses will have serious consequences. The choice is an important one, one that will bring new horizons, but at a frightful cost.

Future Events and Spiritual Achievements: An important test is looming ahead, within forty days. The Lovers will achieve wisdom and a knowledge of the meaning of sacrifice.

Omens and Talismans: This is an auspicious card for scientists.

> Animal Spirit: Goat, Ram
> Bird Spirit: Eagle, Vulture
> Color: White, Deep Blue
> Plant: Dandelion, Clematis
> Tree: Holly, Apple
> Gemstone: Agate, Amethyst
> Metal: Quicksilver (Mercury)
> Direction: West
> Place: Workshop
> Season: Winter

Meditation 41: REVERSAL!

The wise student learns of the Tao
And follows it faithfully.
The mediocre student hears about the Tao
And wanders on and off the track.
The bad student stumbles upon the Tao
And laughs in derision.
Well, that's the way the Way is.
If people didn't laugh at it,
The Tao would be different.

That's why we say,
The shining path seems dark,
The forward path seems to reverse itself,
The pleasant path seems suddenly full of briars,
Stainless purity looks soiled,
Immense goodness appears inadequate.

The greatest square is too big for corners,
The greatest vessel is never finished,
The highest note is beyond hearing.
The greatest thought is out of reach.

The Tao is deep down and nameless.
But it perfectly fulfills nature.

Mystical Key

This is the turning point. The shining path seems dark, for it is here that the struggle is most intense. "The pleasant path seems suddenly full of briars." But this is exactly the moment when true vision can become possible, for it is here that we first begin to truly understand that the Tao is "deep down and nameless."

4

The Return

All things arise from the Tao, and to the Tao must all things return. Thus the Tao is the beginning and the end. It is Yin and Yang in the creative harmony of which the Tao Te Ching speaks.

Meditation 42: Ace of Wands

ACE of WANDS.

The Tao is the Mother of the One.
The One gives birth to Two.
The Two bring forth Three.
And the Three engender the Ten Thousand Things
*   of this World.*
The Ten Thousand Things of this World
Carry the Yin on their backs,
And hold the Yang in their arms.
The Yin and the Yang interact
In creative harmony.

Humanity hates the idea
Of being orphaned, widowed, or of little worth.
Yet these are the very roles the wise leader
Takes upon himself.

Some things are gained by losing them.
Others lost by gaining them.

It's the same old story, but worth repeating:
Those who are violent will be destroyed by violence.

This is the card of Creation.

Mystical Key

The Return opens with the Ace of Wands—a new beginning, a new creation. (The Wand in this picture is exceptionally phallic.) In the picture, the Ace of Wands is also meant to recall the Axis Mundi, the mythic tree or pole around which the world revolves and that supports the firmament. The Axis Mundi gives us the means to "climb to heaven." "The Yin and the Yang interact in creative harmony." A new enterprise is afoot! This Meditation reminds us that All are contained in the One, and the One in the All. We are all children of the Tao, and to her must we return. The Ace is both the highest and lowest card of the deck—the orphan and the king. The wise leader and the one of "little worth" are connected.

Magical Key

Character: The Ace is creative, independent, stable, strong-
    willed, and able to reconcile opposing forces. He has
    tremendous energy and is a good listener. A woman who
    draws this card is very powerful.

Current Circumstances: The beginning of an artistic enterprise.
    Lots of energy and power are available, but they must be
    used wisely, and in the cause of peace. In a negative aspect,
    imminent cruelty and ruin can be indicated.

Conflicts, Dangers, and Limitations: The Ace may be beset with
    envy or greed. Any hardships will make the Ace stronger in
    the end.

Career: Those working in government service or bureaucracy
    can expect a promotion or a salary increase. However, most
    Aces do best in a job where they have an outlet for their
    creativity. Aces don't thrive under close supervision.

Friends and Family: Parents may be domineering. A young fool is
    seeking the Ace out for advice. It is wise to be kind to him.

Finances and Possessions: Although this is a poor time financially, it does not mean that the Ace cannot be happy. This is an excellent opportunity to learn how little money matters.

Health Concerns: The Ace should be careful about diet; metabolism could be improved. Arthritis is a possibility as well.

Romance: The Ace is faithful to his or her partner. The Ace should attach himself to someone who is equally strong-willed; otherwise he may tend to overpower his partner.

Travel: Travel by ship is auspicious now. Take a cruise.

Decision: Do not do this. Do not rely on guesswork.

Future Events and Spiritual Achievements: The Ace will be blessed with grace.

Omen and Talismans: This is an auspicious card for a husband, wife, or eldest son or daughter.

> Animal Spirit: Antelope, Bull
> Bird Spirit: Phoenix, Egret
> Color: White, Golden Yellow
> Plant: Hyacinth, Rhododendron
> Tree: Oak, Peach
> Gemstone: Ruby, Agate
> Metal: Quicksilver (Mercury)
> Direction: South
> Place: Earth, Sky
> Season: Winter

QUEEN of CUPS.

Meditation 43: Queen of Cups

The softest thing on earth
Wears away diamond.
What is without substance
Penetrates solid rock.
Herein, I see the Power of non-action.

It's a difficult concept:
The strength of stillness.

This is the card of Stillness.

Mystical Key

"The softest thing on earth wears away diamond. What is without substance penetrates solid rock." This saying is one of the great keynotes of the Tao Te Ching. In the card, the flowing river winds softly around the stone throne of the Queen, illustrating the verse. The small figure holding the fish on the side of the throne reminds us that eventually the water will wear away the stone.

The Queen bears an incense burner. Traditionally in Western ecclesiastical tradition, incense, the "odor of holiness," was burned to ward off evil spirits. In Taoist religious tradition as well, the incense burner is critical. It symbolizes the gateway between the human world and the world of the gods (Tao).

It is interesting to speculate on the kind of incense she might be holding. Connecting the Queen to her astrological (Venus) and Kabbalistic roots, the scents of jasmine, rose (for Venus), or myrrh (for the Kabbalistic Binah) are indicated.

Although incense was also used as a sacrifice to God, it has had a long history in the Western magical tradition as well. The way of the Tao is silent and still. It is not always the "strongest" who reveals true strength in the end. This card signifies the power of endurance, and the ability to makes dreams a reality. This is the strength of stillness.

Magical Key

Character: The Queen of Cups is a warm, sensual person who makes a perfect romantic partner and spouse, although she may be less satisfactory as a parent. She does well with a large group of people. Her apparent softness, however, masks the fact that she is persistent and tough, and after a time can wear away any opposition. The Queen is an orderly person with a strong sense of justice. However, in a negative aspect, she can be secretive, volatile, and untrustworthy.

Current Circumstances: The Queen may feel isolated, but she has a strong spiritual base to guide her through. The Queen's situation is being attacked in a subtle way, possibly by people wasting her time demanding immediate solutions to all their problems. Flexibility, not stubbornness, is important now. This is a good time for the Queen to participate in charitable activities.

Conflicts, Dangers, and Limitations: The situation is abnormal. However, although the circumstances call for a return to normality, the time is not yet right. Yin and Yang are not balanced; there is too much Yin, even if it appears to be the other way around.

Career: There is no advancement now, but persistence will eventually pay off.

Friends and Family: People will offer their services, and the Queen should accept them.

Finances and Possessions: This is not the time to be concerned about finances or material possessions. They are not ultimately important.

Health Concerns: Vision.

Romance: This is an auspicious time for a wedding.

Travel: The Queen will be taking a long trip over water.

Decision: The Queen should go ahead and make a change. Anxiety or doubts are holding the Queen back.

Future Events and Spiritual Achievements: The Queen will attain both power and a higher consciousness.

Omens and Talismans: This is an auspicious card for people in business, as long as they are persistent.

Animal Spirit: Lion, Fish
Bird Spirit: Pheasant, Flamingo
Color: Yellow, Orange
Plant: Jasmine, Rose
Tree: Apple, Birch
Gemstone: Red Sard, Pearl
Metal: Gold
Direction: North
Place: Earth
Season: Winter

Meditation 44: Seven of Pentacles

Which is more important,
Fame or life?
Which do you hold dearest,
Your body or your fortune?
Which hurts most to lose?

Loving the things of this world too much
Carries a heavy price.
Clinging to fame entails a loss of self.
Grasping after money destroys the person.

Learn contentment and when to stop.
Therein lies long life.

This is the card of Reaping the Harvest.

Mystical Key

The Tao asks us to make a decision about whether we follow the Tao or only the material things of this world. The decision is not a moral one, but a spiritual one. The things of this world are beautiful, but ultimately unsatisfying. Only in losing ourselves do we find ourselves. The Seven of Pentacles is looking at his vine as a producer of money rather than of grapes. The fallen leaves at the bottom of the card suggest that material things eventually rot or become spoiled. Only the treasures of the heart are permanent.

Magical Key

Character: The Seven of Pentacles is ingenious and introspective, but tends to be restless and at the mercy of his moods. He is generous; in fact, he is more generous with others than with himself. He is dignified and very private.

Current Circumstances: Planting the right seeds guarantees the right harvest. Although the Seven has constantly encountered misfortune, he will soon meet with a great opportunity. Ghosts of the past haunt the present.

Conflicts, Dangers, and Limitations: The Seven should not give way to sorrow. It's more important right now to develop the self than to try ineffectually to help others.

Career: The Seven's current job is not perfectly suited to him, but if he is clever, he will find a way to make it work. A business transaction will not work out the expected way. The Seven should seek an interview with someone powerful who can help in advancement. The Seven should not make excuses about his work.

Friends and Family: The family is harmonious, but a "friend" is gossiping.

Finances and Possessions: The Seven can gain a fortune, but of what will that fortune consist? Bad investments of money, time, or spirit are possible. What has been gained should not be discarded. Be prudent.

Health Concerns: Glandular problems and feet. In general, this is a card of health and longevity.

Romance: The relationship will not work out the way Seven hopes. He has made a poor emotional investment.

Travel: Stay at home.

Decision: Do this thing, as long as it is ethical.

Future Events and Spiritual Achievements: A difficult sacrifice will lead to perfect tranquillity and self-discipline.

Omens and Talismans: This is a good card for people in analytic professions. It is also auspicious for persons who live alone, and for those in agriculture.

> Animal Spirit: Elephant, Chameleon
> Bird Spirit: Duck, Ibis
> Color: Silver or Gray, Navy Blue
> Plant: Azalea, Potentilla
> Tree: Flowering Almond, Sycamore
> Gemstone: Yellow Chrysolite, Malachite
> Metal: Copper
> Direction: Northeast

Place: The plains—where heaven meets earth
Season: Midspring

Meditation 45: Nine of Swords

Sometimes
Great accomplishments seem useless;
Fullness appears empty,
Though it is inexhaustible.

Even the straightest road
Can appear crooked.
The sharpest mind
Seem dull.
The noblest eloquence
Sound like stuttering.

When it gets cold, keep moving.
When it gets hot, stay quiet.
This is the way of the world.

This is the card of Useless Regret.

Mystical Key

One of the paradoxes of the human condition is that our reach always exceeds our grasp. No matter how great our accomplishments, no matter how noble our attainments, there are times when we feel it's all for nothing. This card seems to strike the chord of sorrow and despair, but it's really a reminder to keep on the path, and not, as Walt Whitman said in *Leaves of Grass*, to lie awake at night and weep for our sins—or the sins of others. "When it gets cold, keep moving. When it gets hot, stay quiet."

Magical Key

Character: Compassionate, patient, and loving, the Nine
sometimes pays too much attention to matters that, in the
final analysis, are insignificant. The Nine is emotional and

impressionable. She does things for their own sake, not for status.

Current Circumstances: Don't regret what is inevitable. Even though things may appear very bleak at present, escape is possible. Burdens are not so heavy as they appear. Previous wrongs will be righted.

Conflicts, Dangers, and Limitations: There is a dispute, perhaps even a crisis, but you will prevail. Part of your grief stems from your current inability to help others as much as you would like.

Career: This is not the time for the Nine to hide her talents. It's advantageous to be conspicuous, for once. Perform the proper action at the proper time. The Nine should probably not take a job offer in government.

Friends and Family: The darkest suspicions about a person will be justified. One on whom the Nine is dependent completely misjudges her.

Finances and Possessions: A constant battle will rage between riches and poverty. Boasting about money and possessions will result in their loss. Not auspicious for business.

Health Concerns: Insomnia, various other illnesses.

Romance: This card indicates serious misunderstandings in a relationship.

Travel: Travel is difficult right now, but get away if possible.

Decision: Decisions regarding contracts or legal matters should be made with extreme care right now. A misfortune not of the Nine's own making is creating difficulties in this regard. This is the time to do something constructive.

Future Events and Spiritual Achievements: The Nine will receive some uninvited guests. They bring unexpected good fortune. The Nine will achieve spiritual fulfillment.

Omens and Talismans: This is a fortunate card for those in education.

>Animal Spirit: Horse, Aardvark
>Bird Spirit: Plover, Owl
>Color: Purple, Dark Gray or Black
>Plant: Rose, Anemone

Tree: Willow, Blackthorn
Gemstone: Emerald, Sapphire
Metal: Iron
Direction: South
Place: Desert
Season: Spring, Late Autumn

KNIGHT of CUPS.

Meditation 46: Knight of Cups

When the Tao is acknowledged,
Horses return to work in the fields.
When the Tao is hidden from men,
War horses are bred outside the city.

The gravest sin
Is vaulting ambition.
It carries the great curse—
Discontent.

When you know what is sufficient,
You will have enough.

This is the card of Sufficiency.

Mystical Key

All things have both benevolent and malevolent uses. Horses can be used to plow fields or to lead an army. The same is true for knives, poisons, fire, money, and feelings. Following the Tao calls for us to use things for good and not for evil. One way to ensure this is to never overuse anything.

Magical Key

Character: The Knight of Cups is strong and diligent, but he
may also be overambitious or overemotional, carried away
by fantasy. At worst, he is in danger of being shallow and

superficial, living on the surface. It's important for the
Knight to develop more balance and flexibility.

Current Circumstances: Something in the environment is odd,
even wrong and unnatural. There are quarrels and
discontent and a serious error, due to a misunderstanding
of the true nature of the situation. Stemming from the
same cause, the Knight of Cups is not making correct use
of his time, talents, or possessions. When this is corrected,
the Knight's path will be smooth.

Conflicts, Dangers, and Limitations: A sense of desolation and
discontent oppresses the Knight. By giving way to
inappropriate pleasure, the Knight has done something
seriously wrong, and needs to retreat, reflect, and repent.

Career: Although it may seem as if career advancement is slow,
the Knight is on the right path. It's advisable to get the help
of an important person. If things seem unduly difficult,
someone may be obstructing plans, or else the Knight is
wasting time on trivialities.

Friends and Family: The relationship between husband and wife
is harmonious. However, the Knight is isolating himself
from the very people who could help him most.

Finances and Possessions: Commercial activity is favorable.

Health Concerns: Eyes and digestive system, stress. Those
suffering illnesses should try to get more exercise and fresh
air—not stay hidden.

Romance: This is an auspicious card for a romantic adventure.

Travel: This is a favorable card for journeys, especially in the
service of love.

Decision: Do this if it benefits others.

Future Events and Spiritual Achievements: An important
invitation will soon arrive. The Knight of Cups will obtain
visions of his past life.

Omens and Talismans: An auspicious card for those in the
public eye.

Animal Spirit: Donkey, Fish
Bird Spirit: Sandpiper, Seagull

Color: Brown, Silver
Plant: Amaryllis, Snowdrop
Tree: Alder, Apple
Gemstone: Turquoise, Beryl
Metal: Mercury
Direction: North
Place: Fields, Meadows
Season: Spring

Meditation 47: Nine of Cups

Without leaving home,
You can travel the universe.
Without even looking out the window,
You can see the Path of Heaven.
The farther you roam, the less you know.

The wise spirit knows without journeying,
Sees without looking,
Accomplishes without effort.

This is the card of Insight.

Mystical Key

This Meditation reminds us that all we seek can be found within us. The point is to seek deep rather than far. Nine is the Taoist number of completion and fulfillment; in this case, the cup is indeed overflowing.

The Tao proclaims over and over that true wisdom comes from within, not from without, yet this card is strangely ambiguous. Is the character turning his back on the ultimately empty external joys of the world, or is he neglecting his own emotional health? Only the adjoining cards can clarify the issue. The wise spirit must strike a balance. He never turns from experience, but he knows that the deepest experiences can be found "without journeying."

Magical Key

Character: The Nine is gifted in sight, meaning perception and insight. The Nine is idealistic, but can be conceited, and lack deep feelings. He may sometimes take too much satisfaction in his own spiritual accomplishments.

Current Circumstances: There is a lot of quarreling and perhaps even legal disputes, but it will not prove harmful. The Nine should take careful stock of what he has, and enjoy it.

Conflicts, Dangers, and Limitations: Pride in study and accomplishments may only reveal a lack of spiritual attainment.

Career: An influential person will come to the aid of Nine. A forthcoming promotion must be handled carefully; do not assume too much power.

Friends and Family: Although the Nine has many admiring friends, he is often misunderstood. Likewise, he should not believe rumors. Motherhood is indicated.

Finances and Possessions: Do not invest or withdraw funds at the current time. Next month you will see things more clearly.

Health Concerns: This is an auspicious card for health. Skin and hair are of concern. Meditation may be helpful.

Romance: This may not be a particularly favorable card for romance, only because the Nine may be looking in the wrong direction. The Nine may be ignoring the rich treasure of love available to him. He has only to look in front of him to see it.

Travel: The Nine should not take a long trip now, especially over water. This is a time to stay tranquilly at home.

Decision: Wait on the sidelines until the correct moment comes to act.

Future Events and Spiritual Achievements: Success is near. True happiness and peace lie close at hand. The Nine will attain intense joy and material success.

Omens and Talismans: This is an auspicious card for military personnel. This is a favorable card for the eldest son and the youngest daughter.

Animal Spirit: Snake, Rhinoceros
Bird Spirit: Raven, Grouse
Color: Pale Blue, Purple
Plant: Mistletoe, Jasmine
Tree: Cypress, Mulberry
Gemstone: Agate, Topaz
Metal: Bronze
Direction: Southwest
Place: Garden
Season: Fall

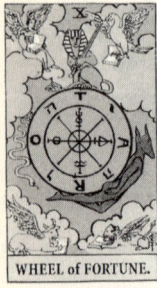

WHEEL of FORTUNE.

Meditation 48:
Wheel of Fortune (X): Yin

Ordinary learning requires accumulating facts,
Learning the Tao means letting them go.
Learning the Tao means diminishment,
The ability to grow small.

He who follows the Tao does less,
Leaves nothing undone.
The wise leader wins the world
By leaving the world alone.

This is the card of Change.

Mystical Key

The Wheel of Fortune bears the alchemical signs for mercury (metal) at the top; sulfur (fire) at the right, salt (earth) at the left, and water at the bottom, from which everything emerges. The Wheel itself is wood—the symbol of renewal and creation. All are suspended in cloud-gemmed air, borne by Anubis, the jackal-god of Egypt. He is the God of Death and Judgment, and guides the soul into the next world. The symbols remind us that the world is sacred and complete as it is. It grows, expands, shrinks, dies, and is reborn into a new creation. The serpent to the left is a highly ambiguous and complex symbol. In this case, it is another manifestation of change (the snake's shedding of his skin) and opportunity for renewal.

The Hebrew letters for Law (*Torah*) and the Tetragrammaton are interspersed on the Wheel.

At the corners stand the traditional symbols for the four Gospels: the lion (Mark), the man (Matthew), the ox (Luke), the eagle (John). (The original description of each of these appears in the book of Ezekiel, as the creatures emerging from a fiery whirlwind. Each appears with wings and his Gospel, which is the customary representation.) The same figures appear again in the World (Meditation 64) but without wings or book. These figures are fraught with many (and extremely variable) symbolic values. For the Tarot, they symbolize the four suits and their accompanying elements: Lion = Wands and Wood; Man = Cups and Water; Ox = Pentacles and Earth; Eagle = Swords and Metal. They also represent the qualities that can get us through the vicissitudes of fortune: strength, yielding, sacrifice, and spirit, respectively.

The sphinx sitting atop the Wheel bears the metal sword to reinforce the power of mercury. Mercury is also known as quicksilver, and is an apt symbol for the ceaseless change of the universe. She also stands for the riddle of human existence.

In the West, many people believe that the only way to go is "up" or "forward." In reality, of course, we know the world doesn't work like this. Fortunes are made and fortunes are lost. "Diminishment" is not an aberration, but part of the natural order of things.

The Wheel of Fortune reminds us that leadership provides a still center for the swirling tides of fortune. The center of the Wheel is so small it has no dimension, yet it governs the whole. "Learning the Tao means diminishment, the ability to grow small." In the wheel of life, too, the larger figure at the top of the wheel inevitably ends up at the bottom. Only by centering oneself, by practicing non-interference, can one achieve the central position that is immune to the ups and down of fortune. Unlike the Magician card, the change doesn't necessarily involve transformation.

Magical Key
Character: The Wheel of Fortune is very popular and a good
listener. She is pliant, non-interfering, and easy to get along

with, although she can be moody and changeable at times. She is not a detail person, but sees the larger picture. The Wheel knows how to conform her life to changes in fortune.

Current Circumstances: This is a time to behave with special caution. Although beset with many changes of fortune, the Wheel will eventually end up on top, especially if she can find a credible spiritual teacher.

Conflicts, Dangers, and Limitations: A great deal of conflict is at hand. How the Wheel enters the conflict determines how she will end up. If she is in danger, she can get herself out of it without help from others. She should not dwell on past mistakes.

Career: The Wheel is an expert in her field. She should not employ an inferior person. The Wheel does best working in the service sector.

Friends and Family: People are drawn to the Wheel, but many and frequent misunderstandings mar relationships.

Finances and Possessions: Investments are profitable if carefully watched. Funds should be kept liquid.

Health Concerns: Except for the usual bout of colds and flu, health outlook is excellent.

Romance: An apparent rejection should not worry the Wheel. Destiny lies elsewhere.

Travel: Travel is inauspicious now.

Decision: Use restraint, especially in times of financial difficulty.

Future Events and Spiritual Achievements: The Wheel will have many reversals of fortune. An unusual shift of fortune, for good or bad, is indicated Eventually, the Wheel will obtain spiritual joy.

Omens and Talismans: This is a fortunate card for the firstborn son or daughter.

 Animal Spirit: Bear, Antelope
 Bird Spirit: Pheasant, Starling
 Color: Black, Pink

Plant: Ivy, Hosta
Tree: Apple, Willow
Gemstone: Amber, Star Sapphire
Metal: Silver
Direction: Southwest
Place: Rivers, Waterside
Season: Spring,

Meditation 49: Justice (XI): Yang

The wise spirit does not follow his own will.
Instead, he acts in the interest of others.
The wise spirit returns good for good.
And he returns good for evil also.
That is the meaning of virtue.

The wise spirit is faithful to those who keep faith
with him.
And he keeps faith even with the faithless.
For that is the meaning of faithfulness.

The wise spirit is shy and self-effacing in the world.
The people of the world look on him as a child.
But it is he who looks after the world.

This is the card of Wisdom.

Mystical Key

Justice follows the Wheel of Fortune in a Taoist reading, just as it follows the Wheel in the pack. While the Wheel of Fortune may be seen as a symbol of Nature's justice, the Justice card puts justice in a societal setting. The figure holds a sword in one hand and scales in the other. The sword evokes the possibility of severe punishment, but it is held aloft, and not in a striking position. Interestingly, although Justice is normally associated with the right (Yang) side, the figure holds the scale of Justice in her left (Yin) hand. This shows that real justice comes from the intuitive, feminine side as well as from the rational "masculine" side. This true justice is not overbearing, and doesn't always come in the form that one expects. It doesn't follow its own will. True justice keeps faith even with the faithless.

Note: In some packs, Justice is number 8 and Strength is number 11. In such decks, the number 8 (4 × 2) is significant, since it clarifies the power of 4, the number of squareness (fairness and justice).

Magical Key

Character: Justice is intelligent and fair, with a gift for balancing the emotional and rational elements. Justice has a strong sense of both duty and compassion, and often uses intuition to seek the fair solution to a problem. Justice is associated with a sense of "smell," which means relying on intuition. She seeks the truth at all times.

Current Circumstances: Justice may be in conflict with others, but must learn to keep a balanced view of things and be fair even to those who are not fair themselves. In a negative aspect, the card can indicate self-righteousness, or suggest that Justice will be the victim of an injustice or lack wisdom. Justice will receive a just reward.

Conflicts, Dangers, and Limitations: Do not engage in conflict. A woman and her children are in danger. A gray-haired person is the enemy.

Career: Justice often works best in a middle-management career. She is a local leader.

Friends and Family: The family is flourishing. A distant friend will appear or send a message.

Finances and Possessions: Taking care of immediate needs, especially for the family, is vital now. It is also a time to give directly to charity. The coming month will be prosperous.

Health Concerns: Health problems causing limping or joint pain will soon clear up. Someone close is pregnant.

Romance: An inauspicious card for romance.

Travel: Go home, or stay home.

Decision: A choice must be made now. Hesitation leads to misfortune. The safest choice is the best one.

Future Events and Spiritual Achievements: Justice will attain
   both wisdom and knowledge.
Omens and Talismans: An auspicious card for those associated
   with law. Also for painters, poets, and sculptors.
   Animal Spirit: Lamb, Dog
   Bird Spirit: Eagle, Bobwhite
   Color: Dark Red, Kelly Green
   Plant: Nettle, Pink
   Tree: Apple, Hazel
   Gemstone: Amethyst, Garnet
   Metal: Bronze
   Direction: Northwest
   Place: Enclosed Garden
   Season: Spring, Autumn

DEATH.

Meditation 50: Death (XIII): Yin

Thirteen are the companions of life.
And thirteen are the companions of death.
And thirteen are the companions of life-in-death.

But the Tao walker
Walks without fear of life or death.
He wears an armor that cannot be pierced—
The horn of rhinoceros is blunted against him.
The tiger's claws have no place to catch hold.

He has no place for death to enter.

This is the card of Rebirth.

Mystical Key

Death has always been an ambiguous card. A skeleton in armor rides a
white, red-eyed steed. He ruthlessly tramples everything in his path,
from kings and priests to women and children. Nothing can escape him.
The paradoxical nature of the Tao assures us that the Death card is one

of great fortune—harboring the return to life. Most interesting is the banner that Death carries: it bears the symbol of the Alchemical Rose— the secret of spiritual transformation!

Curiously, the number thirteen occurs not only on the death card, but in the Tao Meditation concerned with overcoming death. Only the Walker in Tao walks without fear, for he wears an armor that cannot be pierced.

Magical Key

Character: Death is hard on the outside and weak on the inside. This can be positive or negative. If the Yang forces are balanced with Yin, this means that Death is decisive and firm outwardly, and sensitive and flexible inwardly. If the Yang and Yin forces are not in balance, Death is brutal on the outside, but fatally weak on the inside. Correct balance of Yin and Yang are more important for this card than for any other. If in correct balance, the card portends almost unlimited good fortune. If not, the outlook is bad. In any case, Death is intuitive, and he is an excellent communicator.

Current Circumstances: This card is particularly auspicious if it appears during a dark time in the Seeker's life. Death has a secret that should not be revealed to anyone.

Conflicts, Dangers, and Limitations: Rules are not being followed and the situation is chaotic. If involved in a conflict, Death should give way. Death is isolated by opposition; it is urgent to prevent danger.

Career: It's important to cultivate a friendly relationship with the boss. August is a good time to make a career advance. Death works best as a direct aide to the top management. His intuition makes him an invaluable assistant, even at the highest levels.

Friends and Family: Death is in danger of trampling on those closest to him.

Finances and Possessions: This is a good time to purchase land.

Health Concerns: Vision problems or injury to the eye is possible.

Romance: This is an inauspicious card for romance and
   marriage. Death may be drawn to someone inferior.
Travel: Long-distance travel is not recommended.
Decision: Envy and doubt are poor guides.
Future Events and Spiritual Achievements: Death will soon be
   taking leave of something dearly loved. Abrupt, unexpected
   change looms ahead. At first, things will be difficult, then
   easy—a period of good fortune. Expect good luck within
   ten months.
Omens and Talismans: This is a lucky card for a pregnant
   woman or for the eldest son. This is also an auspicious card
   for those engaged in agriculture.

> Animal Spirit: Dolphin, Tiger
> Bird Spirit: Peacock, Ptarmigan, Goose
> Color: Red or Maroon
> Plant: Foxglove, Pansy
> Tree: Oak, Dogwood
> Gemstone: Cat's-Eye, Garnet
> Metal: Lead
> Direction: West
> Place: Mountains
> Season: Winter

Meditation 51: Three of Cups

All things are born from the Tao.
They are nourished by its power.
They are shaped from matter,
Empowered by spirit.

The Ten Thousand Things of this World
All follow the sacred path of the Tao.
Their following is spontaneous, unforced,
For the Tao inspirits them,
The Tao is their protector and provider.
It fulfills without possessing,

Works without claiming,
Leads without coercion.
This is its mystical power.

This is the card of Merriment.

Mystical Key

This is a card of great happiness, a happiness that comes from flowing with the Tao. It's a card of joy and camaraderie, of success without effort. The three dancing figures strongly suggest the Three Graces of Greek and Roman mythology.

However, some interpreters, saturated in Christian mythology, read a somber warning in this card. They see the celebrated harvest as a reminder of the forbidden fruit of the Garden of Eden. This is wrongheaded. Fruit is not always an emblem of sin, and nothing in the card suggests that it should be read so here. Besides, as the Meditation says, "All things are born from the Tao. They are nourished by its power." There is no evil nature, only misinformed actions. The card and the Meditation both suggest that the joyful things in life, while good in themselves, do not bring ultimate fulfillment. "All things are born from the Tao," the dark as well as the light. In a negative reading, it could mean sexual or marital disappointment. It could also mean a failure to take into account certain unpleasant aspects of life without which happiness can be only superficial.

Magical Key

Character: The Three is a happy, optimistic person who
brings happiness to others. She enjoys a life of ease and
luxury. She is skilled in communicating to the point of
eloquence, and has the knack of empathizing with both
sides of a quarrelsome pair. She is happy in her
relationships with both lovers and friends. She has good
taste. In a negative reading, however, emotional
imbalance is possible.

Current Circumstances: The Three is in danger from
unexpected sources. It is very important to be prepared.

Conflicts, Dangers, and Limitations: Quarreling and substance
abuse among people close to the Three are damaging.

Career: The Three does best in a career involving art and media. There are great pressures at work. Progress may be halted because the Three of Cups cannot get in touch with an important person. When she does, the Three has every opportunity to be a great success and an excellent leader. Meanwhile, the Three should keep working hard, even though rewards may be elusive.

Friends and Family: The Three has many friends and happy relationships. Three's best friends are of her own gender. This is the time to show loyalty. There may be an old ghost in the family.

Finances and Possessions: Business enterprises will flourish. The Three's greatest treasures are locked up in her house; they must be kept safe.

Health Concerns: Endocrine system. Generally, this is an auspicious card for health.

Romance: This is an auspicious card for adventurous romance. However, the Three may feel guilty about a past affair. A partner of the opposite sex may be secretly disappointed in the Three.

Travel: It is more favorable to stay home at the present time.

Decision: Go ahead—it will lead to abundance.

Future Events and Spiritual Achievements: A problem will be resolved favorably. Good news. What the Three has lost will be found.

Omens and Talismans: This card is auspicious for a safe childbirth. Also auspicious for a youngest daughter.

    Animal Spirit: Lion, Bear
    Bird Spirit: Hawk, Dove
    Color: Green, Purple
    Plant: Ivy, Mint, Orange Blossom
    Tree: Apple, Spruce
    Gemstone: Diamond, Ruby
    Metal: Silver
    Direction: Northeast
    Place: City
    Season: Spring

Meditation 52: Ace of Cups

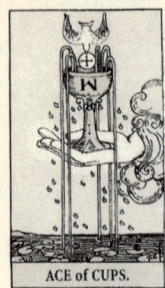

ACE of CUPS.

Back to the origin.
The mother of all things.
To know the mother
Is to know the children.
Wise children remain
Close to the mother.
The mother of all things
Protects all things from death.

By guarding the mouth,
And keeping the breath still,
One achieves life beyond life.
Constant chattering
And feverish busyness
Result in danger.

Seeing the small is Insight.
Being strong
Means yielding.

Rely on the inner light
To be sure.

This is the card of Inner Light.

Mystical Key

The cup (which seems to be the Holy Grail) is full of the original, primordial waters, with the dove of spirit descending on it. The descending dove is the preferred symbol of Christian baptism and stands for the rebirth of the spirit. Alchemically, the dove has a more specific meaning: it represents the "whitening" step of the *materia prima* as it becomes the philosopher's stone.

The Ace of Cups shows the union of original matter and spirit and the moment of birth. All of us are children of the Tao. It may also sig-

nify the beginning of a new romance, for it is through love and its reproductive consequences that we achieve "life beyond life." This card takes
us to the essentials.

Magical Key

Character: The Ace of Cups is sensitive, ambitious, and
original. The Ace is a leader, but at times can be too
blunt or self-centered. Children and young people are
important to the Ace. The Ace also has a strong social
conscience and works hard to effect important changes
for the better.

Current Circumstances: This is a good time to move, either
physically or emotionally.

Conflicts, Dangers, and Limitations: Conflicts can lead to
violence and should be avoided. Guard against
secretiveness. The Ace tends to have an all-knowing
attitude that gets him in trouble.

Career: The Ace of Cups is a hard worker, especially if he
works for himself. This is a favorable card for managing a
career. This isn't a good time to get a new job; learn to enjoy
the one already held. A career in consulting or any other
kind of self-employment is indicated.

Friends and Family: There is dissension within apparent unity.

Finances and Possessions: Abundance. The home needs to be
guarded carefully.

Health Concerns: This is an auspicious card for health.

Romance: The beginning of a rich, healthy romantic
relationship; however, the Ace of Cups needs a particularly
supportive mate.

Travel: Travel to the mountains or one's hometown is
beneficial.

Decision: Intuition is the best guide now.

Future Events and Spiritual Achievements: Unexpected good
fortune from an outside source within thirty days. The person
who has been gone will return. A gift brings bad luck.

Omens and Talismans: This is a very fortunate card for a young
person or a child, or for one in the healing arts.

Animal Spirit: Donkey, Horse
Bird Spirit: Dove, Hawk
Color: Indigo or Dark Blue, Violet
Plant: Hyacinth, Lotus, Water Lily
Tree: Hazel, Birch
Gemstone: Emerald, Beryl
Metal: Gold
Direction: North
Place: Sky, Ocean
Season: Spring, Summer

Meditation 53: Seven of Swords

If I have even a grain of sense,
I'll walk the Tao.
My only worry would be to get sidetracked.

The Tao is smooth and easy.
But people keep getting lost anyway,
Trying to take a shortcut.

When the palace is encrusted with jewels,
The fields are weedy, the granaries empty.

Those who have lost the Tao,
Wear elegant clothes,
And carry sharp swords.
They eat and drink, spend money,
Indulge themselves in material things.
But they are thieves and robbers.
The way they follow
Is not the way of the Tao.

This is the card of Losing the Way.

Mystical Key

The card shows someone who has betrayed the Tao through trickery, unethical compromise, or appeasement. The word "shortcut" refers not only to the attempt to avoid the long path, but to the very act of cutting (as with the stolen swords). "Those who have lost the Tao wear elegant clothes, and carry sharp swords. They eat and drink, spend money, indulge themselves in material things. But they are thieves and robbers."

Magical Key

Character: The Seven is watchful and alert. However, he is possibly unstable.

Current Circumstances: A cloud, possibly a dispute, hangs over the atmosphere. The Seven is taking on too much.

Conflicts, Dangers, and Limitations: The enemy has been successful, probably through trickery or betrayal. But his success will not last.

Career: The Seven should to take a new career path, one involving practical education.

Friends and Family: The Seven is mixing with the wrong people. It's important to gain some social independence from them.

Finances and Possessions: Generosity toward others increases the Seven's own wealth. He may have made an unwise, perhaps illegal, investment. There is an opportunity for profit close by.

Health Concerns: Digestive system. The Seven should not give way to overindulgence.

Romance: The Seven of Swords is not a good card for relationships, which may be in danger of being dissolved.

Travel: A journey over land is indicated. This is a good time to return home.

Decision: The Seven should not take an offer now.

Future Events and Spiritual Achievements: The Seven may fail at the last moment. A guest is coming who will bring excellent gifts.

Omens and Talismans: This is a favorable card for a scholar.
> Animal Spirit: Fish, Dragon
> Bird Spirit: Eagle, Owl

Color: Green, Indigo
Plant: Iris, Violet
Tree: Alder, Cedar
Gemstone: Jade, Jasper
Metal: Iron
Direction: Southwest
Place: Desert
Season: Spring

Meditation 54: Ten of Cups

What is well planted can't be uprooted.
What is closely embraced won't slip away.
The strong family is honored
Through endless generations.

To follow the Tao within
Engenders inner power.
To follow the Tao in the family
Produces virtue.
To follow the Tao in the community
Leads to glorious abundance.
To follow the Tao in the world
Is Tao itself.

Thus the Tao grows manifest
In the self, the family, the community, and the world.
How do I know this is true?
I look.

This is the card of Deep Roots.

Mystical Key

All happiness is rooted in the holy Tao. The Figures show joy both in the heavens and in the earth: they have every joy at their fingertips. The Deep Roots are the basis for transformation.

Magical Key

Character: The Ten of Cups is a good listener, but may be unaware of certain dangers.

Current Circumstances: This is a card of good luck for family, home, and domestic affairs; it is an assurance of happiness and joy, although there may be some problems in day-to-day events. Dreams are prophetic.

Conflicts, Dangers, and Limitations: Beware of anger. The Ten can change his situation for the better. Satiety can also be dangerous.

Career: Someone is looking out for the Seeker's interests. This is a favorable time for a business meeting. Currently, the Ten's work is not productive; it is extremely important to work on professional development just now.

Friends and Family: In a negative reading, it means there is a disturbance in the family order; it can indicate drug or alcohol problems, even violence. The home needs careful guarding now. Loved ones should be persuaded to return home.

Finances and Possessions: Don't take on a big investment or expenditure just now without great thought and planning. Lawsuits are not especially favorable.

Health Concerns: Cardiac system.

Romance: The Ten will find his perfect life partner belatedly.

Travel: This is a good time to travel south, or to the water.

Decision: It's time to make a clear change, as long as the foundation is set correctly.

Future Events and Spiritual Achievements: This card is connected to honors and reputation. Social and professional success is ultimately assured. An award will be won.

Omens and Talismans: The Ten will attain unlimited success in almost any field of endeavor. Especially auspicious for people in politics or education.

Animal Spirit: Fish, Stag
Bird Spirit: Stork, Cuckoo
Color: Citrine, Deep Blue

Plant: Lily, Fern
Tree: Aspen, Birch
Gemstone: Spinel, Alexandrite
Metal: Gold
Direction: East
Place: Lake, Ocean
Season: Fall

Meditation 55: Six of Cups

One steeped in Tao
Is like a baby,
Untouched by wasps
And serpents.
Though his bones are soft,
And his sinews weak,
His grip is firm.

A child knows nothing
About the ways of man and woman,
But his penis is erect.
He can yell all day
And keep in good voice.
Thus he shows the harmony
Between his body and the Tao.
Harmony is the key to the Changeless Tao.
It is enlightenment.

Striving after long life is not the true way,
For it brings with it old age and death.
Keep as a child.

This is the card of Innocence.

Mystical Key

Images of flowers and gardens abound in the Tarot, but this card makes them the centerpiece of the image. The picture shows an almost Edenic scene, a place of refuge and safety, a safety whose source is innocence, which is always in danger of being lost; hence the "wasps and serpents," which can sting or bite without warning.

The flowers are contained in cups, reinforcing the notion that they represent virginity or innocence. Chinese gardens reflect the harmony of the man-made world with the cosmos and with our fellow human beings, and this idea, too, is depicted in this card. This card encourages us to retain our childlike wonder.

Magical Key

Character: An innocent, childlike person. A lover of music. The Six of Cups is a good speaker and communicator. The sympathetic Six is also dedicated to helping other people.

Current Circumstances: A wish is just beginning to come true. There is much mirth. A child does not clutch at the past, but looks forward to the future. Letting go keeps one's body and mind supple. This card is an invitation to live one's life to the fullest, by maintaining a fresh and childlike appreciation of it. The Six may be in the grip of the pleasant past, of which he must let go in order to move forward. Paradoxically, the way to achieve this is to become more childlike oneself.

Conflicts, Dangers, and Limitations: This is a dangerous time; pushing forward too hard can bring great trouble. Take small "baby steps."

Career: The Six is at the beginning of his strength, but it is important to start planning for retirement early. Major problems could result by putting it off.

Friends and Family: Good relationships with the neighbors should be cultivated.

Finances and Possessions: While the financial outlook is not encouraging, the Six does not require money for happiness.

Health Concerns: Alimentary system. Pregnancy is possible for a woman.

Romance: Love is at risk and innocence will be destroyed. Bad omen for relationships, with a possibility of betrayal.

Travel: This is an auspicious card for travel, especially travel to the north.

Decision: Don't undertake anything new or risky.

Future Events and Spiritual Achievements: The Six will achieve wisdom, understanding, and pleasure.

Omens and Talismans: Auspicious for those in the culinary arts and for children and young people.

> Animal Spirit: Dolphin, Toad
> Bird Spirit: Swan, Nighthawk
> Color: Sky Blue, Red/Orange
> Plant: Lily of the Valley, Daffodil
> Tree: Birch, Hazel
> Gemstone: Yellow Diamond, Aquamarine
> Metal: Copper
> Direction: North
> Place: Mountains
> Season: Winter

Meditation 56: Two of Swords

Those who know
Keep silent.
Those who don't know
Jabber endlessly.

The wise spirit
Keeps her mouth closed.
She guards her senses.
She tempers her sword.
She dims her light.
She unravels complexities,
And is at one with the dust of the Way.

In this she becomes part of the mystical Unity.
At this point she is free
From the clutches of friends and enemies,
She is above consideration of benefit or harm.
She is separate from the highest and lowest.
She has achieved the greatest state.

This is the card of Mystical Unity.

Mystical Key

The blindfolded figure balances two Swords. The waxing crescent moon rises behind her. The blindfold, the closed lips, and the crossed arms represent the isolation of the figure from worldly things. Although the blindfold may represent complete vulnerability to fate, the Swords serve as her protection. The crescent moon symbolizes the dimmed light of mystical meditation, the gray dust at her feet and the still water in the background are the Tao. Yet she is not locked into herself, but is part of the Mystical Unity. "At this point she is free from the clutches of friends and enemies."

Magical Key

Character: The Two is imaginative. The Two's inner qualities are just now becoming outwardly apparent. The Two of Swords is a good listener, and her sense of justice can resolve disputes between others. It is important for the Two to get in touch with her Yin side, which is now beginning to emerge strongly.

Current Circumstances: For a woman, the card suggests that she is in great danger. The Two should not engage in plots or secrets now.

Conflicts, Dangers, and Limitations: There is a great deal of opposition from nearly every quarter. The Two needs to learn to assess the nature of the enemy. Ambition is a great danger.

Career: A career in the public sector is very appropriate for the Two.

Friends and Family: The Two is caught between the demands of two opposing friends or family members. She faces opposition from both and must keep aloof from them, following the path she knows to be right.

Finances and Possessions: This is a fortunate time to invest, as long as she carefully reviews her portfolio.

Health Concerns: Renal system, also arm. Any health concerns are minor. Walking would be excellent exercise.

Romance: Women need to be careful about unwanted sexual advances. Men need to stop following women around aimlessly. A quiet, supportive mate is ideal.

Travel: A far, life-changing journey is imminent. It is very important for her to make this trip.

Decision: The answer lies within. The Two has been too indecisive in the past, unable to choose the correct path.

Future Events and Spiritual Achievements: The Two of Swords will attain truth, freedom, and renewed happiness.

Omens and Talismans: This is a fortunate card for those in science or philosophy.

    Animal Spirit: Bison, Butterfly
    Bird Spirit: Lovebird, Woodpecker
    Color: Purple, Sky Blue
    Plant: Lotus, Iris
    Tree: Willow, Apple
    Gemstone: Tourmaline, Carnelian
    Metal: Iron
    Direction: Southwest
    Place: Sea, Ocean
    Season: Midsummer

Meditation 57: King of Pentacles

KING of PENTACLES.

Rule with Justice.
Wage war by using surprise.
Achieve the world by leaving it alone.
How do I know this is true?
In this way:

The more restrictions, laws, and prohibitions,
The poorer people become.
The more weapons among the people,
The more chaos.
The more experts there are,
The stranger things get.
The stranger the times,
The more laws are enacted.
Hence more thieves and robbers.

The wise leader says,
"I'll refrain from action,
And people will take control
Of their own lives.
I'll practice peace,
And people will be restored to honesty.
I'll avoid manipulating the market,
And the people will become wealthy.
I'll have no desires,
And the folk will return to simplicity."

This is the card of Trust.

Mystical Key

More restrictions bring unhappiness and chaos—the very things they were designed to reduce. "The more experts there are, the stranger things get." The wise leader is careful, diplomatic, and self-controlled. He does not push his will onto other people, but allows them to develop their own potential. The symbol of the ox on the King's throne represents the idea of service to others.

Magical Key

Character: The King of Pentacles is both creative and gentle. His high level of intelligence should be nurtured by the best teachers.

Current Circumstances: If the King stays on the current path, he may bring a woman into danger. Dreams are prophetic but veiled in symbolism. It is time to harvest.

Conflicts, Dangers, and Limitations: The King will face many conflicts, but will triumph on account of his moral force. The King has a dangerous enemy who holds a longstanding grudge.

Career: This is an auspicious card for a business leader. The King should make sure that his customers are well cared for. He should bide his time and not allow himself to be misled by illusions. He should expand his horizons, and learn to develop his spiritual side. With the right effort, the King will achieve the highest success in his career.

Friends and Family: The King is in danger of alienating his family. Several people are lying.

Finances and Possessions: This is an auspicious card for finance, although it will take time. He should not expect too much too soon.

Health Concerns: Reproductive system. He should try to get more sleep. Exercise is recommended.

Romance: Not auspicious for illicit affairs.

Travel: Stay at home. The King will celebrate a joyful occasion there.

Decision: This is a dangerous time. The king must take decided action against enemies.

Future Events and Spiritual Achievements: The King will come to an original understanding of the nature of things.

Omens and Talismans: This is a good card for people in the legal or business professions.

Animal Spirit: Ox, Tortoise
Bird Spirit: Phoebe, Martin
Color: Red, Purple
Plant: Narcissus, Grapevine
Tree: Cypress, Poplar
Gemstone: Opal, Amber
Metal: Iron
Direction: Northwest
Place: Fields, Garden
Season: Early Winter

Meditation 58: King of Swords

KING of SWORDS.

The least government keeps people the happiest.
A meddling government makes people rebellious.
Joy is born of sorrow.
And sorrow hides in joy.
How can we predict
The fruit of any action?
What standard can we use?

The normal becomes distorted.
Goodness shades into evil.
The people have no guide.

The leader should mold without cutting,
Carve without disfiguring,
Straighten without forcing,
Enlighten without blinding.

This is the card of Forging the Spirit.

Mystical Key

The Jeffersonian sentiment at the beginning of the Meditation encapsulates the political and social philosophy of the Tao. It calls on the wise leader to trust his people, guide without interfering. Interference by its very nature "distorts the normal." To forget the spirit means to allow the spirit to develop without force.

Magical Key

Character: The King of Swords is diplomatic, watchful, and
protective of those he loves. He is active and powerful,
analytical and fair. He has many creative ideas. People look
up to him. However, he can be manipulative, selfish and
unreliable, perhaps even criminal. He hurts other people
and is a dangerous enemy.

Current Circumstances: It is time to store up what has been
gained. The King may have to retreat in order to advance.

Conflicts, Dangers, and Limitations: The King of Swords is in a
powerful but dangerous position. It is very important for
him not to abuse the trust of others.

Career: This is a good card for a teacher or anyone in a position
of authority. If the King is in a subordinate position, he
should try to keep clear lines of communication open with
the boss. The King has made a dangerous move, but has
managed to get away with it. Someone is vying for the
King's job. This is a good time to seek a better one.

Friends and Family: The King does not have a large circle of
friends, but those he has are loyal.

Finances and Possessions: Business affairs are favorable now.

Health Concerns: Hepatic system. It might be appropriate to try
some medicinal herbs.

Romance: The mother of a male companion is making trouble.

Travel: Travel eastward will be auspicious.

Decision: Go ahead and do it.

Future Events and Spiritual Achievements: The King will achieve
financial success, and spiritual blessings if he helps
someone who is crying out in need right now.

Omens and Talismans: This is a fortunate card for people in
politics or authority.

Animal Spirit: Butterfly, Unicorn
Bird Spirit: Swallow, Falcon

Color: Yellow, Purple
Plant: Orchid, Delphinium
Tree: Hawthorn, Cottonwood
Gemstone: Amethyst, Lapis Lazuli
Metal: Steel
Direction: South
Place: Ocean, Lake
Season: Early Spring

THE EMPEROR.

Meditation 59:
The Emperor (IV): Yang

The key to serving Heaven and others
Is moderation.
Moderation means to return before going astray.
Returning means doubling one's accumulation of
*   virtue.*
With such reserves,
One's abilities become illimitable.
Then only is one worthy to lead.
Being worthy to lead
Means holding firm to the Mothering Tao.
It means having roots that go deep,
Making a strong plant.
This is the Tao of vision,
The Tao of life eternal.

This is the card of Illimitable Ability.

Mystical Key

The Emperor sits on his throne, wearing red and holding the ankh, a
Greek cross (tau) crowned by a circle. The ankh is the ancient Egyptian
symbol of life; it was also a symbol of sexual union, with a circle at the
top representing the Yin principle and the cross representing the Yang
principle. Sometimes it was called the Key to the Nile, not only because

it physically resembled a key, but also because it signified the sexual union of Isis and Osiris, which initiated the annual fertilizing floods of the Nile River. Rivers, of course, are Yin. In ancient China, the emperor was the Son of Heaven, further removed from the people than a mere king, and closer to the gods. He thus became the symbol of divine authority, and the wielder of virtue, hence the Meditation.

In early Coptic Christian mythology, the ankh refers to immortality granted to humans through the sacrifice of Jesus. In this reading, the lower part of the symbol (the cross) represents the generative principle of nature, with the eternal circle superimposed. (The Emperor's counterpart, the Empress, bears the sign for woman, the Latin cross descending from a circle, which is very similar in meaning to the ankh. Together the two signs stand for abundant and immortal life.)

In conventional Tarot readings, this card often has a strongly negative connotation. The beard itself is a distinctively male symbol, and, in medieval days, a man would often "swear by my beard."

The Emperor may refer to the father of the family, or another strong male figure.

In Taoism, the Emperor's long white beard, sign of age and consequent wisdom, is interpreted in a very positive light. Sages, for example, are always depicted with beards.

If there is a good store of Virtue, then nothing is impossible. What is Virtue? The first lines tell you: caring for others and serving heaven. Virtue means humbling oneself to heaven and others. This can be difficult for the Emperor, not because he doesn't care about other people, but because it is always difficult for one in authority to humble oneself. On the other hand, the primary function of the Emperor is to care for his people.

Magical Key

Character: The Emperor's armor may indicate that he has fought for his position, and therefore earned it. It might also mean that he must fight to keep his position. Whether or not he can do so depends on Virtue accumulated in the past. Rulership should depend on virtue and restraint. Control of others begins with self-restraint; otherwise, one is not worthy. The Emperor is a strongly Yang person who wields authority and power. He is protective, responsible, and determined. He is strong, and has powers of self-control. He sees things as they appear to him. He is the soul of reason—except when his will is thwarted. He is protective of *his* rights, *his* turf, *his* ego. He doesn't like surprises, and likes to be in control at all times. Yet the Emperor is also a great civilizing force, and a good person to have around when things go completely out of control. In a negative aspect, the Emperor is a symbol of cold force, male domination, unreasoning Reason, and ruthless power. In this way, he is utterly opposed to the natural flow of the Tao. In fact, the Emperor may have strayed farther from the Tao than any other card in the deck. This does not mean that his cause is hopeless. It means that he must supplement his brilliant reasoning with compassion, intuition, and a metaphoric understanding of life. The Emperor may already have these qualities buried deep within him, as represented by the ankh. He needs to free them from the iron grip of his ratiocination.

Current Circumstances: Someone close to the Emperor will soon be released from a physical or emotional prison. The Emperor should not be afraid to humble himself. He is more in the control of women than he imagines. There is a lot of frustration in the Emperor's life; theft is possible.

Conflicts, Dangers, and Limitations: A lot of rage and passion underlie the Emperor's calm demeanor, and could harm him.

Career: The Emperor will get a promotion. This is a favorable card for leadership in business activities, but the Emperor should make sure to shore up his relationships with subordinates. He tends to be inaccessible.

Friends and Family: This is an important time to take special care of the family. There will soon be a birth.

Finances and Possessions: Prospects are extremely auspicious.

Health Concerns: Digestive system.

Romance: A woman's beautiful face brings trouble.

Travel: It is wise to remain at home.

Decision: Further hesitation leads to regret.

Future Events and Spiritual Achievements: The Emperor will learn wisdom from pain, and hope from hopelessness.

Omens and Talismans: A fortunate card for scientists and athletes.

      Animal Spirit: Fish, Panther
      Bird Spirit: Peacock, Bluebird
      Color: Bright Red, Green
      Plant: Grain, Grape, Lotus
      Tree: Hawthorn, Blackthorn
      Gemstone: Chysoberyl, Pearl
      Metal: Bronze
      Direction: Southeast
      Place: Waterfall
      Season: Summer, Autumn

PAGE of CUPS.

Meditation 60: Page of Cups

Running a country is like cooking a small fish.

Follow the Way,
Whose power controls the demons.
The demons still have their energy,
But it won't be used against others.

The wise spirit
Will thus protect himself and others.
The demons and the wise spirit
Hold each other harmless,
And the power of each
Energizes both.

This is the card of Dealing with Demons.

Mystical Key

(In case you're wondering about the small fish in the first line of the Meditation, the line means the less cooking the better.) This Meditation reminds us not to "stir" things too much—you never know what you might "stir up." The fish in the card not only represents the country, household, or relationship that can be spoiled by too much "cooking." In Chinese thought, the fish usually symbolizes happiness and pleasure. When the fish is combined with a water sign, as here, the pleasure is definitely sexual. Sometimes, however, the fish is the symbol of the principle of darkness, the "demons" now held harmless in the cup.

Each of the Cups Court cards bears a fish motif; you'll need to look closely, but it's there.

Magical Key

Character: This card refers to a creative, imaginative person.
Although he is a good student, the Page is inclined to be somewhat lazy.

Current Circumstances: The Page is beset by many apparent problems. He must learn how to turn these problems into opportunities. This is a time of steady growth, but the Page should not hasten beyond what is timely.

Conflicts, Dangers, and Limitations: The Page of Cups is experiencing a lot of anxiety. Thieves are present, and something has gone awry. It is very important for the Page not to underestimate an adversary now.

Career: A meeting with an important man can influence the Page's career for the better. The Page should not be discouraged if a promotion is withheld. The Page is on the right path.

Friends and Family: Family to the east and friends to the west are auspicious now.

Finances and Possessions: Some unsettling events may cause a decrease in money or possessions.

Health Concerns: Problems include anxiety and sleep disorders. These are mostly minor and will cure themselves.

Romance: An excellent card for romance. Marriage

arrangements may be difficult at first, but they will soon become easy.

Travel: The Page will make a faithful friend on his or her next trip. A river trip could be dangerous. Best travel direction is west to east.

Decision: Follow the advice of a partner or parents for this decision.

Future Events and Spiritual Achievements: A man will bring good fortune. Dreams are prophetic. A traveler will return with rich gifts.

Omens and Talismans: Auspicious card for those in the arts, especially music. This is also an auspicious card for the youngest daughter, and for young men.

> Animal Spirit: Monkey, Fish
> Bird Spirit: Pheasant, Phoenix
> Color: Black, Rose
> Plant: Passionflower, Laurel
> Tree: Alder, Mulberry
> Gemstone: Ruby, Pearl
> Metal: Electrum
> Direction: North
> Place: Cave
> Season: Summer

Meditation 61: Six of Swords

The great nation lies low,
All rivers run to it.
It holds the power of water,
It is the strength of woman.

By stillness
The woman overpowers man.

Just so, the great nation
Yields to the smaller one.

By doing so, it conquers.
The small nation, desiring patronage,
Yields to the great nation.
And by doing so, it conquers.
Both the large and small nation
Yield to serve their needs.
Yielding brings victory.
It is most essential for the great nation
To learn this truth.

This is the card of Yielding.

Mystical Key

A family crosses water in a sword-lined boat. The river is the Tao, into which all things run. It is shallow and easily navigated, as long as the helmsman goes with its flow. "Yielding brings victory. It is most essential for the great nation to learn this truth." This can be a time of painful transition. It is also a political lesson, for the picture reminds us of refugees from small, war-torn countries.

Magical Key

Character: The Six of Swords is sentimental and family oriented. Pride and interference, however, can get the Six into trouble. The Six needs to submit his will to those of others on occasion.

Current Circumstances: The abyss is full to the brim, but not yet overflowing.

Conflicts, Dangers, and Limitations: The Six is prey to unreasonable jealousy and fear of rejection. He must be willing to yield in order to win later on.

Career: The Six's next job will require a great deal of travel. He should follow instructions to the letter.

Friends and Family: The domestic Six is devoted to the family. A brother is in need. A woman friend is in danger.

Finances and Possessions: This is an auspicious card for finances, as long as the Six heeds the words of his financial advisor.

Health Concerns: Eyes and stomach. However, in general, this is a card of physical well-being.

Romance: Someone is about to declare his or her love. The Six is an idealistic lover.

Travel: Journey by water is dangerous. Travel is associated with a job; the first trip will be short, the second long.

Decision: Don't hesitate.

Future Events and Spiritual Achievements: Expect a traveler, a friend from the south. A beautiful young woman will bring good fortune. What is sought will be obtained. Better times lie just ahead. Although there is a great deal of anxiety now, everything will turn out beautifully. An important discovery is near.

Omens and Talismans: This is a fortunate card for someone in the military, the healing arts, or the sciences. The Six will achieve a well-earned success.

    Animal Spirit: Dog, Bee
    Bird Spirit: Pelican, Cardinal
    Color: Red, Yellow
    Plant: Chicory, Water Lily
    Tree: Willow, Holly
    Gemstone: Sardonyx, Yellow Diamond
    Metal: Copper
    Direction: Southwest
    Place: Mountains
    Season: Summer

PAGE of SWORDS.

Meditation 62: Page of Swords

The Tao is the cauldron
From which bubble the Ten Thousand Things.
It is treasured by the faithful follower,
It is a safe harbor for the lost.

The right words will find their target,
The right deeds will earn honor.
Even worthless people benefit from them.

When a king is crowned,
When new leaders take office,
While others run forward with gifts
Of jade and fine horses,
You can offer up the Tao,
And not move a muscle.

Why has the Tao been honored
Since time immemorial?
Because, by its power,
The noble find what they seek,
And the guilty are forgiven.
For this reason the Tao
Is the greatest treasure on earth.

This is the card of Faith.

Mystical Key

This card recognizes the practical benefits that come from following the Tao. Safe harbor for the lost, beneficent influences, the longed-for goal, and forgiveness of the guilty.

Magical Key

Character: The Page is unsettled in his thoughts, and needs to develop more confidence in his own judgment. He tends to be careless.

Current Circumstances: Things appear to be in flux; the Page should remain calm.

Conflicts, Dangers, and Limitations: The Page has hidden enemies—closer than one might think. Secret affairs surround the Page. His strong desire for power could land him in trouble.

Career: Advancement cannot be hoped for at the present time; however, the Page should persevere and all will come out right in the end.

Friends and Family: A traitor is near. The Page should avoid associating only with those whose opinions are agreeable to him. Mingle with many people.

Finances and Possessions: This is a fortunate card for business and investments.

Health Concerns: Eyes and legs. A danger of obsessions and fixations. A relapse is possible.

Romance: This is an auspicious card for marriage.

Travel: Not a good time to travel. The Page should stay peacefully at home.

Decision: This is not a time for vacillation, but a time to negotiate the best deal. The Page has the power and should use it.

Future Events and Spiritual Achievements: Some deep sorrow lies ahead. The Page will not be to blame.

Omens and Talismans: This is a fortunate card for mothers and fathers.

    Animal Spirit: Butterfly, Cricket
    Bird Spirit: Skylark, Raven
    Color: White, Sky Blue
    Plant: Periwinkle, Foxglove
    Tree: Sassafras, Hawthorn
    Gemstone: Sapphire, Black Opal
    Metal: Electrum

Direction: South
Place: Sky
Season: Summer

Meditation 63: Three of Wands

Act without acting.
Work without working.
Taste the flavorless.
Treat the smallest as the greatest,
The few as the many.

Reward injury with kindness.

Master difficult things
While they are still easy—
Even the most complex international affairs
Begin with a word.

Thus the wise spirit gets great things done
By never doing them.

Others take things too lightly—
They make promises they can't fulfill.
The wise spirit anticipates problems.
Therefore he never has to deal with them.

This is the card of Foresight.

Mystical Key

The Tao isn't entirely mystical. In places, it's completely practical. "Reward injury with kindness" is nothing more than Jesus's command to turn the other cheek (but formulated about 600 years earlier). Does this seem too idealistic? On the contrary, by breaking the cycle of pain, one is able to move forward. The Referent, like the figure on the card, will now be able to move forward with his life.

Magical Key

Character: The Three of Wands is faithful to his responsibilities, and is an excellent supervisor. In a bad situation, he may mask fear with contempt. He tends to overstep the limits.

Current Circumstances: This is an auspicious time to move. The past is unfortunate. This is the time to put obsessions about the past behind one, to move forward, not thoughtlessly, but with foresight and taking sensible precautions.

Conflicts, Dangers, and Limitations: Fear and danger surround the Three of Wands. An enemy is violating both oral and written agreements.

Career: This is an extremely auspicious card for business, social work, and trade. Practical knowledge and the advice of others are both important. Promises that can't be kept should not be made. "Master difficult things while they are still easy." This may apply to housework, schoolwork, child rearing, or dog training, but it's wisdom all the same.

Friends and Family: The Three may be envious of his friends, but for the wrong reasons.

Finances and Possessions: Financial progress may be hindered because another person is failing to help.

Health Concerns: Voice, reproductive system.

Romance: The Three should use restraint. An affair is a possibility.

Travel: This is an auspicious time to travel, especially for young women. Travel on the job is likely.

Decision: An impulsive decision, if wrong, will lead to disastrous results.

Future Events and Spiritual Achievements: Something good is beginning within three days. Good fortune comes from the south.

Omens and Talismans: This is a fortunate card for eldest daughters, and for people in authority.

    Animal Spirit: Dog (Especially A Hunting Dog), Moth
    Bird Spirit: Mockingbird, Thrush
    Color: Silver, Dark Blue

Plant: Poinsettia, Columbine
Tree: Cherry, Hazel
Gemstone: Moonstone, Opal
Metal: Lead
Direction: North
Place: Jungle
Season: Spring

THE WORLD.

Meditation 64:
The World (XXI): Yang

It's easy to hold onto resting objects
Just as it's easy to take precautions
Against something before it turns serious.
What is fragile is quickly broken;
Tiny objects are easily scattered.

Deal with events before they happen,
Keep things straight before they turn chaotic.

A massive tree springs from a seedling,
A nine-story terrace emerges from a pile of dirt.
A journey of a thousand miles begins with one step.

Meddling from ulterior motives
Is doomed to destruction.
Grasping an object ensures its loss.
The wise spirit doesn't meddle—
So he is never defeated.
The wise spirit doesn't grasp.
So he is never at a loss.

People tend to ruin things
Just when they're at the point of winning.
They need to focus on the end

At the beginning.
That's the way to stay on track.

The wise spirit is free of desire,
Not bothering to amass precious objects,
Not stubbornly clinging to his own ideas.
He is mindful of what others have lost—
He brings them back to their true values.

He helps all creatures find their own Way,
But he will not use force.

This is the card of Worldly Success.

Mystical Key

For as far back as de Gébelin, the World, or as he called it, the "Universe," represented the first card of the Golden Age. De Gébelin read the cards from highest to lowest. In this reading, the Universe represents the highest state of things. It's not meant to last forever, but, like everything else, is destined to flow downward.

The mandorla, the almond-shaped wreath that surrounds her, is representative of woman, who both receives the creative spark and gives birth to the world. It also is an old symbol for guarding a sacred treasure (this is because of the hard shell of the almond). The Meditation gives the mandorla an ironic twist, since it reminds us that amassing precious objects is a fairly useless activity. The wreath is a symbol of temporary triumph, a motif that reinforces the World's connection with the Wheel of Fortune. The wreath surrounding the character shows that even the World has its limits.

The figure in the center, despite being obviously female, in reality has male characteristics as well—for she carries magic wands in both hands.

The passage may be one of the most difficult concepts of Taoism for Western students to master. We traditionally think of the world as the culmination (and in fact, it is the triumphal, final card of the Tarot deck) and end of all being, but it's only a phase, like everything else. "The wise spirit is free of desire"—especially the desire for the world. The most attractive card can be the most dangerous. The partial Gospel figures, the Lion of Mark, Man of Matthew, Ox of Luke, and Eagle of John without their wings, bodies, or their sacred books reappear here. This suggests an incompleteness, a not-quite fulfillment. This interpretation is opposite to conventional readings of this card, which attribute all good things and only good things to the World.

Magical Key

Character: The World is an active and responsible person, who is sensitive to the needs of others, especially of the poor. He is also a good speaker, with mystical abilities.

Current Circumstances: The World has the power to solve any difficulties in his present environment. However, he may have to hide the full extent of his knowledge in order not to attract too much attention. The World should not neglect the spiritual element. This card, while positive, may only indicate temporary good fortune. The needs of others should be kept in mind. One person's victory entails the defeat of others. Attempts to redo what has already been accomplished will only make things worse.

Conflicts, Dangers, and Limitations: Theft is a definite possibility. Guilt may hinder the World.

Career: This is not a good time to conduct official business. Waiting will bring great rewards.

Friends and Family: A friendly relationship between an older woman and young girl will prove auspicious.

Finances and Possessions: The World is in danger of losing a piece of property.

Health Concerns: Heart.

Romance: Showing too much emotion right now could be harmful. Marriage prospects with someone older.

Travel: Travel is indicated, especially a river journey.

Decision: The World should go ahead with this decision.

Future Events and Spiritual Achievements: Great success and victory will be attained.

Omens and Talismans: This is a good card for a second daughter and for anyone in business.

Animal Spirit: Bee, Lion
Bird Spirit: Oriole, Lark
Color: Orange/Red, Light Blue
Plant: Yew, Astilbe
Tree: Ash, Birch
Gemstone: Lapis Lazuli, Topaz
Metal: Silver
Direction: West
Place: Sky
Season: Early Autumn

QUEEN of SWORDS.

Meditation 65: Queen of Swords

The ancient Tao Masters
Never tried to enlighten people.
It is easier to lead
By keeping people in the dark.

When people are too clever,
They are difficult to manage,
Likewise one who governs by knowledge
Is a scourge to his nation.
One who governs simply is blessed.
These two things provide a clear pattern,
A pattern that leads to Mystical Power.

Mystical Power reaches deep and high.
It brings all things to Return.
And to Unity.

This is the card of Mystical Power.

Mystical Key

The Meditation explains that intelligence alone is not sufficient for good leadership, although it is necessary. The upheld Sword represents unity, and the hand extends a blessing. She may have suffered great pain, but has managed to overcome it. Knowledge and simplicity together attain mystical power.

Magical Key

Character: The Queen of Swords is powerful, highly intelligent, sensual, and perceptive. She is also intensely attractive, and she is kind and patient with uncultured people. Her friendliness can win people over. However, the Queen may be extremely unpredictable and deceitful, and makes a dangerous enemy.

Current Circumstances: Hope surrounds the Queen and there is joy in the atmosphere. It is up to her to help regenerate society. The Queen has been wounded by an evil force, but she is now safe and her worries are baseless.

Conflicts, Dangers, and Limitations: The Queen needs to draw more deeply from her mystical source of power. The Queen's main trouble may occur because she is not aware of the very powerful Yin forces she bears, and she is almost overshadowed by Yang.

Career: Modesty in leadership is important right now.

Friends and Family: The Queen will receive word from a distant friend, who will soon return.

Finances and Possessions: The Queen should be cautious in investments.

Health Concerns: Respiratory system.

Romance: This is a dangerous card for romance.

Travel: Long travel is favored now.

Decision: Any decision made now should be tentative.

Future Events and Spiritual Achievements: The Queen's spiritual attainments will allow her to guide others.

Omens and Talismans: This is a good card for the youngest son and for elected officials.

Animal Spirit: Lion, Butterfly
Bird Spirit: Phoenix, Falcon
Color: White, Red
Plant: Rose, Hydrangea
Tree: Elder, Maple
Gemstone: Bloodstone, Citrine
Metal: Steel
Direction: South
Place: Garden
Season: Summer

Meditation 66: Eight of Pentacles

Why is the sea master of streams and rivers?
Because it lies low and receives their waters.
Just so the wise spirit keeps low,
And draws all people to him.

If the leader would truly lead,
He must follow.
In this way the people
Are not oppressed.
And when he stands before them,
The people are unharmed.
They are happy to follow
One who, without striving,
Has no rival.

This is the card of Creative Service.

Mystical Key
The true leader is one who understand his followers, and who, in serving them, receives his reward. Following and leading are intricately related. The true leader is one whose interest lies with the common folk.

Magical Key

Character: The Eight of Pentacles is skilled, methodical, and hardworking. He is impartial and respected by other people. He works not just for himself, but for others, and the generous Eight will reap his reward. In a negative reading, the Eight could be miserly or stubborn. The card may suggest too much concentration on unimportant details, and relying too much on the way things have been done in the past.

Current Circumstances: Religion is an important influence at this time. The Eight is living alone, either emotionally or physically.

Conflicts, Dangers, and Limitations: An untruth is causing trouble. The Eight is currently at an impasse due to grief or worry.

Career: The Eight will reach his goals as long as he does not deviate from his program. For the experienced, this may be a good time to retire from "center stage."

Friends and Family: Some of the Eight's friends are giving bad advice, which should be ignored. The Eight may have to sever these "friends."

Finances and Possessions: Business affairs are extremely profitable right now.

Health Concerns: Diet is creating a health problem.

Romance: The Eight's partner has unmet needs. The Eight will not attain happiness until he places his partner's happiness before his own.

Travel: Travel is auspicious at this time.

Decision: The Eight should go ahead. He will succeed even if he has previously failed.

Future Events and Spiritual Achievements: The Eight will receive the Sword of Wisdom.

Omens and Talismans: This is an auspicious card for students and outdoors people.

> Animal Spirit: Fish, Deer
> Bird Spirit: Owl, Robin
> Color: White, Orange

Plant: Sunflower, Anemone
Tree: Bay, Sycamore
Gemstone: Ruby, Turquoise
Metal: Silver
Direction: Northwest
Place: Mountains, Rivers
Season: Late Autumn

KING of WANDS.

Meditation 67: King of Wands

Everyone under Heaven
Acknowledges the Tao to be great,
But odd—peculiar.
That's the way of it.
If it weren't so strange,
It would have been found out long ago.

I have three treasures that I value deeply.
One is mercy.
One is temperance.
One is daring to keep low.

Compassion engenders courage.
Temperance allows for generosity.
Humility gives birth to leadership.

Courage without compassion,
Generosity without temperance,
Leadership without humility:
These lead to death.

Compassion wins wars,
And protects defenders.
It is the weapon of Heaven.

This is the card of Leadership.

Mystical Key

Engraved on the King's throne are lions for courage, and salamanders, representative of the transforming power of fire. Courage without compassion is recklessness, and generosity without temperance is being a spendthrift. Leadership without humility is brutality.

Magical Key

Character: In a favorable aspect, the King is strong, honest, just, generous, and courageous. It is an auspicious card for a married person or the father of a family. The King makes a good friend. He has a quirky sense of humor, and understands the curious ways of the universe. In an unfavorable reading, he is brutal, prejudiced, and proud. He may feel oppressed and fearful.

Current Circumstances: The King's good fortune may be temporary, so he should enjoy it now. This is a time to give generous gifts. Plans may not be implemented. There is something oppressing the King, something from which he must distance himself. The King must not believe rumors. This is the time to put into practice what has only been read about. The middle of the month will prove a fortunate time.

Conflicts, Dangers, and Limitations: Greed is causing trouble.

Career: Some of the King's subordinates are completely out of control.

Friends and Family: The father of the family has behaved in a hurtful way, especially toward his son. It is important not to alienate people just now. The King will soon meet someone new.

Finances and Possessions: The financial outlook is very poor at this time, but better for possessions.

Health Concerns: The King is subject to severe depression, which has an adverse effect on his family.

Romance: If this relationship is to succeed, the King must be firm.

Travel: This is an auspicious card for long journeys.

Decision: All the ramifications of the decision should be understood before proceeding.

Future Events and Spiritual Achievements: The King will receive inspiration.

Omens and Talismans: An auspicious card for athletes and people connected with organized religion.

 Animal Spirit: Salamander, Lion
 Bird Spirit: Dove, Thrush
 Color: Olive, Purple
 Plant: Lotus, Nettle
 Tree: Beech, Sweetgum
 Gemstone: Peridot, Onyx
 Metal: Mercury
 Direction: Southwest
 Place: House
 Season: Winter

Meditation 68: Five of Swords

The soldier in Tao in not violent.
The solider in Tao is not angry.
He wins by not antagonizing the enemy.

He leads by serving.
And is skilled with people,
Not weapons.
This is the path of Heaven.

This is the card of Misjudgment.

Mystical Key

The card and Meditation depict someone who has apparently made a conquest, but it is obvious that the victory is neither complete nor honorable. Surely the "defeated" soldiers will return. Both weakness and treachery are indicated.

Magical Key

Character: The Five of Swords possesses many good qualities but neglects them. He tends to give way to anger. He is curious and enjoys meeting new people.

Current Circumstances: The Golden Dawn called this card the "Lord of Defeat." This is a card of loss. The Five will soon reap the disastrous results of an unprincipled act—one that he thought he got away with.

Conflicts, Dangers, and Limitations: The Five of Swords is suffering from repression and narrow, subjective views. Taoists call this state: frog in a well.

Career: This is a good time to form a carefully thought-out business alliance.

Friends and Family: The Five has antagonized the wrong people and lost a friend. The mother of the family has been damaging, but there is little to be done now to change it.

Finances and Possessions: The Five may acquire great possessions, but they bring no joy.

Health Concerns: An injury is possible.

Romance: A misunderstanding is poisoning the relationship.

Travel: Travel is not recommended at this time, but in any case, should not be undertaken alone.

Decision: Indecisiveness is doing the Five great harm.

Future Events and Spiritual Achievements: The Five will experience defeat; only great spiritual effort can turn the defeat into wisdom.

Omens and Talismans: Auspicious card only for those who are unprincipled. A card for villains.

    Animal Spirit: Wild Ox, Frog
    Bird Spirit: Jackdaw, Warbler
    Color: Sky Blue, Violet
    Plant: Chrysanthemum, Cinquefoil
    Tree: Ash, Holly
    Gemstone: Garnet, Moonstone
    Metal: Steel
    Direction: Northeast

Place: Desert
Season: Autumn

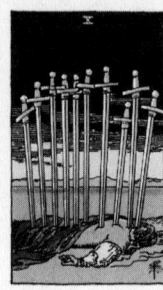

Meditation 69: Ten of Swords

In the art of war,
A good defense
Is a good offense.

It is marching without moving,
Baring one's arms, yet hiding one's strength.
Seizing the enemy before he's aware of your
* presence.*
Holding invisible weapons.

The biggest mistake
Is to underestimate the enemy.
Doing so will cost you your life.

So when the battle is joined,
The peacemaker wins.

This is the card of Treachery and Defeat.

Mystical Key
The sharpness of the Meditation and the sobering picture each tell its
own story, and this card is rightly regarded as one of the most inauspicious in the entire deck.

Magical Key
  Character: The Ten of Swords is constant, but can easily
    misjudge the character of other people. His misplaced
    confidence in them can get him into trouble. The Ten also
    tends to flee from uncomfortable situations instead of
    facing them.
  Current Circumstances: The Ten of Swords has been

backstabbed because he has trusted the wrong people. He has been guilty of underestimating the enemy. Yet even here there is a glimmer of happiness, for the bottom has been reached. The Ten should not try too hard to rectify mistakes of the past; instead, he should cultivate contentment.

Conflicts, Dangers, and Limitations: This card is very unfavorable with regard to relationships or spiritual matters. Obsession and all sorts of excesses lead to serious problems.

Career: The Ten of Swords is surrounded by obstacles at all sides on his job.

Friends and Family: One of them will betray the Ten. This is an especially bad card for the eldest son: someone is plotting against him.

Finances and Possessions: This is a good time for home repairs.

Health Concerns: Back, bones, joints.

Romance: A woman of the Ten's acquaintance will soon be happily married.

Travel: Travel abroad is beneficial at this time.

Decision: The time for action has come. Others should not be allowed to sway Ten's decision.

Future Events and Spiritual Achievements: Return to a pure, uncontaminated state of mind is assured.

Omens and Talismans: A card of great misfortune. Not auspicious for anyone.

    Animal Spirit: Dog, Lion
    Bird Spirit: Dove, Seagull
    Color: Sea Green, Russet
    Plant: Sphagnum Moss, Grape
    Tree: Willow, Oak
    Gemstone: Opal, Cat's-Eye
    Metal: Steel
    Direction: East
    Place: House
    Season: Late Winter

Meditation 70: Four of Pentacles

My words are easy to understand.
Putting them into practice is something else.

They are easy to follow,
But nobody follows them.

Although these words are born of ancient days,
The deeds they enshrine are a sacred pattern.
Yet people are completely ignorant of them.

Those who know me are few.
Thus I am even more valuable.

The wise spirit may wear rags,
But he holds a jewel in his heart.

This is the card of Secret Treasure.

Mystical Key

This card is often mistakenly read as a card of worldly acquisition, and even materialism, but it has a deeper meaning. The jewel the figure holds to his heart is of the earth (Pentacles), but what is often of the earth is not necessarily of the world. In fact, in this case, this powerful pentacle indicates the Tao itself. One Taoist text, Understanding Reality: A Direct Explanation, states, "In the right position in the center is produced the mysterious jewel," which we see in this card. The Tao is under our feet, crowning our head, and most important, held at the heart.

It's an easy enough mistake to make, and it's the mistake the Meditation warns us against. Lao Tzu counsels us that his words "are easy to follow, but nobody practices them." Why is this? Because we insist on setting up a false guide, following gold instead of what gold represents, which is an untarnishable, changeless truth.

Magical Key

Character: The Four of Pentacles represents one who is rooted firmly to the earth. (Four is the traditional number of earth.) He is a strong Yin personality. In a more negative aspect, the Four of Pentacles could be "attached" to the world rather than rooted in the earth. He is honest and steady, but may neglect his spiritual and emotional development for work and a career. He may lack imagination.

Current Circumstances: It is not too late to rectify mistakes of the past. Undertake a study of the self; it can lead to ecstasy. The Four of Pentacles should seek out what is eternally true; only this brings pure joy.

Conflicts, Dangers, and Limitations: Although surrounded by difficulties, the Four can escape them by careful observation of what is really going on.

Career: The Four takes great pride in his work. This is a good time to start a new project—or even a new job, although the Four's conservative nature pulls against it. He will climb to great heights if he can break out of his routine. Working at home is especially recommended. If the Four must criticize others, he should do it constructively.

Friends and Family: The family of the Four is in need. He should not turn his back on them.

Finances and Possessions: The Four of Pentacles may have a tendency toward materialism. If he seeks this route, he will indeed be successful, but poor in spirit, a miserly, discontented, selfish person. Clinging to goods is not following the Tao. It can also signify the loss of money.

Health Concerns: Spleen, stomach.

Romance: The Four should make a concerted effort to control his feelings.

Travel: Not a favorable time to travel.

Decision: The Four should not be afraid to take a risk.

Future Events and Spiritual Achievements: Great joy.

Omens and Talismans: Auspicious for those who are married, and for those in government service.

Animal Spirit: Horse, Cattle
Bird Spirit: Ibis, Warbler
Color: Citrine, Indigo
Plant: Foxglove, Pansy
Tree: Ash, Birch
Gemstone: Agate, Lapis Lazuli
Metal: Copper
Direction: West
Place: Air
Season: Early Spring

Meditation 71: Two of Pentacles

To know that knowledge is ignorance
Is to be ignorant, and to believe
That ignorance is knowledge
Is a mental disease.

To be sick of sickness
Is the cure.
The wise spirit avoids sickness
By being sick of it.

That is the way to health.

This is the card of Balance.

Mystical Key

Our culture has lauded the supreme rationalist as the highest of all thinkers. But "supreme" leads to "extreme"—to imbalance. Rational thinking is only one side of the human equation. One needs to expect the changes that naturally come in life; they will then be easier to deal with.

Magical Key

Character: The Two of Pentacles is good with smooth words, but is not always trustworthy. The Two gets along well with

others, but can be a hypocrite and a deceiver. The Two
prefers peace at any price, and is both tactful and
diplomatic, sometimes at the cost of truth.

Current Circumstances: There are difficulties in achieving a
goal, which may be misdirected. The Two should cultivate
attentiveness. A gift will be arriving.

Conflicts, Dangers, and Limitations: There is a problem with
starting a new project; the Two may be trying too hard.
There are bad influences that must be removed. The Two
tends to be self-conscious without need.

Career: A change of job is a definite possibility. Flexibility in
dealing with superiors is a trait to strive for.

Friends and Family: Friends are envious, but they will not be
able to harm the Two of Pentacles.

Finances and Possessions: Wise investing will ensure wealth.

Health Concerns: Lungs and large intestine. Balance is the
key to health. Drugs, junk food, tobacco, and sexual
promiscuity are to be avoided, since all produce an
imbalance in the body that can result in health
problems.

Romance: This is an auspicious card for both romance and
marriage. Partnerships will be strong.

Travel: The Two of Pentacles will soon take a beneficial trip.

Decision: Wait until next spring to do this.

Future Events and Spiritual Achievements: The Two must wait a
while for the goal to be accomplished. Change will be
harmonious and the Two will eventually achieve bliss and
the gift of foresight.

Omens and Talismans: Auspicious for those in the healing arts,
and for those working with animals.

    Animal Spirit: Pig, Fish
    Bird Spirit: Dove, Blackbird
    Color: Gray, Yellow
    Plant: Dianthus, Phlox
    Tree: Alder, Pine
    Gemstone: Emerald, Jade
    Metal: Copper

Direction: Southeast
Place: City
Season: Winter, Spring

THE TOWER.

Meditation 72:

The Tower (XVI): Yang

When we are not in awe of the awesome,
We are in mortal danger.

We shouldn't live in narrow dwellings
And do useless work.

If you don't meddle,
You won't be hurt.

The wise spirit knows this well.
He cares for the treasure,
But leaves it to others.
He loves himself,
And prizes the treasure within.

This is the card of Chaos.

Mystical Key

We are in mortal danger. The Tower, symbol of our pride in our ability to reconstruct the cosmos, has been struck by lightning, which represents supernatural (possibly evil) power. Two figures (archetypal human beings) have been pitched from its heights. So has a golden crown, symbol of human grasping and dominion. The Tower reminds us of both the Tower of Babel and the expulsion of Adam and Eve. We have been torn from the sacral realm. "If you don't meddle, you won't be hurt." This line is a direct reference to those who try to force the universe into a new structure of their own devising. We must again learn the "awe of the awesome."

Conventionally, the Tower is held to refer to the ultimate futility of human endeavors. After all, the higher one climbs, the more likely one is to be struck by lightning. The irony is that this result should have been expected when one tried to touch the sky.

And yet, there is a positive note in all this. For chaos leads ultimately to liberation and reorganization. Thus the Tower is in its way an alchemical symbol—the lightning doing its part to break down matter into spirit. The Tower can represent all that is both soaring and tragic in our nature. Only those who dare greatly and risk everything are worthy of the name "hero."

On a wider social level, the Tower can indicate war and terrorism. (I drew this card on September 11, 2001—the day of the infamous attack on the World Trade Center and the Pentagon.)

Magical Key

Character: The Tower is both ambitious and courageous, but possibly arrogant. She must free herself from all prejudice and be open to the abilities of people from every class.

Current Circumstances: The Tower is in danger of attack from those who are envious or who bear a grudge. However, no matter what tragedy the Tower endures, a new and stronger personality will arise from her foundations. There is an evil that must be expelled. The Tower is undertaking a project that, unless properly held within natural bounds, will fail. This applies to financial ventures, career moves, and personal life. Change is essential—now. The old order will be tossed aside so that a new one may arise. The Tower's life is in upheaval. There is great danger everywhere; the true situation is unknown.

Conflicts, Dangers, and Limitations: Your mind is your own worst enemy.

Career: A current means of making a living will not remain profitable. The Tower needs allies to make a position of leadership work better.

Friends and Family: The sudden loss of a friendship is possible.

Finances and Possessions: The Tower may attain abundant, though often temporary, wealth.

Health Concerns: Kidney, bladder, and reproductive organs.
Diet and exercise are critical.

Romance: A sudden breakup is possible.

Travel: This is an extremely inauspicious card for travel.

Decision: There is a hidden dragon. Do not act.

Future Events and Spiritual Achievements: The long-term future
is very unclear. A great deal depends on how the Tower
responds to misfortune and tragedy. The Tower will achieve
fame, but in an unexpected way.

Omens and Talismans: The Tower is not an auspicious card for
anyone.

> Animal Spirit: Cat, Cattle
> Bird Spirit: Raven, Grackle
> Color: Russet, Light Red
> Plant: Nettle, Bleeding Heart
> Tree: Birch, Elder
> Gemstone: Sapphire, Chrysoprase
> Metal: Iron
> Direction: North
> Place: Air
> Season: Early Fall

JUDGEMENT.

Meditation 73: Judgment (XX): Yang

Recklessness leads to death.
True courage gives life.
Which is more beneficial?
It is sometimes hard to know
Which is heaven's will.
Even the Tao Master cannot be certain.

The way of heaven overcomes without strife;
It is silent, yet it always answers.
It doesn't call on us,
Yet the people obey.
It moves effortlessly.

The net of heaven is vast,
And its meshes are wide.
Yet nothing escapes it.

This is the card of Consequences and Renewal.

Mystical Key

The archangel Gabriel blows the trumpet signifying the end of days and the Last Judgment. The human figures in the card appear to welcome its appearance, showing that they have accepted the path of the Tao and followed it to its ceaseless fulfillment. The card bears witness to the truth that renewal is a fact of life, and that despite even the grimmest tragedies, rebirth is assured.

Magical Key

Character: Judgment is independent, fair, and indomitable. He has a secret power over others, and others look to him with respect, and possibly a little fear.

Current Circumstances: A criminal case needs to be investigated further in order to prevent a serious miscarriage of justice. Something is hidden. There is a great opportunity today. Judgment needs to repent evil actions, and forgive other people theirs. The end of the month is an auspicious time.

Conflicts, Dangers, and Limitations: Ignorance and immaturity are blocking the way.

Career: It is important to select the right people for a project—and then give them a free hand. Sluggishness is hindering a beginning.

Friends and Family: Judgment may feel cut off and separated. Although admired by others, Judgment can be feared as well.

Finances and Possessions: Gradual accumulation of wealth and possessions is likely.

Health Concerns: Liver and gall bladder. In addition, the utmost cleanliness of the body and mind are important just now.

Romance: A quiet romance is auspicious now.

Travel: Travel with a loved one is recommended.

Decision: Proceed gradually.

Future Events and Spiritual Achievements: Judgment will be judged by his actions. No one can escape the "net of heaven." Judgment will have many descendants.

Omens and Talismans: An auspicious card for those in law.

> Animal Spirit: Dog, Crab
> Bird Spirit: Vireo, Seagull
> Color: Violet, Maroon
> Plant: Bleeding Heart, Buttercup
> Tree: Ash, English Yew
> Gemstone: Alexandrite, Ruby
> Metal: Gold
> Direction: South
> Place: Fields
> Season: Late Spring

THE HANGED MAN.

Meditation 74: The Hanged Man (XII): Yin

When people no longer fear death,
They cannot be threatened with it.
Only those who fear dying
Fear the death penalty.

The Great Executioner awaits everyone.
If you try to do the job yourself,
You'll suffer the consequences.
Those who try to cut wood
Like the master carpenter
End up slicing their own hand.

This is the card of Fearless Sacrifice.

Mystical Key

The figure hangs by his left leg from a branch, or the top bar of a Tau (Greek) cross. His right leg is bent so as to repeat the cross motif, or in another interpretation, the number 4, sign of the earth. (The upper portion of the Hanged Man's body suggests a triangle—the heavenly sign 3).

His hands are tied behind his back. In Christian tradition, Saint Peter was crucified upside down, and the man's calm expression and halo lend credence to this interpretation. In a similar vein, the great god Odin was supposed to have hung upside down from the World Tree for nine days in order to receive the power of spells or prophecy from the runes, a kind of Norse Tarot. The shining circle behind the Hanged Man's head represents the "golden blossom" of Taoism that grows from the head and symbolizes the highest spiritual attainment.

In a Taoist reading, this is a card of mysterious incongruities. "The Great Executioner awaits everyone." The serene expression of the Hanged Man seems totally at odds with his situation. This is the transforming card that alters the meaning of nearly every card that comes in contact with it. The Hanged Man changes everything. Favorable cards turn inauspicious when coupled with the Hanged Man—unfavorable cards have a reverse meaning. He is making a sacrifice that costs him his life—but for what end? More than any other card in the deck, the Hanged Man is ambiguous, and requires a careful reading. The Hanged Man is a very dangerous omen for those in public life; it can signify serious dissension, even revolution. It was customary in Italy, where the Tarot was probably first devised, to hang traitors upside down, often by one foot, and one Italian name for this card, the Traitor, should not be ignored in analysis. (More recently, Mussolini, his mistress, and one of his generals were strung up this way after their assassinations.)

Magical Key

Character: Is the Hanged Man a saint—or a traitor? or both?
The character of the Hanged Man is extraordinarily
complex. He has connections with the Hermit, the Fool,
and the Magician. He may be a victim or a savior, a hero or
a villain. The depths of his character can be explored only
in relation to the surrounding cards.

Current Circumstances: Obstacles and disruption surround the Hanged Man. He is making a great sacrifice. If the sacrifice is for noble ends, great good can come from it: this is signified by the flowering branch above. Much lies in the balance—a suspension of activities, a stasis, may be hindering the Hanged Man from accomplishing his goals.

Conflicts, Dangers, and Limitations: Bad habits are getting the Hanged Man into trouble. These habits must be reversed. He is in a crisis situation, even if he isn't aware of it. (In fact, the Hanged Man may feel as if he is stuck, and that in itself is a crisis.) Ignorance is to be avoided.

Career: The Hanged Man is having difficulty making progress. He is being held back by others, and by a fate he can only partly control.

Friends and Family: The relationship between father and son is difficult. The Hanged Man is charismatic, and has a wide circle of admirers, but almost none of them truly understand him.

Finances and Possessions: The Hanged Man obtains true riches by sharing wealth and comfort with the poor.

Health Concerns: Heart, liver, and small intestine.

Romance: The Hanged Man is generally a loner—but when in love, his passion is great and undying.

Travel: Travel is favorable now. Minor concerns should not be a hindrance.

Decision: The most critical decision of the Hanged Man's life will soon arise. The correct choice is the most courageous one.

Future Events and Spiritual Achievements: The Hanged Man will attain purified real knowledge.

Omens and Talismans: An auspicious card for spiritual people.

    Animal Spirit: Rabbit, Horse
    Bird Spirit: Lark, Redbird
    Color: Red, Yellow, Dark Blue
    Plant: Lily of the Valley, Buttercup
    Tree: Walnut, Buckeye
    Gemstone: Jade, Amber
    Metal: Gold

Direction: South
Place: Mountains
Season: Autumn

Meditation 75: Five of Pentacles

People are starving.
Those in power eat up their money in taxes.

The people rebel against a meddlesome
  government,
Rebel against leaders who serve their own ends.

These people no longer fear death,
Because for them life isn't worth living.
So they laugh at death.

When life hangs by a thread,
People are willing to cut it.

This is the card of Compassion.

Mystical Key
One of the great myths about the Tao Te Ching is that it has no social consciousness. This is simply not true. The Tao is always allied with the lowest, the poorest, and the weakest members of a community, for from them, paradoxically comes its strength. A community or a nation that preys on its weakest members grows weak in return. It will be uprooted and torn apart. Oppression gives birth to rebellion.

Magical Key
  Character: The restless Five has objective awareness, but may
    lack the compassion that is absolutely essential to his
    salvation. The Five may not develop compassion for others
    until he needs it himself; this is the very lesson that he
    needs to achieve enlightenment.

Current Circumstances: Circumstances are very difficult now. A person of great power and ability is at hand, but his motives are misunderstood by the people. The Five is safe and protected, but under constraint. The expected person will be late. Egotism is to be avoided.

Conflicts, Dangers, and Limitations: All the Five's troubles stem from lack of compassion. The Five of Pentacles must be aware of his own attitude toward the weaker members of his family, community, and nation. "When life hangs by a thread, people are willing to cut it." This card can signal the loss of job or indicate a health problem. It may also mean being an outcast from a circle of friends, or much effort with little result. In the most positive reading, this card represents those who have given up the things of this world for the things of the spirit, much as the Buddha cast off his riches for the rags of a mendicant and the holy friars of the Middle Ages became beggars in the service of God. In Chinese myth, one of the Eight Immortals, the soul-traveler Li-t'ieh-kuai, walks with a crutch. Likewise, those who draw this card have a far-ranging spirit.

Career: Official business will not be successful. The Five should speak up about job concerns.

Friends and Family: The Five may be plagued by forever-borrowing friends and family. For the best outcome, he should do the generous thing.

Finance and Possessions: An inauspicious card for money matters. Seeker could end up in poverty if not careful.

Health Concerns: Pancreas, liver, and spleen. Outdoor activities are helpful.

Romance: The sexually attractive Five of Pentacles tends to be a flirt, and to have many relationships. In these relationships, the Five requires a lot of freedom.

Travel: The Five of Pentacles loves and benefits from travel.

Decision: Wait. Consider how the decision affects others.

Future Events and Spiritual Achievements: The Five will have many problems in the beginning, but in the end will achieve the full development of his potential.

Omens and Talismans: This is an auspicious card for people in
entertainment and sales.

    Animal Spirit: Ox, Rabbit
    Bird Spirit: Blackbird, Kingfisher
    Color: Green, Black
    Plant: Lily, Buttercup
    Tree: Beech, Mistletoe
    Gemstone: Turquoise, Aquamarine
    Metal: Tin
    Direction: North
    Place: Hills, Mountains
    Season: Winter

Meditation 76: Four of Swords

A living person is soft and flexible,
The dead are rigid and hard.
Young plants and flowers are tender and supple,
Dead ones are dry and stiff.

A rigid sword will snap,
A dry tree crack.

The hard, stiff, and strong inevitably fall.
The soft, flexible, and supple will flourish.

This is the card of Flexibility.

Mystical Key

Chuang Tzu says, "The life of man is only breath. When it is gathered,
there is life, when it disperses, there is death. Since life and death are
companions, why fret over them? All creatures are one. The life they
love seems wonderfully vibrant, the death they hate seems a foul rottenness. Yet the rottenness turns to vitality, and life to death. In this world
there is only one breath." This is the kind of knowledge that brings
serenity.

Magical Key

> *Character:* The Four of Swords is thrifty, but his outlook is too
> limited. He is dedicated, but he must learn to become more
> flexible; compromise is important as long as he can hold on
> to his principles.
>
> *Current Circumstances:* There is a temporary truce amid a great
> deal of conflict. Legal problems may be indicated. A
> falsehood needs to be countered.
>
> *Conflicts, Dangers, and Limitations:* Hatred is holding the Four
> back from achieving everything he desires. Aversion is to be
> avoided. The Four should avoid making any major changes
> until he is calm and knows exactly what to do.
>
> *Career:* Although the Four of Swords will overcome his enemies
> (who may be business partners), it will be at a terrific cost
> to himself. The Four should hire an assistant. He should
> consider taking a vacation, going into retreat, or just taking
> some time off to reassess values.
>
> *Friends and Family:* Someone will step in to provide assistance.
>
> *Finances and Possessions:* An unexpected bonus is a possibility.
>
> *Health Concerns:* Adrenal glands, arteries. The Four of Swords
> is overstressed, and his health is suffering as a result. He
> will be cured, although perhaps it will come slowly.
>
> *Romance:* The Four is a deep lover, but very controlled.
>
> *Travel:* This is an extremely inauspicious card for travel.
>
> *Decision:* Reject the offer—it is not advantageous. Do not make
> new plans now.
>
> *Future Events and Spiritual Achievements:* The Four will attain
> peace after conflict.
>
> *Omens and Talismans:* This is a good card for military personnel
> and scientists.
>
>> Animal Spirit: Bear, Elephant
>> Bird Spirit: Lark, Egret
>> Color: Yellow, Light Blue
>> Plant: Astilbe, Lilac
>> Tree: English Yew, Locust
>> Gemstone: Amber, Beryl

Metal: Iron
Direction: East
Place: Ocean
Season: Summer

Meditation 77: Six of Pentacles

The path of Heaven is a tightened bow,
What was high is low.
What was low is high.

If the bowstring is too long,
It's cut.
If it's too short,
It is lengthened.
This is the way of Tao.

But the way of humanity is different.
Those in power take from the weak.
They stuff their own coffers.

Only those who walk in Tao
Have enough treasure to give to all.
The wise spirit accomplishes his work
Without notice.
He doesn't flaunt his power.

This is the card of Magnanimity.

Mystical Key

The Meditation points out that the treasure of Tao is the treasure of all of us. The wise spirit knows that he must share his wealth to enjoy it fully. This refers to spiritual as well as material wealth.

Magical Key

Character: The Six of Pentacles is serene and considerate. He is self-sacrificing and has strong convictions.

Current Circumstances: The Six is generous in giving to others, friends as well as enemies. This giving should include spiritual as well as material gifts. This is the time to take care of the small and insignificant. The Six should seek assistance only from those who can really help.

Conflicts, Dangers, and Limitations: Danger comes from the north. The Six should avoid being controlled by desire. He is also subject to moodiness due to his sensitive nature.

Career: Things are very inauspicious. Leave should be requested.

Friends and Family: The Six is generous to friends, although they are giving bad advice that should be rejected.

Finances and Possessions: Bad debts are a definite possibility.

Health Concerns: Endocrine system.

Romance: Jealousy is destroying a relationship. Compassion may make repairs.

Travel: Winter travel is auspicious.

Decision: No important actions should be taken at present.

Future Events and Spiritual Achievements: The fate of the Six is to control the destiny of others.

Omens and Talismans: This is a favorable card for a wife or mother.

> Animal Spirit: Hare, Snake
> Bird Spirit: Owl, Blue Jay
> Color: Violet, Sky Blue
> Plant: Chrysanthemum, Buddleia
> Tree: Holly, Hickory
> Gemstone: Emerald, Blue Topaz
> Metal: Silver
> Direction: East
> Place: Desert
> Season: Winter

Meditation 78: Eight of Cups

Water seems weak
But of all things on earth,
It is best for wearing away
A cliff.
Everyone knows this.
No one puts it into practice.

But the wise spirit knows
That one rebuked by the world
Is fit to rule.
And one who takes on the grief of his country
Is its lord.

This is a paradox, isn't it?

This is the card of Paradox.

Mystical Key

We are coming close to the end of the Tao, and paradoxically we are beginning a new journey. This is the nature of the Tao, which never truly has an end. Although it appears as if the character is turning away from the feelings and emotions represented by Cups, in reality he is on a new and upward journey. The land he is leaving is unproductive and swampy—he is better off in a new place. He must turn his distaste into a search for new meanings.

Magical Key

> Character: The Eight of Cups is a born leader and is very
> competitive. He has good insight into other people, and
> understands what makes them tick. However, he may be
> plagued by corruptive forces and become lazy.
>
> Current Circumstances: Although difficulties are beginning to
> pile up, this is a transitional phase. It's important to work

together with other people to help solve a social problem. Factionalism is dangerous.

Conflicts, Dangers, and Limitations: An ungenerous spirit puts the Eight at risk of losing everything. He must avoid possessiveness. The Eight of Cups is wearied by his old lifestyle.

Career: A career in the arts, especially the literary arts, is wise. This is the time to join with a community of others.

Friends and Family: The family's enterprises are successful. Old relationships are stagnant.

Finances and Possessions: A joint venture with friends will be beneficial.

Health Concerns: Thyroid gland.

Romance: This is an auspicious time for marriage.

Travel: Adventurous travel is indicated.

Decision: Do not hesitate.

Future Events and Spiritual Achievements: Danger lies near at hand. Don't abandon plans without a very good reason. The Eight will receive inspiration, and will exchange material success for deeper happiness.

Omens and Talismans: This is a fortunate card for poets.

Animal Spirit: Fox, Tortoise
Bird Spirit: Wren, Peacock
Color: White, Azure
Plant: Iceplant, Lupine
Tree: Willow, Palm
Gemstone: Pearl, Opal
Metal: Tin
Direction: West
Place: Sky
Season: Autumn

Meditation 79: Nine of Wands

After the dust of battle settles,
People still hold grudges.
How is true peace begotten?
The wise spirit asks nothing of others,
But fulfills his obligations unilaterally.
Inferior people insist on the compliance of others.

The Tao plays no favorites,
But flows with virtue.

This is the card of Acceptance.

Mystical Key

The fearless figure has fought a difficult battle, but the struggle is not over. Now he must let go of his anger and pain. "The Tao plays no favorites."

Magical Key

Character: The Nine of Wands is gentle by nature, but does not make empty threats. He is a person of great strength, and should not be underestimated.

Current Circumstances: The people the Nine seeks are not trustworthy. This is the time to call on reserved strength. It's hard to let go of hatred, just as it's hard to let go of love. "The wise spirit asks nothing of others." Hanging on to love or hate is draining. Most people insist on a tit-for-tat mode of exchange; however, this attitude often creates a greater strain than reward. The philosophical way is to "fulfill one's obligations unilaterally."

Conflicts, Dangers, and Limitations: The Nine experiences much sorrow, often due to disappointed ideals. He should not give way to exhaustion, but should persevere.

Career: The Nine does well in scholarly and socially responsible careers.

Friends and Family: An older man may pose danger.

Finances and Possessions: This is a time for conservative investments.

Health Concerns: Pituitary gland. If the Nine is ill, he will soon recover.

Romance: The Nine tends to make an idealistic lover, but marriage may not be auspicious.

Travel: The Nine benefits from a great deal of travel.

Decision: Do not do this now—the time isn't right.

Future Events and Spiritual Achievements: Expect trouble. Valuable possessions are in jeopardy. The Nine will attain wisdom.

Omens and Talismans: This is a fortunate card for artists, writers, and people in the helping professions.

    Animal Spirit: Horse, Scorpion, Basilisk
    Bird Spirit: Heron, Bobolink
    Color: Blue, Green
    Plant: Echinacea, Hosta
    Tree: Hazel, English Yew
    Gemstone: Star Sapphire, Carnelian
    Metal: Bronze
    Direction: East
    Place: Mountains
    Season: Autumn

Meditation 80: Four of Wands

A small country with few people
Is blessed by not needing much technology.
They love their life, and don't travel far.
They have transport, but don't need it.
They have weapons, but leave them alone.
They choose knotted ropes over complex writing.
They take pleasure in their food, their clothing, their homes.
They rejoice in a simple life.

> The next community might be so close
> Our little country can hear their chickens
>   cackling,
> And their dogs barking.
> But they'd never bother to go there.

This is the card of Strong Foundations.

Mystical Key

If the Tao Te Ching begins in mystery, it ends in simplicity. The perfect life is one of close community, but joyful satisfaction in what one has. The Taoist Book of Balance and Harmony tells us further that "In building the foundation, it must be steady and stable" ("Building a Hut," a Taoist treatise). It is interesting that some of the final words of the Tao Te Ching concern building, which is always a commitment to the future, a future that is open to the water, the landscape, the air, and the heavenly moon. Build the foundation simply and well, and everything else will follow. Only the strong foundation can bear the ever-changing water-path of the Ten Thousand Things.

Magical Key

Character: The Four of Wands is a perfectionist with the highest ideals and the work ethic necessary to achieve his goals. He is hardworking, but in a negative aspect can be rigid and unwavering.

Current Circumstances: The Four of Wands has perfected his work. The Four should establish his home as a firm foundation for his life. This will provide him with a happy, close, and highly regarded life. The ideal home is simple, peopled with close companions, and all-sustaining. So is the ideal life.

Conflicts, Dangers, and Limitations: In an unfavorable aspect, the card suggests that the Four of Wands may not have adequately prepared his foundations, or that his existence is stagnating. He may also have chosen the wrong goal.

Career: The Four tends to be a tough boss; he should take some time to appreciate the good qualities of others, even though

they differ from his own. Bad habits may hinder chances
for success.

Friends and Family: One who appears to be an enemy is not.

Finances and Possessions: Although the Four is hesitant to
invest, this is the time to make a good investment.

Health Concerns: Endocrine system, feet or toes.

Romance: The Four likes to be in control of romantic
relationships, and feels lost if he is not.

Travel: Although the Four is not fond of travel, he should find it
a broadening experience.

Decision: Do not do this—it's wrong.

Future Events and Spiritual Achievements: In three years,
the Four will achieve his goal and an unsought
wisdom.

Omens and Talismans: This is a favorable card for those in
crafts and the building trades.

> Animal Spirit: Lamb, Frog
> Bird Spirit: Swallow, Robin
> Color: Yellow, Red
> Plant: Rose, Orange Blossom
> Tree: Hazel, Cherry, Plum
> Gemstone: Topaz, Beryl
> Metal: Gold
> Direction: East
> Place: Home
> Season: Summer

Meditation 81: Final Meditation

The truest words aren't the most enchanting.
The most enchanting words aren't true.
People of truth don't argue.
People who argue aren't true.
The walkers in Tao are not scholarly.
The scholarly can't feel the Tao.

The wise spirit doesn't accumulate.
He gives.
The more he gives, the more he has to give.

Though the blade of Heaven is sharp,
It never cuts.
And the Master of the Tao
Is the Work of the Tao.

This is the Freedom to Live.

Mystical Key

The glory of the Tao and the Tarot is that they don't command action—
they offer us freedom and opportunity to create a new life. So often are
we enclosed in a prison of our own making that we are blind and deaf
not only to the beauty of nature, but to the spiritual treasures we carry
within us. The Tao and the Tarot, through symbol, poetry, and picture,
open us to the infinite possibilities that lie within us, flow through us,
and lead us onward. They show us who we are and what we can achieve.
We are all the Fool and the Emperor, the High Priestess and Death,
Judgment and the Magician. Whether we carry the Cup, the Sword, the
Wand, or the Pentacle, we can be open to a new and richer vision, a
nobler life, and a purer spirit. The past and present, friends and family,
health and finances, effort and luck, the outer life and the inner spirit—
all form a seamless web of adventure, pain, sorrow, joy, and sacrifice that
is the riddle of human existence.

Part Three

Beneath the Waves

5

Basic Techniques:
Principles of Divination

Neither the Tarot nor the Tao Te Ching can "tell your fortune." It won't do to approach oracles or sacred literature as if they were the newspaper astrology column, something to be glanced at and forgotten. Such an attitude not only defeats the whole purpose of divination, but puts the Seeker at spiritual risk—not the risk of damnation, but the risk of being stuck forever in a mundane, secular world devoid of spiritual truths.

Divination is a complex mix of magic and mystery that encourages us to discover within ourselves and the world around us the keys to wisdom, compassion, and joy. Our fate depends on two factors: nature and nurture. Neither one alone "controls" a person's life. To gain the best of the both, Taoists "go with the flow," by which they recognize themselves as part of nature. However, dedicated Taoists also cultivate and nurture their inner being by meditation, study, and resolve. This is what we mean by "nurture," the practice of tending to our spiritual needs.

Getting an accurate reading takes practice, and careful attention. A good reading requires intense focus on the cards, which in a broad sense represent the outer world, and then meditation on their meaning as it applies to oneself. If you do only one, you're not getting the fullest benefit from the exercise. People who maintain that the Tarot doesn't "work" for them are seldom investing the practice with the serious meditation it deserves. Deep meanings, by definition, do not lie on the surface—you have to dig deep to find them. Approached in the right spirit, the Tarot and the accompanying Taoist Meditations can bring you into deep harmony with both your inner and outer worlds.

This is an adventure unlike any other, and it has curious, paradoxical lessons to teach. The best leader of people is the truest follower of Tao. Wealth of material brings poverty of spirit. Looking inward opens the largest window on the greatest view. Emptiness is the crucible of creation. Some of these insights may be not immediately apparent; if they were, everyone would hearken to them. These are not axioms to be learned—they are truths to be lived. The readings of the Tarot can show you exactly and specifically how they apply.

Taoist Meditation

I want you to think of reading the Tarot cards as a kind of meditation. Unlike some Hindu and Buddhist meditation practices, Taoist meditation is not an endurance contest. As soon as you get tired of it, stop. Never force yourself, trying to find some "breakthrough." You may "stumble" on the Tao when you least expect it. Or it may find you.

Taoist meditation (*kuan*) means looking inward. It is often imagined as following the breath as it circulates throughout the body. In classical Taoist thought, the pupils of the eye are pure Yang, while the hidden circulating breath reminds us of the Yin inherent in the Tao itself. So when we follow the Yin breath with our Yang vision, we are practicing an ancient Taoist alchemy whose aim is keeping Yin and Yang in perfect balance.

Another way of thinking about *kuan* is called "focusing on the One," imagined as a small, pure light. For interpreting Tarot cards, *kuan* means both developing the right question (Yang mode), and being open to the answer (Yin mode). If you fail in either aspect, the exercise can't provide the insight you seek.

On the whole, however, both these "still-sitting" meditations reflect the Yin aspect of the Tao. More active, or Yang meditations, are Taoist martial arts like *t'ai chi chuan*. (I encourage you to experiment with these meditations as well, under the guidance of an accomplished master.)

The Tarot as Writing

Chinese writing is ideogrammatic, which means it is based on pictures rather than letters. In fact, you don't even have to know spoken Chinese in order to understand the written language, which bypasses words and goes straight to the heart—just like the Tao itself. This "nonlinear" system of writing can present a concept—or a feeling—as quickly as a painting, and with as much complexity and open-endedness. As Alan Watts has pointed out in *The Watercourse Way*, the writing of the Chinese is almost the Tao-made-visible.

But for those who are not fluent readers of Chinese, the Tarot cards provide invaluable help. The Tarot cards are also largely ideogrammatic and nonlinear. They too are concepts and feelings made visible. This is one reason the Tarot cards are useful in focusing attention on the Taoist Meditation. The visual impact of each card is immediate, but its true meaning slowly uncoils as you read through and think about the Meditation. Each illuminates the other.

The Tarot and the Alchemical Tradition

As I mentioned in the first chapter, Tarot has a long and celebrated connection with Western alchemy. The Rider-Waite pack is full of such alchemical symbols. But what is alchemy, and how does it connect with Tarot cards?

Alchemy, both Eastern and Western, is a curious art than has both material and spiritual goals. At first glance, alchemy seems to be thoroughly based in materialism. And it is true that Western alchemy was developed to change base elements like lead into gold through a series of purificatory steps. The final purpose of this operation was said to be the cure of all diseases.

Taoism has its own alchemical system, whose material goal is to ensure physical immortality, or at least a very long life. (Two hundred years was considered a good starting point, with real adepts reportedly managing to make it into four figures.) In Eastern alchemy, gold was not the end point of the process, merely another material to work with—like mercury and arsenic.

However, more philosophically oriented alchemy, both Eastern and Western, reflects a spiritual emphasis. For Taoists, the purpose of this "internal alchemy" is to transform the body into spirit. In a similar vein, the purpose of true Western alchemy is to arrive at a true spiritual knowledge, the so-called pushing back of darkness into the realm of light. (Taosts tend to seek the truth hidden in shadow, but the results are similar.) All these concepts are united in the Tarot.

(The very first card of the Major Arcana, the Magician, is obviously an alchemist. He holds his magic wand in his hand, and before him lie the four symbols of the earthly elements. He himself is fire, the magical catalyst that turns one element into another.)

Reading the Cards: Basic Technique

The art of card reading is known as cartomancy. This ancient practice is governed by many rules that impress on the reader the significance of the undertaking. In cartomancy, we are dealing primarily with symbols, which should be distinguished from signs. In signs, each image "means" something else. In symbols, however, the image opens out into a multi-layered universe of meaning, ideas, and actions. A symbol always "means" what is seems to mean, and much more besides. How much more, and exactly what, depend on the Seeker, and the experience and insight she can bring to the image. There is never a one-to-one correspondence between an image and an idea—the card is merely a "pointer" that shows us what path we might take to our destination.

Asking the Right Question

The most important element in a fruitful reading is to ask the right question. Of course, I can't tell you what that is—but you can. The best questions are those that draw the answers out of yourself. If you ask, "Will Lorenzo marry me?" you are asking the wrong question. You'll be getting an answer—but a limited answer that doesn't take into account the most important factors. The Tarot, with its seventy-eight complex cards, was not designed as a simple fortune-teller, and doesn't work best that way. If, on the other hand, you ask, "What kind of person should I marry?" you'll be nearer the mark. For in that case, you are offering yourself the opportunity to draw from the Tarot the deep truths about yourself and your life.

Many people prefer, at least sometimes, to go into a reading asking a "nonquestion," thus remaining open and attentive to whatever the Tarot and Tao Te Ching have to reveal. There are advantages and disadvantages to this approach. The main advantage is that we are much more ready to "hear" whatever the cards have to tell us; the major disadvantage is that such an attitude may not prepare us carefully enough to make use of what we do hear.

Once we frame the right question—we wait for the answer. But where does the "answer" come from? Both physics and common sense tell us that the future is embedded in the past. Part of the "answer" lies in our present circumstances, and part of it lies in our responses to that situation. Again, the external (Yang) and internal (Yin) meet in the kind of creative encounter that gives birth to truth.

Preparation for Reading

I call this "inviting the spirit." There's nothing weird, supernatural, or even especially psychic about this, for the spirit I want you to invite is your own. All the powers and tools you need to interpret the Tarot are carried in your own heart. You only need to allow them to work. Reading Tarot, like interpreting all dreams and omens, requires an open heart, not a closed mind. Your purpose must be pure. If you come to Tarot looking for a way to get ahead, injure others, or soothe your ego, you've come to the wrong place. You are not asking for any gift but wisdom, and that lies within you. The Tarot can only help you find it.

For most purposes, Tarot reading works best when the Reader and Querent are two separate people—the Yin and Yang. Like a river, a reading should ideally flow between two banks to keep it flowing smoothly and on course. The interaction between the Reader and the Querent gives the reading structure and purpose. Without such a structure and purpose, the reading can be like flood spilling everywhere, not fertilizing the fields, but drowning them.

If you do attempt to read your own cards, choose a time when you are quiet and expect no interruptions. The cards don't care, but you obviously can't devote your full intuitive powers to a reading with the kids screaming, dogs barking, and neighbors begging for sugar and flour. Turn off the phone, and give yourself some time to "get in the mood." An ideal time might be after a warm bath or following a relaxing or invigorating walk. *Never* attempt a Tarot reading when you are angry, terrified, manic, or sad. You will not get an accurate reading.

Storing and Handling the Cards

Tarot cards should be kept in a special place, and encased in a silk or velvet bag. This not only keeps the cards clean, but helps remind the "owner" of the pack that they are special cards, intended for special use. It's also important for the Seeker himself to handle new cards frequently and thoroughly, so as to imprint the cards with one's "aura."

Shuffling

Shuffling the cards thoroughly is critical to obtaining a good Tarot reading. Since every suit represents a different element, the shuffling of the cards represents the mix of the elements. "Chance" plays its role here, as it does in nature. To achieve randomness, you must shuffle the deck at least nine times. (This mathematical curiosity takes on more interest when we consider that nine is a sacred number among Taoists.)

In some systems, the Reader shuffles the cards, in others the Seeker. I believe it works best if the Seeker shuffles the cards. This not only imparts some of his aura to the deck, but more important, helps the Seeker focus his attention on the question and the process of searching for the answer.

The cards should be shuffled until the Querent feels that it's "right." Another signal that it's time to stop may be if the cards just won't meld. Then the cards should also be cut—using the opposite from the Querent's governing hand. Thus, right-handers should cut the pack with their left hand and vice versa. This represents the equalizing of forces—the Yin forces are symbolized by using the opposite hand.

The Question of Randomness and Determination

No random collection of cards represents some preordained, unalterable arrangement of Fate. Obviously, you can shuffle and re-deal the cards and get an entirely different bunch, although the same few cards tend to reappear over and over again. However, different cards, carefully read, will give the same reading. The key is the skill and concentration of the Reader. And although anyone can learn to read Tarot cards well, it does require some practice.

If the cards seem contradictory, *do not* reshuffle them except under extraordinary circumstances. Life is contradictory, and contradictory forces are at work within us; this is not necessarily a deplorable thing. Make a further, more concerted attempt to clarify their meaning. Examine the pictures or Meditations again, and see if a personal meaning, not present in the mystical or magical meaning I have provided, suggests itself. Careful observation will reveal an important theme running through the cards. The purpose of good Tarot reading is not to uncover a fixed future but to empower the Seeker to understand himself and make good choices.

Laying Out the Cards

Once you have decided on the layout, set down the cards. It is not necessary to lay them facedown and then turn them over, although you may, if it makes the layout feel more manageable. But you can't interpret any card until you understand its place in the whole layout. As you get more comfortable handling the layouts, you will be able to assess the cards in a larger, more closely integrated context.

The Question of Reversals

In conventional Tarot readings, a card that presents itself in reverse is often given the opposite meaning of its standard reading. Taoism does not recognize oppositional forces, since it understands that all forces serve one end. Apparent opposites are, at most, complementary forces, which in the end become one. The great symbol of Taoism, the Yin/Yang Circle (*Tai Ji Tu*), does not have a "right side up." Everything is circular.

Therefore, a card that presents itself in reverse in a Taoist reading does not carry an opposite meaning to a right-side-up card. *Instead, a reverse indicates that the card's divinatory meaning may be hidden or obscured now from the Querent's life.* Conditions do not currently prevail to bring it forth, or perhaps the Referent is psychologically or spiritually unable to see how the meaning of that card is working itself out in his life. In most cases, a reverse card indicates some "blindness" on the part of the Referent. The card itself, however, retains its primary meaning. The Querent is encouraged to look deeper—often into himself—for the complete meaning of the card.

Most cards in the pack have both a positive and a negative aspect, depending on where the card falls in the reading. For example, a generally positive card can be said to have a bad aspect when it turns up in the Conflicts section. The interpretation applied to each card includes both positive and negative aspects. Not every aspect of the card applies to its appearance in a particular reading. Try to use only the part of the card that specifically applies. For instance, if you are reading the "Romance" slot, it doesn't matter if the card says that a trip is indicated. Only the part about romance applies to that slot.

The Question of Proximity

An individual Tarot card does not stand alone, single and inviolate, as if in an isolation chamber. Each card is influenced, modified, or reversed by cards that stand in immediate proximity to it. To get the fullest reading, the cards should be considered as related to one another. Like the Tao Te Ching, the Tarot is a contextual system. The influence each card bears on another depends partly on its position in the reading, and partly on the cards that stand near it. The keys to understanding the influences are experience and intuitive, thoughtful reading, always bearing in mind the Meditation that goes with each card. For example, whether the Moon exerts a strengthening or weakening influence on the card that followed or preceded it depends on the nature of the slot. In some cases, which are obvious on a reading, the Moon may indicate that the following card's influence is secret or hidden. At other times, it may indicate that that influence is changing. Only concerted practice, meditation, and experience can clarify the meaning of the card.

This is one reason why Tarot reading is an art, and why it is the source of such rich insight.

Examining the Cards

Especially when you are first beginning Tarot through Tao, you'll need to examine each card carefully. Study the symbolism, and read the accompanying description and explanation. As the image of each card sinks into your consciousness, and its multitude of meanings becomes clearer, it won't be necessary to "read" them at all. They will already be inscribed in your mind.

When reading the cards, do not be hasty in drawing conclusions. Accurate readings depend on meditation and intuition. Chuang Tzu tells an interesting tale about a certain Chu Chiao Tsu, who was having some trouble deciphering a tricky point in Taoist doctrine. He noted that even Confucius couldn't figure it out. Chang Wu Tsu, the great Taoist master, responded, "These words would have confused even the Yellow Emperor, so how could Confucius understand them? Moreover, you are too quick to draw conclusions. You see an egg, and immediately you listen for the crowing of a full-grown cock." The wise person allows time for events to work themselves out. If a reading is mysterious, don't worry it like a dog with a bone. Contemplate the meditations that accompany the cards and let the future ripen of its own accord.

Important Symbols of the Tarot

As a universal divination system, the Tarot draws its symbols from the natural world and from universal human symbolic structures. Many of these appear in several cards, often with slightly different meanings. Some of the most common of these symbols are animals (mythic and real), armor, circles, cities, clouds, crosses, crowns, flowers, fruits, hands, the moon, pillars, plumes, serpents, stars, the sun, thrones, triangles, water, and wings. These appear over and over again. So do archetypal characters like the king, the queen, the juggler, the beggar, and the fool. Images of struggle, dancing, work, deliberation, and death also occur. In many cases the meaning of such cultural symbols is obvious; in other cases perhaps not. I discuss each of the main image devices as they appear, but I also invite the reader to consider how these images affect him and what they might mean in his or her own life.

The Spiritual Meaning

Beyond both the public and private meanings of the Tarot cards is a spiritual meaning. Over the centuries, as we have seen, people have used the

Kabbalah, Egyptian magic, and other resources to draw forth this meaning. But for me, only Tao provides the completing Yin qualities to the Yang of the Tarot, and its rich mysteries stand in perfect counterbalance to the beautiful magic of Tarot. One way into this reading is to meditate mindfully on the accompanying Meditation. Only by this method can the Seeker draw out the deepest meaning of the Tarot. The postreading Meditation "completes" the reading, and the reading should not be considered finished until then. Read the Meditation aloud slowly, and let the images it evokes take root in your mind. This meditation is, of course, done privately.

Yin Cards, Yang Cards

Because the Tarot represents the universe as a whole, the Tarot cards contain both Yin and Yang symbols. Pick up a pack of Tarot cards, and glance through the Major Arcana. They fall quite naturally into Yin (feminine, dark, mysterious) and Yang (masculine, bright, logical). People who possess true Yang are strong, tough, decisive, sharp, energetic, and fearless. But when the Yang becomes corrupted by incomplete mixing with the Yin force, the strength becomes aggression, firmness becomes stubbornness, and courage turns to recklessness. People with true Yin are yielding, flexible, self-mastering, open, and modest. But when the Yin force is corrupted by too little Yang, the yielding becomes weakness, simplicity degenerates into shallowness, and modesty turns to passivity.

The Magician, the Emperor, and the Hierophant are as obviously Yang as the High Priestess, the Empress, and the Moon are Yin. Some cards are a bit more secretive. The Hanged Man reveals itself as Yin, for instance, only after some meditation. But on the whole, the Yin/Yang orientation of the Major Arcana is so clear that after a moment's reflection, people tend to unerringly divide them correctly.

The appearance of a Yin card, even a totally Yin card like the High Priestess or the Empress, does not necessary mean that the Referent is a woman. It means that Yin forces are at work in the reading. The more Yin cards drawn, the more secret or hidden influences are at work in the Seeker's life.

Yin Signs: Cups; Pentacles; O Fool, II High Priestess, III Empress, VIII Strength, IX Hermit, X Wheel of Fortune, XII Hanged Man, XIII Death, XIV Temperance, XVII Star, XVIII Moon.

Yang Signs: Swords; Wands; I Magician, IV Emperor, V Hierophant, VI Lovers, VII Chariot, IX Justice, XV Devil, XVI Tower, XIX Sun, XX Judgment, XXI World.

The Major Arcana

The Major Arcana often represent persons, usually aspects of the Seeker herself or, less frequently, people of influence in her life. Their element is fire. Fire is the very principle of transformation. This accords with modern chemical knowledge, which tells us that substances cannot be changed except through heat (some sort of energy exchange). In many ways it seems the opposite of water, and in traditional schemes, water "trumps" fire by "putting it out;" they are complementary forces. Both are deeply connected with the idea of transformation—water because it itself is transformed into its three physical forms of liquid, steam, and solid, and fire because it has the ability to transform all other substances. One sacred Taoist text, "The Union of Fire and Water," says that when the senses run outward, that is fire; when they are gathered inward, that is water.

Traditionally, Tarot adepts have considered Tarot cards, especially the Major Arcana, as archetypes of our collective unconscious: the primal Mother, the eternal Virgin, the Knightly Warrior, the Sacrificial Victim, or the great King. Others represent natural objects: the Sun, the Moon, or the Star. Still others embody abstract concepts like Judgment, Strength, and Temperance. Some are comforting, while others, like the Tower and Death, seem distinctly unpleasant. But the Tarot, like the Tao, plays its tricks. The grimmest-looking card is not always a card of misfortune. In addition, the personal or spiritual meaning of a card may overrule or subvert the public, communal one. And no single, isolated card can ever delineate the entire character, past and present, of the Seeker.

To further complicate things, the public, communal meaning is never the whole meaning. Sometimes a particular card may have a special meaning or private association for the Querent himself. In this case, the personal reference may be more important than the traditional divinatory meaning. It's a mistake, however, to assume this is this always so. The cards represent millennia-old archetypes whose meaning is not necessarily obliterated by an alternate or contrary personal reference. Both need to be taken into account and carefully evaluated.

The Major Arcana are the most potent cards in the deck and, in a reading, a card of the Major Arcana with a meaning contradictory to that of a neighboring Minor Arcana card is always the stronger force. (That doesn't mean it will prevail, however. It just means that it's the stronger force. In a Taoist reading, it's sometimes the weaker force that will prevail.) When many Major Arcana show up in a reading, it's an indication that the Querent is in the grasp of powerful forces that he must learn to control.

The Minor Arcana

The Minor Arcana generally have to do with current conditions and present actions, whereas the Major Arcana symbolize the more permanent elements of destiny.

Most writers on the Tarot are of the opinion that the Minor Arcana have only "fortune-telling" properties, while the Major Arcana have connections to deep spiritual truths. This is probably an oversimplification. While it is true that the Minor Arcana received pictorial presentation later than did the Major Arcana, it does not follow that they are devoid of "deeper" meanings simply because their pictures are newer than those of the Major Arcana. The pictures on the Minor Arcana of most modern decks closely follow Waite and Colman Smith's original designs. This in itself shows that something about those designs strike a deep chord in the human psyche. The decks that have struck out on their own to develop new designs, usually for both the Minor and Major Arcana, just demonstrate how fruitful a ground the Tarot is for expressing the complexities of the human imagination. The cards themselves are only starting points for the Reader's interaction with the symbolic order of things, in whatever form it takes. For this purpose, the Major and Minor Arcana can be equally important. However, it is true that the very names of the

Major Arcana (the Magician, the High Priestess, the Wheel of Fortune, and so on) open more doors into the psychic world than does the "Four of Wands," for instance.

In general, the Minor Arcana is more difficult to decipher than is the Major Arcana. In addition to interpreting each card, one has to take into account both suit and number, both of which have acquired rich layers of meaning throughout the centuries.

The Suits

A preponderance of any suit in a reading indicates a certain sphere of influence, powers, and threats to the Querent. Although each suit is associated with a specific element, each is also touched by all the others.

Swords

Swords is a pure Yang suit. Swords are associated with everything male—from warfare to phalluses. Many Swords in a reading may signal conflicts, but they may also represent a powerful, energetic, astute, vibrant person of either sex.

Swords are linked with metal, of course, although some Western interpretations of Tao give Swords the element air. This is because, for one thing, ancient Western systems did not consider metal an element (and air is not an element in the Chinese scheme), and also because the energetic action of Swords takes place in the air. Since air is equated with spirit, it makes sense to think of Swords as the blade of Spirit. In ancient Chinese iconography, Swords were emblems of fighting off demons, so he who bears the Sword is a warrior on the side of truth.

A Sword that occurs in a negative spot suggests that the Referent will have the power to successfully struggle against the demons. Swords represent courage and high spiritual ambition. This is a good suit for leaders, soldiers, and people in authority.

Swords became the modern suit of Spades, thus also connecting them with the traditional element earth. So although Swords are linked with sexual and physical energy, a high number of Swords indicates that the Seeker has invested a deeply spiritual quality into his or her sexuality.

The Sword represents the Tao itself. The Taoist Book of Harmony and Balance contains the poem, "The Sword of Wisdom" [Cleary 453, Vol. 2]. Part of it reads:

Ever since adepts handed on
The secret of the sword,
The true imperative has been upheld
Completely, truly adamant.

If someone asks me about
Looking for its origin,
I say it is not ordinary iron.
This lump of stillness;
When you obtain it, it rises up.

Forging it in a glowing fire,
Through repeated efforts,
It is refined
And forged into steel.

When students of the Tao
Know this secret,
The spirit of light is intensely powerful,
And devils of darkness vanish.

The fact that the Sword is chosen as symbol of Tao is a key to the awareness that the Tao is not always to be regarded as passive, quiet, and still. The Page holds the Sword, but doesn't use it—it has the power of pure potentiality.

A large number of Swords suggests the following about the Seeker:

Mode: Yang
Element: Metal
Season: Spring
Power: Intellectual
Realm: Air
Color: White/Silver

Cups

Cups, which once represented the chalice of the Roman Catholic mass, became Hearts in modern decks. Many cups in a reading signify the importance of feelings and emotions. Cups can be made of any element—metal, wood, earth (pottery)—but the element they hold is water, symbol of the sacred Tao.

Cups are associated with water, the ultimate Yin sign. They represent the Feminine (and the Tao) in its purest form. In Western interpretations, Cups also represent the emotions, another Yin attribute. Large numbers of Cups in a reading are very auspicious in a Taoist interpretation, for they symbolize water, the primal element of Tao. From the most ancient times, water was used to combat evil forces. Indeed, most Western religions use water as a purificatory device. This is also the most auspicious suit for love and happiness.

A large number of Cups in a reading suggests the following about the Seeker:

Mode: Yin
Element: Water
Season: Winter
Power: Emotional
Realm: The Human Heart
Color: Black

Pentacles

Pentacles (also called coins or disks) turned into Diamonds in modern decks. A high number of Pentacles in a reading indicates a concern with money, earthly matters, and business. This is an auspicious suit for business people. The higher Pentacles are also favorable for relationships, marriage, and family.

Pentacles are the jewel of the earth and, like the Unmanifest Tao, lie secret. Pentacles represent the earth, another powerful Yin sign, but with a Yang aspect. This is the suit of earthly power, money, and success. Pentacles represent creativity and good career possibilities in the Earthly Realm. But "earthliness" has another significance. It means abundance, and as such, fertility and creation. According to most mythologies, earth is the material from which human beings were made.

Yet their starry shape reminds us of the spiritual quality inherent even in this most earthly of elements. Pythagoras and his circle used the Pentacle to symbolize mind/body harmony.

A large number of Pentacles in a reading suggests the following about the Seeker:

Mode: Yin/Yang
Element: Earth
Season: Autumn
Power: Body
Realm: The World
Color: Yellow/Gold

Wands

Wands, sometimes called Scepters, became clubs in modern playing card decks, thereby losing some of their rich symbolism. Wands can be a flowering branch, a weapon, a scepter, a magic wand, or a burden, but a Club is a club and that's about it. Traditionally, Wands have been assigned to the element of fire, but in Taoist approaches, their most natural element is Wood, whose activity is growth and creation.

Wands, while also phallic (the Wands of the Rider-Waite deck really do emphasize this aspect of the suit), are rather Yin in their creation symbolism. Wands are made of wood, which is rooted in the earth, but blossoms in the air. Wands represent creative fruitfulness. Wands are the symbolic representation of the Cosmic or World Tree, the Axis Mundi, the pole that connects Earth to Heaven. This is an inheritance from the most ancient shamanistic tradition. Some of the Wands also bear forest symbolism, with its obvious connotations of complexity, romance, and half-light, a place of fear and danger to the uninitiated, and of solace and refuge to those who understand its ways.

A preponderance of Wands in a layout signifies an extremely imaginative, enterprising, and creative person. If all the Wand Court cards appear, it indicates that the Seeker will fulfill his creative potential. A lack of Court cards suggests that the Seeker needs to work harder to accomplish his creative goals.

Wands are the creative power of the earth. They are auspicious cards for all workers, crafts persons, and artists.

A large number of Wands in a reading suggests the following about the Seeker:

Mode: Yin/Yang:
Element: Wood
Season: Summer
Power: Creativity
Realm: Spirit
Color: Green/Blue

Numbers

ACES: The Suit in its purest form. The cumulous clouds, from which the hand merges in all four suits, represents, in Taoist thought, a union of the Yin and Yang forces. In a negative sense, many Aces can represent chaos, imbalance, and conflict. When many Aces appear in a reading, it indicates that the Seeker will shortly begin a major life change. Aces also signify the center, creation, and beginning. As Meditation 42 says, "The Tao is the Mother of the One. The One gives birth to Two. The Two bring forth Three. And the Three engender the Ten Thousand Things of this World."

TWO: The opposite, duality, a balance. In Western myth, Two brings forth an evil third, but Taoism sees that they are merely external aspects of the Unmanifest Tao, and certainly not evil. When many Twos appear in a reading, it indicates that there is a lot of Yin/Yang conflict that needs to be balanced more carefully.

THREE: A masculine number. The creation of spirit out of matter. Possible dissension or quarreling. Yet the Three is also a magical number of great power in almost all cultures. Many Threes in a reading indicate a conflict that will produce a fruitful result.

FOUR: Completion. This is an earthly number, which is why the Emperor bears a Four in the Major Arcana. Many Fours in a reading indicate strength, honor, completeness, and stability. The persons represented by the Fours of any suit are builders of strong foundations, so much so that they tend to be too conservative.

FIVE: Ambivalence. Five is a lucky number in Taoism and in Chinese culture—but frequently an unlucky number in standard Tarot readings. Yet Five is also the number that represents our humanity, for it signals a dimension above mere matter. Metaphorically, the four limbs and head of a person also stand for the number 5.

In classical culture, Five is the number of Justice. Thus, when Fives appear in a reading, it means justice will be done. Whether this is lucky or not depends on the past behavior of the Referent. Many Fives can indicate uneasiness, corruption, sensuality, and restlessness, a breakdown of affairs, even the presence of occult forces.

In Chinese and Taoist thought, however, five (*wu*) is a sacred number. There were five elements, five tones, five compass points, five spices, five kinds of animals, five classical books, five kinds of creatures, and five kinds of virtue. Fives interact well with others.

When many Fives appear in a reading, it indicates that the Seeker is under a great deal of stress and conflict. The ultimate result of the conflict depends on the hints provided in surrounding cards.

SIX: Reconciliation or equilibrium, especially in love relationships. In Western tradition, it is the number of Aphrodite, goddess of love. This number is sometimes considered the number of blessing. For some it represents the human soul. Many Sixes indicate a life of service and compassion for others.

SEVEN: Both limitation and wisdom. Many Sevens show that the Seeker is an inveterate lover of truth and wisdom. The Seven may be detached and overintellectual. This card refers to the wisdom of limitation—understanding one's limits. Temporary stoppage. In a favorable reading, many Sevens show a search for self-knowledge.

EIGHT: Expansion, renewal, spiraling upward. Balancing opposition. Many Eights in a reading suggest excitement, change, and growth.

NINE: Integration. In Taoism, it is the mystical number for totality. It is significant as the square (higher power) of three. Nines of any suit are powerful. The number of chapters in the Tao Te Ching is eighty-one: nine times nine.

TEN: Culmination. Three or more tens denote great strength.

The Court Cards

Court cards tend to represent people, rather than events or qualities. Sometimes the card may refer to the Seeker himself; at other times it may refer to a family member, significant other, boss, or even an enemy. Many Court cards in a reading signify the importance of other people in the Seeker's life.

PAGE: The Page is an androgyne, who unites the characteristics of male and female, and can stand for both. This same quality is found in many Tarot cards. The appearance of the Page often signifies transition from one state or condition to another. The more Pages that appear in a section, the more powerful the change will be. Traditionally, Pages are associated with the body and things related to our physical being. A Page can also indicate the influence of a child.

Many Pages in a reading suggest a person of physical or sexual prowess.

KNIGHT: All the Knights are mounted, of course, and the relationship between the horse and the Knight signifies the relationship between the ego and the id. The appearance of many Knights, or the appearance of a Knight next to a King, signify material wealth. Knights are also associated with mental quickness. Yet Knights have another, more spiritual meaning. In shamanistic China, the birthplace of Taoism, horses signified flight into the spiritual world. Many Knights in a reading signify a person who is both mentally alert and spiritually awake.

If the Knight appears next to a Queen, or, most auspiciously, an Ace, the Seeker is a person of spiritual attainment. If the Knight appears next to the Page, the Quest is just beginning, but will succeed.

QUEEN: The appearance of many Queens in the reading signifies health and long life. They represent the matriarchal power of a civilization. Many Queens in a reading signify a person of powerful emotions (Swords and Wands) or emotional sensitivity (Cups and Wands).

KING: Rulership—a leading quality. Kings represent the patriarchal power of a civilization. They are associated with will. Many kings in a reading signify a person of powerful will. The King of Cups signifies a powerful emotional will, Pentacles a financial or business will, Swords a mental or spiritual will, and Wands a creative will. If the King is in an unfavorable slot, the entire reading becomes much less favorable.

Creating a Personal Mandala

By meditating on the Omens section of your reading, or by pulling a special card either at random or that speaks to you through its image or Meditation, you can create a personal mandala made up of the colors, animals, plants, and symbol of your card. This mandala can be created with paper and paint, sewn, appliquéd—whatever suits your talent and inclinations. If you are not talented artistically (like me!), you can imagine a design and describe it in words to use as a meditative device or as a personal symbol.

This exercise helps you develop connections that you may not have noticed previously. It helps you think about your strengths, your weaknesses, and your spiritual path. You can test your creativity and spiritual knowledge by using all the signs of the Omen, or you may wish to create a simpler emblem by choosing only a few. You may want to include part of the Tarot card (even just its name) or use the Meditation or images it suggests personally to you. This practice will help you engage directly with the Tarot and the Tao Te Ching, and bring you into a fuller understanding of what they have to offer.

6

Reading the Cards

Classical Taoist Divination Patterns

There are thousands of ways of laying out Tarot cards. Layouts like the Celtic Cross, Le Grand Jeu, the Tree of Life, and the Horseshoe have been in common use for centuries. In this book, I offer four extremely powerful layouts, based on ancient Taoist oracles, whose origin goes back more than 3,000 years: they are the earliest divination oracles in the world. These are fluid, timeless patterns based not on someone's whim, but on the eternal workings of nature. They speak to everyone who has ever contemplated himself in a mirror, gazed at the stars, or followed in spirit the flow of a river.

YES AND NO—or the One-Question Reading

For extremely simple one-answer (yes/no) readings, no layout is necessary. Simply shuffle and pull a card. I don't recommend this layout for a question of life importance, since such circumstances have too many variables.

YES. Swords and these Major Arcana (Yang cards): I Magician, IV Emperor, V Hierophant, VI Lovers, VII Chariot, IX Justice, XV Devil, XVI Tower, XIX Sun, XX Judgment, XXI World.

NO. Cups and these Major Arcana: Pentacle (Yin cards): II High

Priestess, III Empress, VIII Strength, IX Hermit, X Wheel of Fortune, XII Hanged Man, XIII Death, XIV Temperance, XVII Star, XVIII Moon.

But be careful. Some cards like the Tower have unfortunate connotations, so even if "Yes" is the answer you want, the ultimate result may be unlucky. This is why it's better to ask a more complex question.

Probably. Wands. The higher the card—the more nearly "Yes."

Probably not. Pentacles. The higher the card, the more nearly "No."

Maybe. The Fool: The answer is unknown—for the Fool says, "What's the difference between yes and no?"

You may also ask the Tarot a question relating to career, friends and family, health, travel, romance, or the like. Simply frame the question, draw the card, and check the accompanying divination for that subject. Again, the answer you receive will be an oversimplification of what you would get in a full reading.

Waterdrop Reading

In this reading you choose or draw one card and read the accompanying Meditation, Magical Key, and Mystical Key. Just as a drop of water contains the chemical properties of the river, but not the dynamic ebb and flow of the current, the Waterdrop Reading encapsulates the major significance of the question, but cannot offer the nuanced understanding that a more thorough reading can give.

If you wish to let the Tao take control of the choice, draw a card randomly. If you wish to participate more actively, select a card whose name or meaning speaks deeply to you.

Celestial Palaces: The Script of Heaven

Taoists know that we are all born from the stars. For them, the stars represent the far spiritual outreaches of the cosmos, just as water represents what lies closest to the body. The Script of Heaven is an attempt to connect what is farthest away with what is closest at hand.

The constellations are the rivers of the sky. They flow across the heavens in an unerring pilgrimage whose solemn procession is highlighted, not disturbed, by the wandering planets and rogue comets that cross their path.

In Chinese, this system of divination is known as *Tzu-wei Tu-Su* (System of the Ruling Star *Tzu-Wei* and the Numerics of the Bushel Stars). The Bushel Stars comprise the Big Dipper (the Northern Bushel) and another constellation known to Chinese astrologers as the Southern Bushel. In Taoist thought, the stars of the Big Dipper have special attributes, and influence health, longevity, and even human destiny.

The positions of the stars (or, in our case, the cards) are placed into twelve "Celestial Palaces," akin to the "Houses" of the Western system. The Palaces are "read" counterclockwise.

Place a card in each Palace, facedown. Experienced readers may turn them up, but novice readers tend to be overwhelmed with the amount of information provided. It's easier to concentrate on the meaning of the cards if they are read one at a time. None of the individual meanings should be interpreted as if they were carved in stone or written in blood. Insufficient shuffling and inattention can produce inconsistent results.

These slots correspond with the Magical Keys, with the exception of "Decision," obviously left out because the entire reading centers on decisions.

First Palace: Character. This card explores basic personality traits. For this slot, select the "Character" heading for the card drawn. Depending on the question asked, the character may refer to the Seeker, or to a Referent (someone the Seeker is asking about), a boss, a family member, or a significant other.

Second Palace: Current Circumstances. This slot refers to the physical, social, and emotional environment in which the Seeker finds himself. Sometimes it contains small pieces of practical advice.

Third Palace: Friends and Family. This slot refers to the Seeker's family and circle of acquaintances. The term "friends" is a loose one. As the cards may indicate, some of the friends may not be so friendly after all. The same is true for family.

Fourth Palace: Helpful Meditation. Carefully read and reflect on the meditation that accompanies the card drawn. For example, if the Six of Wands is drawn, the corresponding meditation is Meditation 31. This slot points the reader to a Meditation that may clarify his past, explain the present, and guide the future. It is one-quarter of the way through the reading, and it is intended to throw light on what has gone before and what is to come. The Meditations call on you to meditate on both the card and the Tao Te Ching. Together, these elements of the Manifest and Unmanifest Tao bring forth realizations. Do not neglect this part of the reading—it holds the key to your spiritual development.

Fifth Palace: Finances and Possessions. This slot refers to the present and projected material wealth of the Referent or Seeker.

Sixth Palace: Health Concerns. This slot refers to general health concerns of the Referent. Nothing in the reading is meant as a prediction, or even a suggestion, that the Referent will become ill. It merely means that he or she should take special care in the particular area(s) referred to.

Seventh Palace: Travel. This slot indicates whether travel would be advisable at the present time. Sometimes the slot specifies a distance, a time, a direction, or even an environment or destination.

Eighth Palace: Romance. This slot is reserved for the Seeker's romantic relationships, and in some cases, marriage predictions.

Ninth Palace: Career. This slot covers promotions, salary increases, unemployment, and job transfers.

Tenth Palace: Conflicts, Dangers, and Limitations. This slot warns the Seeker about obstacles, both internal and external, that may keep him from reaching his goal.

Eleventh Palace: Future Events and Spiritual Achievements. This slot briefly sums up the tendencies of the preceding cards to make a prediction about future events. If the warnings of any of the preceding cards are heeded by the Seeker, the future outcome will be affected.

Twelfth Palace: Omens and Talismans. These constitute
important portents and talismans. However, it's important to
note that they are attached to the card, and not necessarily
to the Seeker, except inasmuch as he identifies with them.
These significant omens are usually auspicious, but in some
cases may prove inauspicious. All, however, will be
important for the Seeker's development. In many cases, two
examples are provided, each of which may serve a different
function or turn out to be important in different areas or
during different times of the Seeker's life. For example, one
omen might be a healing plant intended to provide nurture
and sustenance for a vulnerable part of the Seeker's body.
These omens are not necessarily meant to "match" the
image, Meditation, or other omens. For example, simply
because the Color is blue, it doesn't necessarily follow that
the Gemstone has to be blue also. These talismans have
occult significance whose meaning is derived from Eastern
and Western alchemy, ancient Celtic and Chinese oracles,
and other divination techniques. The connection with the
card and the Meditation is nevertheless very strong.

Celestial Palaces

First Palace Character	Twelfth Palace Omens and Talismans	Eleventh Palace Future Events and Spiritual Achievements	Tenth Palace Conflicts, Dangers, and Limitations
Second Palace Current Circumstances			Ninth Palace Career
Third Palace Friends and Family			Eighth Palace Romance
Fourth Palace Helpful Meditation	Fifth Palace Finances and Possessions	Sixth Palace Health Concerns	Seventh Palace Travel

Resources

For those who wish to further explore the magic of Tarot and mystery of Tao, I recommend the following works:

Tarot

Banzhoff, Hajo. *Tarot and the Journey of the Hero*. York Beach, ME: Samuel Weiser, Inc., 2000.

Campbell, Joseph and Richard Roberts. *Tarot Revelations*. San Anselmo, CA: Vernal Equinox Press, 1987.

Cavendish, Richard, *The Tarot*. London: Michael Jordan Ltd., 1975.

D'Agostino, Joseph. *Tarot: The Path to Wisdom*. York Beach, ME: Samuel Weiser, Inc., 1994.

Gad, Irene. *Tarot and Individuation: Correspondences with Cabala and Alchemy*. York Beach, ME. Nicholas-Hays, Inc., 1994.

Crowley, Aleister. *The Book of Thoth*. York Beach, ME: WeiserBooks, 1974.

Giles, Cynthia. *The Tarot: History, Mystery, and Lore*. NY: Simon and Schuster, 1992.

Kaplan, Stuart R. *The Encyclopedia of Tarot*, Vols. I, II, and III. Stamford, CT: U.S. Games Systems, Inc., 1986.

———. *Tarot Classic*. NY: U.S. Games Systems, Inc., 1972.

MacGregor, Trish and Phyllis Vega. *Power Tarot*. NY: Simon and Schuster, 1998.

Ozaniec, Naomi. *The Illustrated Guide to Tarot*. NY: Sterling Publishing Co., 1999.

Papus. *The Tarot of the Bohemians*. Translated from the French by A. P. Morton. London: Studio Edition, Ltd., 1994.

Pollack, Rachel. *Seventy-Eight Degrees of Wisdom: A Book of Tarot*. London: Thorsons (an imprint of HarperCollins), 1997.

Sterling, Stephen Walter. *Tarot Awareness: Exploring the Spiritual Path*. St. Paul: Llewellyn Publications, 2000.

Taoism

The best way to learn more about Taoism is to study the primacy sources. These include the Tao Te Ching and the Chuang Tzu, both available in many translations. Other Taoist classics are included in Thomas Cleary's collected translations: *The Taoist Classics* (Bopston: Shambhala, 2000) in four volumes.

Blofeld, John. *Taoism: The Road to Immortality*. Boston:Shambhala, 1985.

Clark, J. J. *The Tao of the West: Western Transformation of Taoist Thought*. London and New York: Routledge, 2000.

Cleary, Thomas. *Vitality, Energy, Spirit: A Taoist Sourcebook*. Boston and London: Shambhala, 1991.

Eberhard, Wolfram. *A Dictionary of Chinese Symbols: Hidden Symbols in Chinese Life and Thought*. London and New York: Routledge, 1986.

Kaltenmark, Max. *Lao Tzu and Taoism*. Stanford: Stanford University Press, 1969.

Nan, Huai-Chin. *Tao and Longevity: Mind-Body Transformation*. Translated by Wen Kuan Chu. York Beach, ME: Samuel Weiser, Inc., 1984.

Roth, Harold D. *Original Tao:Inward Training*. New York: Columbia University Press, 1983.

Sawyer, Ralph D. and Mei-chün Lee Sawyer, translators. *Ling Ch'i Ching: A Classic Chinese Oracle*. Boston and London: Shambhala, 1995.

Watts, Alan. *The Watercourse Way*. NY: Pantheon Books, 1975.

Welch, Holmes. *Taoism: The Parting of the Way*. Boston: Beacon Press, 1957.

Wong, Eva. *The Shambhala Guide to Taoism*. Boston and London: Shambhala, 1997.

———. *The Teachings of the Tao*. Boston and London: Shambhala, 1997.